God after Metaphysics

INDIANA SERIES IN THE PHILOSOPHY OF RELIGION
MEROLD WESTPHAL, GENERAL EDITOR

God after Metaphysics
A Theological Aesthetic

John Panteleimon Manoussakis

INDIANA UNIVERSITY PRESS
BLOOMINGTON AND INDIANAPOLIS

This book is a publication of

Indiana University Press
601 North Morton Street
Bloomington, IN 47404-3797 USA

http://iupress.indiana.edu

Telephone orders   800-842-6796
Fax orders   812-855-7931
Orders by e-mail   iuporder@indiana.edu

MANUFACTURED IN THE UNITED STATES OF AMERICA

Library of Congress Cataloging-in-Publication Data

Manoussakis, John Panteleimon.
    God after metaphysics : a theological aesthetic / John Panteleimon Manoussakis.
       p.   cm.   — (Indiana series in the philosophy of religion)
    Includes bibliographical references and index.
    ISBN 978-0-253-34880-7 (cloth : alk. paper) 1. God—Knowableness.
    2. Experience (Religion) 3. Christianity—Philosophy. 4. Orthodox Eastern
    Church—Doctrines. I. Title.
    BT102.M36 2007
    231—dc22
                                                            2006035932

1 2 3 4 5 12 11 10 09 08 07

Τῆς Παναγίας, ἀχράντου, ὑπερευλογημένης, ἐνδόξου Δεσποίνης ἡμῶν Θεοτόκου καί ἀειπαρθένου Μαρίας.

So, following the saintly fathers, we all with one voice teach the confession of one and the same Son, our Lord Jesus Christ: the same perfect in divinity and perfect in humanity, the same truly God and truly man, of a rational soul and a body; consubstantial with the Father as regards his divinity, and the same consubstantial with us as regards his humanity; like us in all respects except for sin; begotten before the ages from the Father as regards his divinity, and in the last days the same for us and for our salvation from Mary, the virgin God-bearer as regards his humanity; one and the same Christ, Son, Lord, only-begotten, acknowledged in two natures which undergo *no confusion, no change, no division, no separation*; at no point was the difference between the natures taken away through the union, but rather the property of both natures is preserved and comes together into a single person and a single subsistent being; he is not parted or divided into two persons, but is one and the same only-begotten Son, God, Word, Lord Jesus Christ, just as the prophets taught from the beginning about him, and as the Lord Jesus Christ himself instructed us, and as the creed of the fathers handed it down to us.

—The Fourth Ecumenical Council of Chalcedon (A.D. 451)

It is nothing less than the loud assertion that this mysterious Maker of the world has visited His world in person. It declares that really and even recently, or right in the middle of historic times, there did walk into the world this original invisible being; about whom the thinkers make theories and the mythologists hand down myths; *the Man who made the World*. That such a higher personality exists behind all things had always been implied by the best thinkers as well as by all the beautiful legends. But nothing of this sort has ever been implied by any of them . . . The most that any religious prophet had said was that he was the true servant of such a being. The most that any visionary had ever said was that men might catch glimpses of the glory of that spiritual being; much more often of lesser spiritual beings. The most that any primitive myth had ever suggested was that the Creator was present at the Creation. But that the Creator was present at scenes a little subsequent to the supper-parties of Horace, and talked with tax collectors and government officials in the detailed daily life of the Roman Empire, and that this fact continued to be firmly asserted by the whole of that great civilization for more than a thousand years — that is something utterly unlike anything else in nature. It is the one great startling statement that man has made since he spoke his first articulate word . . . it makes nothing but dust and nonsense of comparative religion.

—G. K. Chesterton, The Everlasting Man

Contents

ACKNOWLEDGMENTS

The core of the present work was formed as a result of my research and writing for my doctorate in philosophy at Boston College (2001–2005). During that period of gestation, my work profited immensely from the tutelage of Richard Kearney, the Charles B. Seelig Chair in Philosophy, who oversaw, with paternal affection and unfailing encouragement, every small step taken on my way to completion. Professor Jean-Luc Marion has gifted this work with many great insights that bear the unmistakable stamp of his genius, but above all, he has given me the gift of his friendship. I am indebted to him for reading my work from the very first sketches to the final form, and for introducing me to many different systems of thought that have proven of paramount importance to the development of my own thought, among which I feel compelled to mention that of Hans Urs von Balthasar. I am also grateful to Gary M. Gurtler, S.J., for countless hours of conversation; without his advice the shortcomings of this work would have been more obvious than they might be now. To my first mentor in academia and a friend in life, Nicholas Constas, I owe more than I could ever be able to acknowledge. During the last years at BC I have learned from my teachers but also from my students, many of whom, I am sure, are not even aware of their input and contribution to my work. Among them — too many to be listed here — I should thank Christopher Murray for his unexpected, and sometimes all too mystical for me, insights.

I would also like to acknowledge the decisive support of a Charlotte W. Newcombe Dissertation Fellowship (2004); regardless of the honor of becoming the recipient of such a prestigious award, their generous support provided me with a year of undivided dedication to writing. Thanks are due to Merold Westphal and Kevin Hart for reading the manuscript and making a number of useful suggestions, and to my sponsoring editor, Dee Mortensen, for her unwavering attention to this project. Finally, because none of all this would have ever been possible without his indispensable support and friendship, I would like to thank Dr. George Pelayo. *Non intratur in veritatem, nisi per charitatem.*

On the Feast of the Annunciation, 2006

ABBREVIATIONS

Ad Theo	Gregory of Nyssa, *Ad Theophilum*, GNO III
An et res	Gregory of Nyssa, *De Anima et resurrectione*, PG 46
Cant	Gregory of Nyssa, *In canticum canticorum*, GNO VI
CE	Gregory of Nyssa, *Contra Eunomium libri IV*, GNO I and II
CH	Dionysius the Aeropagite, *De Coelesti Hierarchia*, in *Corpus Dionysiacum* II, ed. Günter Heil and Adolf Martin Ritter (Berlin: Walter de Gruyter, 1991)
DN	Dionysius the Aeropagite, *De Divinis Nominibus*, in *Corpus Dionysiacum* I, ed. Beater Regina Suchla (Berlin: Walter de Gruyter, 1990)
Hex.	Gregory of Nyssa, *Apologia in Hexaemeron*, GNO IV 1
GNO	Werner W. Jaeger et al., *Gregorii Nysseni Opera* (Leiden: Brill, 1960–1996)
Inscr	Gregory of Nyssa, *In inscriptions Psalmorum*, GNO V
PG	J. P. Migne, *Patrologia Cursus Completus, Series Graeca* (Paris: 1857–1866)
Sanct Pasch	Gregory of Nyssa, *In sanctum Pascha*, GNO IX
Trid spat	Gregory of Nyssa, *De tridui . . . spatio*, GNO IX

God after Metaphysics

Introduction

The guiding question of this work is "How can we think God *after* meta-physics?" I would like, however, to add immediately a caveat: the word "after" here does not necessarily mean "against" or "without." I take "after" in the following three senses: (a) as posterior *(post)* in order, chronological or otherwise, (b) as accordance *(secundum)*, in the sense that we say that a painting is after Rubens, and (c) as pursuance *(petitio)*, in the sense of one "going after" something, or "being after" someone — a quest, but also a questioning. This means that the thought of God sought here is to be at once, according to the metaphysical tradition *(secundum)*, and yet different or otherwise *(post)* than this tradition. This can occur only through a questioning *(petitio)* of our conceptual cluster of divine attributes such as being, omnipresence, omnipotence, omniscience, actuality, and eternity. I do not pretend to replace the old metaphysical categories with some other ones, newly discovered perhaps, outside or beyond metaphysics. What I seek, instead, are certain *topoi* within the history of philosophy, notions or paradigms that are usually less emphasized and often overlooked or forgotten. The thinking of God that will emerge through such a topology is that of a personal God rather than a conceptual one; a God to be reached through the relationships generated by the *prosopon* and the icon; a God that exists in the temporality of the *kairos* and appears in the sudden moment of the *exaiphnes* (part 1); a God who is better understood by the doxological language of praise and in the music of hymns rather than by the systematic *logos* of theology (part 2); a God, finally, that touches us and scandalously invites us to touch Him back: inaugurating an entirely new order of knowledge as the hiatus between the Self and the Other, the abysmal subject/object dualism effortlessly vanishes in the chiasm of the touch (part 3).

The term "aesthetics" also, as it is used in the subtitle and throughout this work — it should be immediately emphasized — has little to do with the beautiful as understood by that branch of philosophy that deals with the notion of beauty and the fine arts (inaugurated by Alexander Gottlieb Baumgarten in the late eighteenth century). It is rather used in its original Greek sense of *aisthanomai*: to feel by means of one's senses. This is the meaning that the term "aesthetics" has in Kant's first *Critique*, for example. In the very beginning of that section of *The Critique of Pure Reason* entitled "Transcendental Aesthetics," Kant defines "aesthetics" as "sensibility," that is, "the capacity (receptivity) for receiving representations through the mode in which we are affected by objects" (A19). Following Kant's definition, then, we could describe *Theological Aesthetics* as precisely that field which Kant's "Transcendental Aesthetics" had always excluded: that field that would consider God as a *possible* "object" of experience (B73). A field that would explore the possibility of God to be given; an "intuition" of God, if you like — be it maximalistic or minimalistic — an intuition that would not be immediately paired with understanding to produce concepts, but rather, it will leave behind whatever concepts understanding has formed in order to relocate the encounter with God in this *capacity to receive* — a capacity performed by our senses. Theological Aesthetic presented here, then, aspires to bring God back to the human flesh, and by doing so, by reenacting the incarnational event (precisely thanks to the historical Incarnation), we will be able to respond to Kant's challenging axiom that "intuitions without concepts are blind" (A51/B75). (The first part of this work, thus, quite properly, discusses a blind vision.)

At the same time, however, it is the rapture of the beautiful, or as the Greeks understood it,[1] the call *(kaleo)* that the beautiful *(to kalon)* has first extended to us that enables our response in terms of sensibility and receptivity, in terms of aesthetics. This double principle of aesthetics, as the perception of the sensible and as the attraction that the sensible exercises in order to be perceived, constitutes the theoretical backbone of Hans Urs von Balthasar's *The Glory of the Lord*,[2] a work that bears as a subtitle the indication "A Theological Aesthetics." As homage to von Balthasar's thought and in acknowledgment of my indebtedness to it, I have chosen to keep the same subtitle for the present work.

"Aesthetics," Heidegger writes in the epilogue to his "Origin of the Work of Art," "treated the artwork as an object, as indeed an object of *aesthesis*, of sensory apprehension in a broad sense. These days, such apprehension is called an 'experience.'"[3] The casting, however, of the beautiful as the "object" of the aesthetic experience, even more, the very concept of such an aesthetic experience, has brought art to its death. Again, as Heidegger writes, "experience is the element in which art dies." On this assessment Heidegger cites Hegel's proclamation of art as "a thing of the past."[4] Was not, perhaps, the death of art a precondition of its objectification and its subsequent elevation into a "science," that is, into aesthetics? Could not, in other words, art become a science only if first it had become an object?

The death of art is brought about by the forgetfulness of the beautiful, or more precisely, by our "deafness" to the call of the beautiful *(to kalon)*. In another work where Heidegger discusses art, he writes,

> As soon as man lets himself be bound by Being in his view upon it, he is cast beyond himself, so that he is stretched, as it were, between himself and Being and is outside himself. Such elevation beyond oneself and such being drawn toward Being itself is *eros*. Only to the extent that Being is able to elicit "erotic" power in its relation to man is man capable of thinking about Being and overcoming oblivion of Being.[5]

This is a remarkable passage — if only because Heidegger seems here to attribute an erotic quality to Being. Even so, however, how is it possible for Being to elicit an erotic attraction in man? Heidegger borrows his answer for Plato's *Phaedrus:* as that which is beautiful. "Hence it is the beautiful that snatches us from oblivion of Being and grants the view upon Being."[6] The beautiful as the most manifest *(to ekphanestaton)* is also the loveliest *(to erasmiotaton)* (*Phaedrus,* 250d); this dual character results in the ecstasy (quite literally as ek-stasis, "being outside of oneself") described by Heidegger in the passage above. Without this erotic ecstasy one could never see the manifestation of the beautiful (but, perhaps, only the "beautiful" object of aesthetics) — and without perception one would never leave oneself behind, drawn in this rapture of beauty.

Opposed to the experience of "aesthetics" (understood precisely as science of the experience of the object of art), I propose this double character of *aesthesis* (as an ekstasis enabling manifestation and a manifestation leading to ekstasis) which would require the articulation of a new paradigm, quite contrary to that of experience, namely, that of counter-experience[7] (especially for a *theological* aesthetic, as the one that concerns us here, since God could never give Himself as an object for our experience). If in the structure of artistic experience we find the vestiges of Platonism, in aesthetic counter-experience we encounter the antinomy of the Incarnation. Indeed, the inversion of Platonism, which Nietzsche sought with such intensity, was achieved only with Christianity.[8] If it is the hierarchy of the sensuous to the supersensuous that sums up Platonism (as the inferior relation of a copy to its original), then the Christology of Chalcedon cannot be seen as anything less than a fatal blow against it. For the Incarnation does not merely invert the Platonic scheme by placing the sensuous "above" and by bringing the supersensuous here "below" (as many immanentist philosophies nowadays claim to do), or even by abolishing the supersensuous altogether for the sake of the sensuous — such inversions would have left Platonism intact insofar as they maintain the hierarchy of a "below" and an "above."[9] Christianity goes further than that: when Paul asserts Christ as "the image of the invisible God" (Col. 1:15) he does not wish to reiterate the Platonic model of a visible image reflecting its invisible original (the Ideas). Rather, what Paul says is far more radical — he declares that without image there can be no original, as without the Son there is no Father. He says that the Father has chosen to make Himself manifest in the Son with Whom He is One. One does not have to take these claims in their doctrinal authority in order to appreciate their import for philosophy.[10]

* * *

A few words about the structure of this work are in order. Since my goal was to draw a sketch of a theological aesthetic, as defined above, and moreover an aesthetic that would have drawn its principle from the event of the Incarnation, it made eminent sense to follow what can be taken as the very axiom of the Incarnation, namely, the preamble of John's First Epistle: "Him, who was from the beginning, we have seen with our eyes, and we have heard and our hands have touched." Therefore, I decided to divide the work into three parts, one for each of the senses mentioned in John's verse: seeing, hearing, and touching. Next, it remained to decide how many chapters each of these parts would have. Playing with a tradition that distinguishes for each sense the sentient, the sensible, and the medium of the sensing (for example, for the sense of sight, the eye is the sentient, the visible is the sensible, and visibility, or light, the medium of seeing), I assigned to each part a number of chapters equal to the subdivisions of the sense that it represents: three for seeing (part 1), three for hearing (part 2), but only two for touching (part 3), as touch is the only sense that lacks a proper medium, and even more it operates by traversing anything mediating between the tangible and the tactile.

Once I had the structure of the work in place, like a skeleton that needed only to be clothed with flesh and blood, a trip to Madrid presented me with a final clue: during a visit to the Prado Museum I came across the so-called "room of the five senses." That is how the allegorical paintings of Brueghel came to preface each of the parts of this work. Although there are many things that I have learned from these paintings — not least among them, allegory and anagogy — I am most indebted to them for teaching me how to show what cannot be shown by hiding it in plain view. In Brueghel's work I had found an ancestor in the theological aesthetics — what he had conceived and accomplished in terms of his painting the present work aspires to do for philosophy.

* * *

This text makes evident that the two main resources utilized in the following discussion are phenomenology and hermeneutics. The three key structures of this work — seeing, hearing, and touching — function as different horizons within which the phenomenon of God is to be given in accordance (or not) with the consciousness's operations of intentionality and intuition. In any case, the basic layout of my analysis is faithfully phenomenological, even when it ventures to trespass phenomenology's limitations, insofar as its terms and tools remain those of Husserl and his epigones.

At the same time, I do allow myself recourse to the Scriptures, which will be often cited and frequently discussed in the pages of this work — but not necessarily because I see in them the embodiment of any doctrinal truth, but rather because they are texts that, in our tradition, have informed our concepts and ideas about God. The sacred script, more than any other text, calls for hermeneutics, as the long tradition of scriptural commentary and interpretation undoubtedly attests, and that is how I approach and read such texts here.

In spite of these disclaimers, the adjective "theological" has to remain in the subtitle of this work. For the subject matter is, at the end, God; neither one of the religious phenomena, nor religion in general, but God Himself. This, however, should not necessitate the classification of my analysis under the label of "theology" (understood as its own distinct science). By no means is God the exclusive privilege of theology. Since Aristotle's *first philosophy*, if not earlier, God has been a concern, and a central one, indeed, for philosophical thinking. The fact that God figures preeminently in metaphysical thinking is not to be credited, as hastily assumed by many, to the "hijacking" of metaphysics by the Christian Church, but, according to Heidegger, it is due to the inception of metaphysics itself: "the theological character of ontology is not merely due to the fact that Greek metaphysics was later taken up and transformed by the ecclesiastic theology of Christianity. Rather it is due to the manner in which beings as beings have revealed themselves from early on."[11] It is this original revelation of beings in the epochal history of Being that compels us today to think and rethink God *after* Metaphysics through *aesthesis*.

What is at stake, in other words, is an effort to disengage God from His metaphysical commitment to the sphere of transcendence *(epekeina)* by learning to recognize the ways He touches our immanence *(entautha)* — an Incarnational approach through and through. At such an idea, I think, hints Heidegger's reading of an anecdotal passage reported by Aristotle; it relates how some strangers, who had come to visit Heraclitus, found the thinker sitting

near a stove, warming himself. To their surprise and disappointment at finding him in such ordinary circumstances, Heraclitus is said to have extended
the following welcoming words: "Even here there are gods." Heidegger concludes:

> *Kai entautha*, "even here," at the stove, in that ordinary place where every
> thing and every circumstance, each deed and thought is intimate and com-
> monplace, that is, familiar, "even here" in the sphere of the familiar, *einai
> theous*, it is the case that "the gods come to presence."[12]

PART ONE. SEEING

*Him—who was from the beginning— . . . we have seen
with our eyes.*
    —1 John: 1

ALLEGORY 1

The "key," so to speak, in the three allegorical paintings by Brueghel lies invariably in those paintings depicted within each painting. In order to unlock their meaning the viewer needs to look for those "privileged" paintings that Brueghel "hides" within his works. This is, furthermore, the case with every allegory: it invites us to read it (and understand it) on its own terms — from within, we could say, and not by exterior means — as, for example, in the case of an allegorical text: its "solution" should be sought within itself.

In the case of Brueghel's paintings, the painter (or rather the painting in question itself) poses and, at the same time, solves the enigma. The key of the riddle lies within it, hidden in plain sight.

In the first painting I have chosen to discuss here — "Sight" — the process is almost self-evident. Painting itself is one of the visual arts and as such should be included in this celebration of the visual. Therefore, there is nothing surprising, at first sight at least, in finding more paintings within the painting about painting (alongside statues and busts representing sculpture, telescopes and sextants for astronomy, geometrical diagrams and instruments, and, in short, every other thing that appeals to the eye).

However, one painting (Painting B) holds a special position within Brueghel's composition. It is probably the painting that the painter would like to show us, the one that he wishes to call our attention to, but instead of his doing so himself (such a move would indicate a certain lack of tact) he depicts a personage of his painting (a young winged cupid) holding it and offering it to Aphrodite's inspection.

What is this painting all about? It depicts, as a closer look makes clear, the well-known story of the blind man's miraculous healing as recorded in the gospel. How fitting, indeed. At the center of the allegory of sight, an instance of blindness is offered to the speculative gaze of Aphrodite (and ours).

This is nothing short of a stroke of genius on Brueghel's part. In a painting that asphyxiates with objects of vision, that, even further, reproduces visibility's very conditions (the distant landscape that unfolds through one of the room's doors, the interior of the room itself, given in skillful perspective), in that space that includes, substitutes, and exhausts the visual, there the painter places, at its center, the poignant reminder of vision's own limitation: *blindness*.

Let's unfold this tangle of gazes. The painting opens in front of the spectator's gaze offering us everything that the eye can see. In the painting itself, the main personage, Aphrodite, does not look back at the spectator, or, in fact, at any other thing of the many that surround her, but only at this one: a painting about someone who sees nothing. The reduction is a simple one: from the many to the one and from the one to none.

However, insofar as the painting within the painting is about the *healing* of the blind man, his eyes are, for the first time, opened, and his gaze meets the One—thanks to Whom he can now see. In this sense, the blind (and healed) man holds a position symmetrical to Aphrodite's, who is also "blind" to everything around her apart from the one painting showed to her by Eros. Between the vision of the blind man and the "blindness" of Aphrodite we could locate with precision the cut that separates Brueghel's composition into two halves. There we find the exact point of inversion, where vision is blinded and blindness is granted sight. That is the "blind" spot of the painting, the point zero of visibility, where the painting closes itself off and from which the painting opens again up *(punctum caecum)*. Here is how we could render the relation between the two paintings schematically:

Painting A ──────────────────⟶ Painting B

Many ⟹ One ⟹ None   None ⟹ One ⟹ Many

Looking at Brueghel's painting we realize now that our gaze rehearses and repeats the same itinerary: from the many (the plethora of objects depicted in the painting) to the one specific painting that Aphrodite's gaze directs us to.

Then, we are invited to undergo an experience of blindness through the blind man's loss of sight only so that our eyes can open again, at the healing moment, in the One and by the One, through Whom the many (possibilities of seeing the world) are given again anew.

A last question before we leave Brueghel's allegory: why Aphrodite and why Eros? What does the painter's selection of these two personages invite us to think of?

I have already spoken of a sort of a reduction or anagogy that leads us from the many toward the one—a movement parallel to the *scala kallonis* described by Plato in the *Symposium*. Like the lover in Plato, the viewer of Brueghel's work is led from the multitude of beautiful things, through the erotic ascent, toward the Idea of the Beautiful itself (personified here by Aphrodite). However, Brueghel goes a step further than Plato, by supplementing the erotic ascent (from the many to the one) with its counterpart, that is, the kenotic descent of the Lover, Who "comes down to the World" (from the one to the many).

In the first level (Painting A), sight is operated by us (as viewers, that is, the privileged *subject* of the painting); in the second level (Painting B), sight is given to us as a gift, through a blind vision, where we discover ourselves on the inverted side of visibility—as seen, rather than as seers. It is such a vision that I shall discuss in the next three chapters.

one
The Metaphysical Chiasm

Den ihr verehret,
Werdet ihr schauen.

—J. W. von Goethe, *Faust II*, Act V (11,932–11,933)

This field where philosophical thinking runs the greatest risk of losing itself (but also the field where it receives the greatest promise to regain itself) is that which concerns the question of God. The thought of God is, par excellence, that which does *not* belong to thought:[1] the "idea" of God goes beyond the horizon of thinking and exhausts the abilities of thinking. And yet, the thought of God, as a question and as a problem posed to philosophy, is raised always within philosophical thinking, which it endlessly confronts.

The thought of God: what brings forth such a thought if not thinking itself? There are instances in the history of philosophy when the phrase "the thought of God" is mostly understood as an objective genitive: in those cases, the thought of God is *my thought* about God — God is nothing more than the object of that thought. Indeed, the objectification of God is symptomatic of the inability of metaphysics to think God precisely as the possible impossibility of thought, that terminal point where thought "needs to jump lest it falls."

In a sense, for metaphysics God (that is, the idea of God) appears always within the mind; "appears," so to speak of course, because "within the mind" nothing can really *appear*. When one reads what philosophers have to say

13

about God, one is often left with the impression that philosophy (or at least that tradition whose constitution Heidegger criticized as "onto-theo-logical") believes only in the human who creates God "in his image and his likeness" (Gen. 1:27). To a certain extent this is justified; as we will see (in chapter 5), Gregory of Nyssa would advise caution regarding our concepts of God, for everything our intellect conceives about God is ours and not God's. Even Revelation, one could argue, appeared "veiled" in flesh — in what is *ours*. That is why Bernard of Clairvaux writes, "what is seen in Him is ours, but what is heard from Him is His" (*Commentary on the Song of Songs*, XXVIII, 3). The task, therefore, for seeing will be a diacritical one: our vision has to learn to distinguish in Him what is *not* ours.

That "thought of God" is nothing else but the masqueraded thought of man about himself. It is a thought that, after Aristotle, is doomed to think itself. Could we, however, dare to imagine such a thinking that does not contain the thought of God but comes "face-to-face" with Him? Could we ever imagine such a case where God is located within the mind but appears to it? An appearance in which consciousness finds itself surprised by Him who suddenly (ἐξαίφνης) appears? Could we, in other words, think of the phenomenon of God? What could such a phenomenon possibly be like, and how could it be given to consciousness? Could it be ever possible for the I to have *an experience of God*?[2]

The Possibility of the Phenomenon and the Phenomenon of the Possibility

Such an experience will have to satisfy two different — and antithetical — premises. The first mandates that in order to have an experience of God, God would have to be presented to my senses (after all, *omnis cognitio incipit a sensu*). The second, on the other hand, rules out what the first premise speculates as a possibility: any experience of a God palpable by my senses, any such phenomenon that has come under the possessive grasp of my mind has already become *mine* and thus cannot be God anymore — all I am left with is an idol.[3]

Phenomenologically, the tension between these two premises is famously expressed in Husserl's "principle of all principles":

> that *every originary presentive intuition is a legitimizing source of cognition,* that *everything originarily* (so to speak in its "personal" actuality) *offered to us in "intuition" is to be accepted simply as what it is presented as being,* but also *only within the limits in which it is presented there.*[4]

There are two simultaneous gestures in this principle that need to be taken in a Chalcedonian manner, that is, without division, but also, without confusion. The first is the question of *the possibility of the phenomenon*; anything has the right on its own to present itself to my consciousness, and this presencing alone, its very appearance, is "sufficient reason" for phenomena to be accepted as such. The second gesture, which runs in parallel with the first and makes it possible, is precisely the question of *the phenomenon of the possible* itself; what gives anything "sufficient reason" to appear and makes that appearance possible is a "zone of reason" within which each phenomenon, in order to be such, needs to make its appearance. "The question concerning the possibility of the phenomenon," Marion writes, "implies the question of the phenomenon of possibility" (103). What Husserl says epigrammatically in the "principle of all principles" is (1) that with no intuition given to intention there is no possibility for any phenomenon to appear, but also (2) with no intention to receive that intuition there is no phenomenon of any possibility of an appearance. The one is grounded in the other.

And that seems to be the core of the problem, a problem that was radicalized when phenomenology undertook the so-called "turn" to theology. Previously it seemed to make some sense that in order for something to appear it had to "appeal" to my intentional horizon, and thus it had to be grounded on the constituting I. Soon, though, one realizes that such grounding (whatever the appearing "thing" might be: objects, concepts, and fellow humans alike) means that the phenomena are all seen by the I in some kind of symmetry to its own self, a symmetry that indicates, even further, a kind of appropriation. Thus the world becomes a private spectacle for consciousness, a consciousness that is also the absolute director and the exclusive audience of this performance. Husserl himself was aware of the "grave objection" that already arises here, the objection that, as he writes in his *Fifth Cartesian Meditation*, the meditating I will eventually become nothing more than a *solus ipse*.[5] In the ipseity of the I, thus understood, where the I reigns self-same and autistic, there is no room for the Other. The Other suffers injustice and violence, and if the Other under consideration happens to be the wholly Other, the Other par excellence, then things become all the more complex. To ground the groundless and to limit the limitless, to reduce the infinite to finite proportions — what else can better describe this paradox? If God is to remain God (that is, *tout autre*, as Derrida has put it) and not to become an idol erected by my perception and imagination, He needs to prevent Himself from appearing altogether, He rather needs to safeguard His aloofness, so to speak, the height of heights that Levinas so often ascribes to Him or, as others have phrased it, "the right to refuse to appear, [the] right to preserve itself as transcendent and thereby maintain its identity."[6] Thus, the possibility of a religious phenomenon, the possibility of God to appear, is rendered impossible; God Himself *is* (the) impossible. Anything more would amount to an attempt to reduce the otherness of the Other to the sameness of the same.

And yet this reduction is precisely what Husserl adopts as his strategy in order to show that transcendental phenomenology would not degenerate into a transcendental solipsism! A *reduction to one's own ownness*. One can hardly imagine a bolder and more baffling movement. Paul Ricoeur sheds some very helpful light on this issue when he writes:

> for the sense "Other" is drawn from the sense "me" because one must first give sense to "me" and to "my own" in order then to give sense to the "Other" and to the "world of the Other." There is something "alien" (*étranger*) because there is something "own" (*propre*), and not conversely.[7]

The emphasis, I believe, in Ricoeur's comment should not be placed merely on the precedence that the "ownness" takes over the "otherness" but rather in the much more important dependence of the latter on the former, a dependence that furthermore is *inconvertible*. If there is an Other there, it is because there is a "me" here — that is, a dative for the Other's manifestation. That dependence, when applied to the problematic of the possibility of God's phenomenality, simply means that if God is ever given a chance to appear, this would be because of *me*. God, as the ultimate religious phenomenon, is *in need* of the human self as this very *lieu* that gives place to God. Every human self, thus, is understood as the sacred *topos* of God's epiphany.

I understand that a statement like this — an anathema for some — cannot go without some explanation. We will have to take up the thread of our thoughts from the beginning then, and re-pose the question of the possibility within the methodology of phenomenology.

Possibility as such in Husserl is essentially governed by imagination. The possibility of the possible to appear within the intending horizon of my consciousness is determined by the modality of the "as if":[8] that is, the border limits of possibility coincide with the borders of the Subject's imagination. Such a conclusion would immediately mean that everything that falls outside the farthest limits of my imagination is to be understood precisely as the impossible. The impossible, then, has zero possibility ever to appear to me, since it cannot find a ground within either my actual or imaginary experience, and thus it has to be excluded from phenomenology proper. The impossible is, therefore, the non-phenomenon, the *a-phanton*.

That is where the problematic of God's phenomenality is situated. In the case of God, the possibility of His appearance itself is determined by the limits of a horizon (and that is what "horizon" means: the limit), a horizon, furthermore, that by necessity is always *mine*, the horizon of the meaning-constituting I. Everything outside this horizon is thus not only unimaginable and impossible but also *meaningless*. The conviction that nothing could appear beyond this horizon — or, which amounts to the same thing, that even if something were to appear it would be "nothing to me" (*Critique of Pure Reason*, B132) — reflects a Kantian judgment that presupposes the bifurcation of reality into phenomena and noumena. Things stand differently, however, with Plotinus, who, in a celebrated passage from the *Enneads*, writes: "the sun rising over the horizon gives itself to the eyes to see. But from where will he of whom the sun is an image rise? What is the *horizon*, which he will have to surmount when he appears? He will have to surmount the Intellect that contemplates him" (V, 5, 8: 6–10, Armstrong's translation modified). Here consciousness itself is the very horizon that is overwhelmed and surpassed (a theme that deeply resonates with Marion's saturated phenomenon) by what can appear only by means of such overwhelming and surpassing. For when "he" (as Plotinus insists) comes, he comes "as one who did not come" (V, 5, 8: 15), and the *nous* that sees him sees him only "when it does not see" (V, 5, 7: 29).

Nevertheless, I will somehow have to "see" God in order to have His appearance registered as experience. I will have to "see" Him either with the senses of my body or in the free play of my imagination. Why? Because these are the only two ways that any Other — including the wholly Other — can possibly appear to me. To continue with my reading of the *Fifth Cartesian Meditation*, the reduction to the sphere of "ownness" (which was Husserl's first step toward the "opening" of the consciousness to the presence and experience of the Other) becomes, a few pages later, *incarnated* to my body:

> Let us assume that another man enters our perceptual sphere. Primordially reduced, that signifies: In the perceptual sphere pertaining to my primordial Nature, a body is presented, which, as primordial, is of course only a determining part of myself: an "immanent transcendency." Since, in this Nature and this world, my animate organism is the only body that is or can be constituted originally as an animate organism (a functioning organ), the body over there, which is nevertheless apprehended as an animate organism, must have derived this sense by an *apperceptive transfer from my animate organism* . . . It is clear from the very beginning that only a similarly connecting, within my primordial sphere, that body over there with my body can serve as the motivational basis for the *"analogizing" apprehension* of that body as another animate organism. (§50, 110–111)

But it is not only the sphere of perception (or apprehension in this case) that, through appresentation and the analogous pairing of bodies, can give me a hint into the otherness of the Other. In the sphere of imagination also I can, through free variation, expose myself to possibilities that open up the mode of *otherwise: If I were there*, which soon comes to take the proportions of an *If I were the Other*:

> As reflexively related to itself, my animate bodily organism (in my primordial sphere) has the central "Here" as its mode of givenness; every other body, and accordingly the "other's" body, has the mode "There" . . . By free modification of my kinesthesias, particularly those of locomotion, I can change my position in such a manner that I convert any There into a Here . . . I do not apperceive the other ego simply as a duplicate of myself and accordingly as having my original sphere or one completely like mine. I do not apperceive him as having, more particularly, the spatial modes of appearance that are mine from here; rather, as we find on closer examination, I apperceive him as having spatial modes of appearance like those I should have if I should go over there and be where he is. (§53, 116–117)

The analogical apprehension of the Other reminds us of the *analogia entis* of scholastic philosophy, but that is exactly where the problem lies: I cannot apperceive God analogically in the same way that I see the (human) Other since such apperception will do injustice to God due to the fundamental asymmetry that exists between me and God.[9] To mention just one example in order to illustrate the difficulty: I have a body that allows me, by analogy, to "experience" the Other's perception of his or her body. God, however, is bodiless[10]—an observation that, no matter how self-evident it may sound, nevertheless poses the following crucial set of questions: how can I, a finite consciousness, perceive the infinite? In which ways, if any, could the I have an intuition of the infinite, the impossible, the unimaginable? In which mode could the infinite give itself to my intention? There is a passage from the book of Kings that may give us some answers:

> Then the Lord said to Elijah: "Go outside and stand on the mountain before the Lord; the Lord will be passing by." A strong and heavy wind was rending the mountains and crushing rocks before the Lord — but the Lord was not in the wind. After the wind there was an earthquake — but the Lord was not in the earthquake. After the earthquake there was fire — but the Lord was not in the fire. (1 Kings 19:11–12a)

What we have in this description is a paradigmatic case of failure in achieving the necessary adequation between intention (Elijah's expectation to see God passing by) and intuition (the appearance of God that is given nowhere). The possibility of the phenomenon needs the underlying phenomenon of possibility. Without the matching of these two modes, Husserl insists, there is no evidence produced: the Lord was not there, and Elijah's intentionality remains unfulfilled. God did not give Himself there, where He was most expected: the strong wind, the earthquake, the fire. In the scriptural story God appears at last but in a way that signals the paradox, and the impossibility perhaps of His manifestation: "After the fire there was a tiny whispering sound. When he heard this, Elijah hid his face in his cloak" (I Kings 19:12b–13). God therefore appears and yet He remains nevertheless *imperceptible*. A tiny whispering sound of wind, a breeze in other words, is precisely what passes unnoticed, that which does not announce itself. It signifies a bare minimum of givenness (in other words, a minimalistic phenomenology that, paradoxically, can provide the ground for a maximalistic aesthetics, as the one we are exploring in this work). And yet, even in this way, it must be something harmful enough for Elijah, the scripture tells us, to hide his face in apprehension.[11]

There is a series of questions involved here that we can start untangling beginning with the scriptural passage just cited. If one looks in the Bible for other occasions of divine manifestation one can find a whole variety. Let us take the example of the Pentecost (in the narration recorded in the book of Acts): God appears there in a totally different way from the gentle whispering wind in Elijah's cave, although it is again a wind, this time a "strong, driving wind" that is heard throughout the city as it breaks down from the sky suddenly (ἄφνω, a variation of ἐξαίφνης, Acts 2:2–3). It seems then that God can choose from a whole repertoire of epiphanies, from an idol to an icon and from a trace to a saturated phenomenon. None of these, however, will ever give us the entire God-phenomenon as such, in that all of the theophanies to be found in Greek, Judaic, or Christian sources, no matter how opaque or elusive, are made possible by means of an *as if*—that is, they are made possible by means of hypothesis, imagination, representation, signification—all of which are modalities operated by the I. Revelations and apparitions of God, saturated or otherwise, still have to be perceived somehow and by someone. They have to be seen and felt somatically (to return to the Husserlian principle), they have to become *incarnated* in certain figures, schemes, colors, sounds, and smells if they want to be epiphanies at all (*epi-phany* is what appears, *phainesthai*, to or upon someone and, thus, still a phenomenon).[12] Prophets and mystics speak of their visions in metaphors, in similes, and in narrations—that is, they process them through language in order to be experienced by them and communicated to others. All these, though, constitute horizons, conditions as they are, that exclude the possibility of any "pure," unconditional giving of God:

> We believe that the apparition of the transcendent nature (τῆς ὑπερεχούσης φύσεως) took place always according to the degree of capacity (κατὰ τὸ μέτρον τῆς δυνάμεως) of those who received the divine epiphany. For it was greater and more divine to those who were capable of reaching such heights, but it was lesser and rather ordinary (σμικροπρεπεστέρα) to those who could not contain more.[13]

Gregory is setting here a principle that will become the canonical position not only of mystical experience but of all experience of God: God always gives Himself, but He does so by respecting each one's unique disposition.[14] He never gives more than one could receive or less than one would be pleased with. He is to be found in exceptional phenomena (where one would expect His presence) but also there where He is unexpected, in ordinary everydayness. It was this proportionality of divine manifestation that prompted God's ultimate Revelation (a paradoxical revelation, as it hides what it is supposed to reveal) in the flesh of a Nazarene Man:

> If, indeed, it was possible for all of us to be in the darkness in which Moses saw the invisible things, or if it was possible to be lifted up in the third heaven like the sublime Paul and be taught in paradise about the things that are ineffable and beyond reason, or [if it was possible] to be taken by fire in the ethereal sphere like the zealot Elijah, without the weight of the body drawing us down, or [if it was possible] like Ezekiel and Isaiah to see on the throne of glory Him who is carried by the Cherubim and praised by the Seraphim, then, *there would have been no need at all for God's epiphany in flesh* [οὐδ᾽ ἂν ἐγένετο πάντως χρεία τῆς διὰ σαρκὸς τοῦ Θεοῦ ἡμῶν ἐπιφανείας].[15]

Inverse Intentionality

Phenomenology, however, ought to allow only one exclusion, and that is the exclusion of exclusion. This seems to be Marion's wager throughout the *Saturated Phenomenon*, where he takes the decisive step to invert the Husserlian model and, thus, to envisage a phenomenon saturated with intuition — that is, an intuition that exceeds and overwhelms any intention:

> Having arrived at this point, we can pose the question of a strictly inverse hypothesis: in certain cases still to be defined, must we not oppose to the restricted possibility of phenomenality a phenomenality that is in the end absolutely possible? To the phenomenon that is supposed to be impoverished in intuition can we not oppose a phenomenon that is saturated with intuition? To the phenomenon that is most often characterized by an effect of intuition, and therefore by a deception of the intentional aim and, in particular instances, by the equality between intuition and intention, why would there not correspond the possibility of a phenomenon in which intuition would give *more, indeed immeasurably more,* than intention ever would have intended or foreseen? (112)

A few paragraphs later he gives a more detailed definition of what we should expect a saturated phenomenon to be: "it will therefore be *invisible* according to quantity, *unbearable* according to quality, *absolute* according to relation, and *incapable* of being looked at according to modality" (113). One can legitimately object to this parade of negations that push phenomenology, and along with it all human experience, to its limits by asking: Does anything remain to be seen, perceived, or experienced? And how can we go ahead and live our life once we take a look at this deserted scene, saturated as it is, with excess? Indeed, we cannot live. "Thou canst not see my face, for no man shall see me and live" (Exod. 33:20). This is an age-old question, a dream saturated with agony, an anxiety that has haunted the prophet's vision: "Who may abide the day of His coming, and who shall stand when He appeareth?" (Mal. 3:2). Accordingly, it would be hard to imagine the subject of such an experience surviving the overwhelming confrontation with the excess of the saturated phenomenon. Marion himself is aware of this danger, as he recognizes a certain degree of blinding caused by the intensity of the unbearable spectacle (114). In that way, unconditional, horizonless, and unmediated "experience" of God can become the only possible impossibility since, if it were ever to take place, it would result in the vanishing of the subject. Elijah hid his face, and so did Moses; perhaps they knew better.

Therefore, it would seem that if we were to have an experience of God we are left with the following two options: either God is reduced to the modalities of the *as* and the *if,* conditioned by the Subject's imagination and experience (but then, we are running the risk of turning God into an idol), or He is to appear unconditionally in all His excessive glory but at the subject's own risk.

However, is the subject absolutely indispensable for my experience of God? What necessity dictates that experience in general is limited by my subjectivity? The middle voice of experience (both *experior* in Latin and πειράομαι in Greek are deponent verbs) indicates that the subject acts, but, at the same time, it undergoes (reflexively) its own action, as if it were its own object. A more philosophically accurate grammar of experience should require the subject to be placed not only in the nominative (I) but in the accusative (me) as well.

Jean-Paul Sartre's discussion of a typical instance of intersubjective encounter provides some useful evidence toward a reevaluation of the role of subjectivity in my experience of the Other. In Sartre's phenomenological analysis of the look we witness a reversal of the fundamental principle of seeing. Given that every look is reciprocal, Sartre writes, when I see the Other there is always the possibility to be seen by the Other as well. As far as I see the Other like this man who passes by the benches in a public park or as this beggar at the corner of the street, I see him or her as an *object*. The Other becomes really Other only at the crucial moment that *I am seen by the Other*. When I cease seeing the Other and allow him or her to see *me* (in a wonderful exchange of reciprocal gazes), then the Other leaves the realm of a thing among other things and regains his or her status as a "subject" in relation and communion with me (who, in turn, I become decentered and vulnerable in my relation with the Other).[16] *Then, when what I do* not *see stands higher than what I see, then the Other is allowed to appear.*[17]

The look of the Other surprises us. It forces us to become suddenly aware of ourselves: "First of all, I now exist as *myself* for my unreflective consciousness. It is this irruption of the self which has been most often described: I see *myself* because *somebody* sees me."[18] In the look of the Other it is not only the Other who is given to us, but in the most paradoxical way, our very own self becomes apparent.

Thus the ego undergoes a split into the constituting I and the constituted Me. The first two possibilities of God's appearance already described above appealed to the constituting I and are regulated by it. There, I am the subject and God is expected to appear as the object of my consciousness, in the mode of the "as if." The saturated phenomenon, however, in overwhelming the subject with excess, could offer us a first glimpse of a phenomenological account of non-subjective experience. Such an experience will pave the way to a third possibility for God's appearance, one that is opened up by the look of the Other, where it is God that acts as the subject to whom the I appears — yet this "I" is no longer the constituting I, but rather an I that has been put in the accusative, that is, the constituted Me.

Could this, then, be a third way that will allow God to appear without compromising His otherness? Could we think of a phenomenology where the I does *not* look and does *not* see but experiences the Other's look? When the I instead of seeing is seen, when it discovers itself caught in the horizon of God, when it is the I that appears to God and not God that appears to the I? Could it be, then, that I can finally "see" God even if it is with eyes *shut*?[19]

I am, thus, able to gaze upon God's countenance but only as *videre videor*,[20] or even better, as *videntem videre*.[21] As far as we remain within the realm of *videre* we are seeking to see God by reproducing the modality of *intelligere* (comprehension): to see is to know, and our claim to *see* God is the masqueraded desire of our failing attempt to *know* God. To "see" God, however, in the moment of being seen *(videor)* by Him means to pass from the mode of *intelligere* to that of *sentire*: to "feel" God as one feels someone when touched (as discussed in the third part of this work). We cannot "touch" something without, at the same time, by the very same gesture, being touched back. In the touch there is an irrevocable reciprocity that surpasses by far any evidence produced by seeing. A reciprocity that offers us a "knowledge" more secure and indubitable than any conceptual abstraction. A reciprocity that situates the knowledge of the Other back into my body and, by means of this body, the distance from the Other is somehow bridged and the difference from the Other becomes less.

In his exposition of concrete cases of saturation, Marion, discussing the phenomenological appeal of painting (under the heading of "the Idol"), writes that "only a *face*" can look at us "because it alone comes to expose itself in the mode of encounter."[22] In the encounter with the Other, "the other takes the status of a me other than me . . . it is necessary, in order to appear to me as such that the other manifests me in exercising on me an intentionality as original as mine. In this way the *face* arises — a *counter intentionality*."[23] For Marion the Other can appear to me only in "another way"—other than the way of an "idol"; he names that way (the way of counter-intentionality) "that of the icon."[24] That is why it is in the chapter on the icon that Marion returns to the theme of counter-intentionality in order to flesh out more fully its ways of operation. There Marion, once he has rehearsed the paradoxical logic that governs the different types of saturated phenomena, groups "the icon of the other person" under those phenomena "that cannot be looked at," according to their modality, phenomena "that escape all relation with thought in general."[25] And he explains:

> I cannot have vision of these phenomena, because I cannot constitute them starting from a univocal meaning, and even less produce them as objects. What I see of them, if I see anything of them that *is*, does not result from the constitution I would assign to them in the visible, but *from the effect they produce on me*. And, in fact, this happens *in reverse* so that my look is submerged, in a *counter-intentional* manner. Then I am no longer the transcendental *I* but rather the witness, constituted by what happens to him or her. Hence the para-dox, inverted *doxa*. In this way, the phenomenon that befalls and happens to us *reverses* the order of visibility in that it no longer results from my intention but from its own *counter-intentionality*.[26]

Perhaps this explains the uneasiness that we often feel when we look at an icon. The uneasiness that comes from the realization that He has seen us even before we looked at Him, that it is His gaze that first addresses us and not ours turned on Him, and that this gaze, a piercing gaze that springs forth from the enlarged eyes and penetrates our bodies, will follow us as we go through our days. Referring to the icon at this point of our discussion is far from accidental. Artistically, it has been noted, the icon embodies this turn from the point of *seeing* to that of *being seen* in a unique way. This turn is aptly expressed by a shift in perspective whose technical name, *umgekehrte Perspektive*, suggests just that: the inverse or inverted perspective.[27] To the inversion of the classical phenomenological model (intentionality) corresponds the inversion of the classical representational perspective. The model that the iconic technique inverts is the one that the Renaissance had mastered: the background of the painting is delineated by a horizontal line into which every point vanishes — thus the false impression of depth takes effect. Anything close to the observer assumes its "real-life" dimensions, but to the extent that it distances itself away from that privileged point of view, it is engulfed by the voracious distance that yawns between the viewer and that remote horizon. The icon, on the other hand, projects this horizon outwards, behind and beyond the viewer toward whom it always extends itself. There is nothing — no horizon — to be seen behind the depicted person in the icon, because the horizon is now on the other side, *our* side (as predicted by Plotinus in the passage quoted above). But by relocating its perspective, by exteriorizing it, the icon demands *not* to be seen — if anything, it is the icon that sees. The icon, strictly speaking then, refuses to be the *object* of our observation (it is not accidental that an icon invariably depicts a *subject*, that is, a *person*), it denies our claims to turn it into an object for our eyes, it is *we* — as accusative us — who appear to the icon and not vice versa.

Since at least the early 1980s, Marion's work has been decisive in helping us to endow terms like "icon" and "idol" with a distinctive value in philosophical currency. The opening chapter of his *God without Being*[28] announces that icon and idol "disclose a phenomenological conflict — a conflict between two phenomenologies" (GWB, 7). Both terms signal "two manners of being for beings" (GWB, 8), two rather antithetical ways according to which a being appears to be. Their difference is spelled out by Marion as follows: "Whereas the idol results from the gaze that aims at it, the icon summons sight in letting the visible be *saturated* little by little with the invisible" (GWB, 17; my emphasis). Anticipating, thus, his later analysis of the saturated phenomenon,[29] he writes of the icon not only as that mode of visibility that presents the invisible (while remaining such) but also as the precise *inversion* in the mode of seeing (akin to an inverted intentionality): "[T]he gaze no longer belongs here to the man who aims as far as the first visible, less yet to an artist; such a gaze here belongs to the icon itself, where the invisible only becomes visible . . . The icon regards us, it *concerns* us" (GWB, 19; emphasis in the original).[30]

Icons are only one example of how and where we can experience the look of God. It is also to be found in every other fellow human that we encounter in our everyday life. The wholly Other (*tout autre* à la Derrida) is incarnated into *this* Other.[31] His or her face bespeaks the authority of God's look, the same inexhaustible quality that comes from beyond and challenges our actions: it is the face of the Other that prohibits violence and demands respect. Marion attests to an affinity between the icon and the face: "The icon opens in a face . . . One even must venture to state that only the icon shows us a face (in other words, that every face is given as an icon)" (GWB, 19). Hence the interchangeable usage of the terms *eikon* (icon) and *prosopon* (face, person) in patristic theology (we will return to the relation between these two terms and their position in patristic thought in the third part of this chapter).

The face of the Other creates that space where relations take place. It is not an accident, then, that Husserl, as soon as he opens the discussion to the analysis of transcendental intersubjectivity, abandons the terminology of the *monad*, a term borrowed from Leibniz, and adopts that of the *person*. Paul Ricoeur aptly registers this change:

> It also appears that the person is completely constituted only at this level [of transcendental intersubjectivity], which represents a source of interiorization for these cultural worlds. Thus, the person, in Husserl, is synonymous neither with the ego nor even with "man" (Husserl always speaks of man in relation to the psyche, consequently still on the naturalist level). Rather, *the person is correlative to the community* and its "habitual properties."[32]

Community is the mode of existence of the person, and, accordingly, a person exists only as belonging to a community. But how can the look of the Other be related to the communal existence of the person? A person *essentially* designates a being that is open to the Other's look. To fully comprehend this intrinsic relation between the mode of being-a-person and the mode of being-seen-by-the-Other we will need only to refer to the etymology of the Greek word *prosopon* (πρόσωπον). The term *prosopon* (the Greek equivalent for person) denotes a self open to the look of the Other and, even more, constituted by that look. Personhood is not a once-and-for-all given that we individually possess, but rather a process of creation occasioned by a continuous and mutual exposure to the Other.

A Hermeneutics of the *Prosopon*

Aesthetics

We usually translate *prosopon* as "face" and hence as "person." Indeed, *prosopon* is the face and the person, but it means much more than that. Let us say that the term is used exclusively with the verb "to be" and never with the verb "to have." It only makes sense to say that someone *is* a *prosopon*. To say that someone *has* a *prosopon* diminishes the term into something that someone possesses, namely, a mask. What does it mean to be a *prosopon*? "Pros" means *toward, in front of,* and "opos" (the genitive of the noun ὤψ) means a face, and especially an eye (as in our word "optics"). As such, to be a *pros-opon* means nothing more than *to be-toward-a-face,* to stand *in front of someone's face,* to be present in her or his presence and in her or his vision.

We should not let go unnoticed the fact that in classical Greek literature the term *prosopon* only rarely occurs in the form that we are using here, that is, in its singular form. Homer, for example, seems to prefer the plural form, *prosopa,* even when he is referring to a single person (e.g., *Iliad* VII.211–12). The plural upsets the strict rules of grammar and the structure of syntax, since the single subject of a sentence is modified by a noun in the plural. This is only one example, but it has dramatic effects when we observe its various instances throughout the poetry of Homer (e.g., *Iliad* XVIII.414, *Odyssey* XIX.361) and Sophocles (*Electra* 1277, *Oedipus at Colonus* 314). The Greek language is too strict to allow such an anomaly to occur without good reason. Perhaps, since *prosopon,* by definition, cannot exist solely as one person, it always needs (and always refers to) at least another person and the relationship between them. Being-toward-a-face always presupposes the Other, in front of whom we stand. This Other, in turn, by standing in front of me, has to be a *prosopon* as well.

Both components of the term show some interesting characteristics. First, let us examine the preposition "*pros.*" To be a *pros*-opon means to be on your way toward the Other. This also situates my being in a perpetual *ek-sistence* (i.e., existence as ecstasy), a stepping-out-of-myself and a being-toward-the-Other. *Prosopon,* as a term that indicates the reciprocal movement toward the Other, underscores the ecstatic character of the personal *(prosopic)* relationship. The gaze and the face of the Other, in front of whom I stand, invite me to this exodus to the unknown, unknowable, and yet promised land of the Other. The step toward this land, however, also amounts to a step away from everything familiar, from myself, a self that I am called to leave behind me. The abandonment of the Same for the sake of the Other locates my existence as this passage from what I once was, but am not any more, to what I am to become but am not yet. Between these two poles I belong nowhere as I am to be found in none. *Prosopon* strongly implies the reciprocity of gaze through which the self is interpellated by the Other and, ultimately, "othered." The passage toward the Other leaves my existence vulnerable to the fear and trembling of the infinite possibilities that await me. In this sense, the dynamic (i.e., full of potential) character of the person makes "the possible" a personal *(prosopic)* category par excellence. Personhood, far from being a synonym for selfhood or identity, is never to be understood as a fait accompli or a once-and-for-all given that somehow we possess. Rather, to be a person suggests a process continuously occasioned by the unreserved exposure to the Other.

Perhaps we could grasp better the semantics of the *prosopon* by juxtaposing it with its opposite. The antonym of a *prosopon* is described in the Greek language by the term *atomon*. *Prosopon* and *atomon* seem to be the two diametrically opposite poles that exhaust the existential possibilities open to a human being. To be an *atomon* means to be in fragmentation (from the privative prefix "a-" and the verb *temno*, to cut; therefore, the a-tomic is that which cannot be cut any further). As in the English language, the in-dividual is one who has been "divided" so many times that he or she has reached this point where no further split is possible. The individual stands in sharp opposition to the *prosopon*. Where the latter gathers and unites, the former cuts off, separates, alienates, and negates. Where, then, does the individual belong? One could say that it belongs to Hades, the place of non-being, the underworld, the place where there is no *seeing*. Ἅιδης properly names the place where there is neither gaze nor face, where the possibility to see the Other, face-to-face, has disappeared and along with it the dynamics of being a *prosopon* and of being as such. Hades is surrounded by the river Lethe; *a-letheia*, therefore, has no place there. This is the reign of existential death. As Kearney, reversing Sartre, puts it, the only hell in this scenario is that of self condemned to self. "The empty choosing will. The idolatry of each-for-itself."[33]

Ethics

Kierkegaard calls the individualism of the *atomon* the demonic. In his discussion of anxiety about the good, he makes clear that the demonic is defined by the very rejection of relationship and communion. "The demonic is unfreedom that wants to close itself off," solipsistic enclosedness (*det Indeslut-tede*) that "closes itself up within itself."[34] In contradistinction to the ecstatic movement of the *prosopon*, the demonic remains withdrawn in this lonely prison made up by the fragments of a mirror that reflect back the selfsame images of itself. Condemned to this monotonous existence, we should not be surprised by Kierkegaard's apt observation that monologue and soliloquy are the modes of demonic expression and that the discontinuity of the sudden[35]—always the same, without memory or expectation—becomes the form of its manifestation.[36] A last but telling point: the demonic does not "partake of communion" (*communicere*), which means that it does not communicate, but also (and it is Kierkegaard himself who invites us to think of this sense) that it does not receive communion.[37]

With regard to the ethical considerations of personhood, then, let us say that the *prosopon* resists being used as a tool or as the means toward an end. In the *prosopon* we are not allowed to see the Other as serving the fulfilment of our intentions or our desires. There are two types of desire that we need to differentiate with regard to the *prosopon*: the desire *of* the Other and the desire *for* the Other. A lover of pleasures, who sees in the Other a body given for his satisfaction, sees *only* that (and therefore, he misses the person, for he reduces the otherness of the Other into his own desire). Similarly, the money lover, who sees in the Other the means of making a profit, reduces the person to a customer or a client, stripping him or her of any other personal characteristic.

These descriptions formulate modes of seeing the Other as "this" or "that," in which the Other "is," or rather "becomes," what I desire him or her to be. Our desire prevents the Other as such from appearing, or according to Heidegger's expression, to "show itself in itself" (*Being and Time*, 28). Thus, our desire finds in others "only what we ourselves put into them" (*Critique of Pure Reason*, Bxviii). And that means that, in my desire of the Other, the otherness of the Other is lost, the Other gradually ceases to be any other (different) from me. Insofar as the Other reflects back my desire, he becomes the narcissistic idol of myself. I am freed from this desire only by the desire *for* the Other (in opposition to the possessive genitive of the "of," the "for" here hits at the ecstatic movement of the *prosopon*: outside of oneself and toward the Other, so one can finally meet the Other, not in the "here" of my sameness but "there" where the Other resides).

Poetically, the *prosopic* relationship has found its best expression so far in Paul Celan's saying *Ich bin du, wenn ich ich bin* (from the poem "Lob der Ferne"). This is a cry of almost erotic anguish that the *prosopon* addresses to its Other, recognizing in him or her the source of itself — "I am *you*, when I am myself," or as Paul writes in his *Letter to Galatians*, "I no longer live, but Christ lives in me" (2:20). *Contra* Heidegger's analysis of authenticity, what constitutes the core of my authentic existence is not the "mineness" or the "ownness" (*Eigentlichkeit*) of the being that concerns me "which is always *mine*" (*Being and Time*, 42), but rather, the Other and the paradoxical understanding that I *am* only insofar as the Other is. Or, put differently, I am mine only insofar as I am his.[38] That is why, to the ecstatic/erotic confession of the *prosopon*, the voice of the Other can respond with these strange words: *sis tu tuus et ego ero tuus* — "be yours and I will be yours as well" (Nicholas of Cusa, *De Visione Dei*, vii, 25).

Religion

Already through the title of his work, *De Visione Dei*, Nicholas of Cusa lets the ambiguity of the double genitive to be heard — for this will become the very ambiguity of *the vision of God*, to be defined as a seeing (of God) and being seen (by God):

> What other, O Lord, is your seeing, when you look upon me with the eye of mercy, than your being seen by me? In seeing me you, who are the hidden God, give yourself to be seen by me. No one can see you except in the measure you grant to be seen. Nor is your being seen other than your seeing one who sees you (V, 13).[39]

The principle behind this understanding of the vision of God is that of the inverted intentionality. I can see God only by means of being seen by Him. It is far from being an accident, then, that Nicholas of Cusa takes an icon as the point of departure and, indeed, the center of his speech. A speech that does what it says and effects what it describes, for as soon as his speech turns to the subject of the vision of God, Cusanus delivers his entire essay not anymore as a speech *about* the icon, but as a speech addressed *to* an icon. For Cusanus, the theology of God's vision cannot be separated from a theology of the icon.

Cusanus's text seems to allude to a passage in Genesis where Hagar, Abraham's maid and mother of Ishmael, encounters God. The passage reads as follows: "Then, she called the name of the Lord who spoke to her, You-Are-the-God-Who-Sees; for she said, Have I also here seen Him who sees me?" (16:13). The Greek text of the Septuagint has ἐνώπιον εἶδον for the name of God. And Hagar names the well by which God spoke to her "Beer-lahai-roi," which is also rendered into Greek as ἐνώπιον εἶδον. The word *enopion* (ἐνώπιον) literally means "face-to-face" (according to Liddell-Scott), and it shares the same etymological root as *prosopon* (πρόσωπον). The God who speaks to Hagar and whom she calls The-God-Who-Sees is a personal God, namely, a God who allows His face to be seen by him or her who, called into being by this face-to-face relationship with Him, is given the status of a person (*prosopon*). To "see" His Face consists precisely in being seen by Him.

But who is this face?

> The Biblical experience of God in both the Old and the New Testaments is characterized as a whole by the fact that the essentially "invisible" and "unapproachable" God enters the sphere of creaturely visibleness, not by means of intermediary beings, but in himself . . . This structure of Biblical revelation should neither be sold short nor overplayed . . . It could be overplayed by the view that all that God has instituted for our salvation, culminating in his Incarnation, is in the end only something preliminary which must finally be transcended by either a mystical or an eschatologico-celestial immediacy that would surpass and make superfluous the form of salvation, or, put concretely, *the humanity* of Jesus Christ. This last danger is not so far removed from the Platonising currents of Christian spirituality as one would hope or want to believe: *the impulsive search for an immediate vision of God* that would no longer be mediated by the Son of Man, that is, by the whole of God's form in the world is the conscious or unconscious basis for many eschatological speculations . . . *The Incarnation is the eschaton and, as such, is unsurpassable.*[40]

We do recognize in this "impulsive search for an immediate vision of God" our own desire to see God and to see Him immediately. What von Balthasar emphasizes in this passage is that there is never and never will be an *immediate* givenness of God, insofar as a mediator (i.e., Christ; see 1 Tim. 2:5) is given to us. We can "see" God, so to speak, only in and through Christ (we recall here the saying "no one comes to the Father but through me"; John 14:5). And this seems to be the paradox. Because in Christ we *don't* see God. We think that the "folly of Incarnation" (the fact that God "appeared" in flesh, concealing, as it were, His appearance under flesh) plays with the double mode of any seeing of God: in seeing God one can see only oneself. This can very well be the case with Christ: when I see Christ, one could argue, I see only someone *like* me, a mere human being. And this is indeed the case, but not the entire truth. In seeing God, I must come to recognize the Other(-ness) of other human beings. This last thought has far-reaching consequences. If, as von Balthasar strongly states, I can see only God in Christ and no other "vision" would ever be given to me, that could, then, mean that I can see only God in the other human being ("in *the humanity* of Jesus Christ"). The entire gospel seems to serve as a pointer toward such an understanding: phrases like "as often as you did it for one of my least brothers [the hungry and thirsty, the stranger and sick, the ones in prison] you did it for me" (Matt. 25:40) ring now with a more literal sense.[41] On the other hand, one would not want to trivialize the uniqueness of Christ's person by extending the same attributes (God's mediator, Word incarnate) to everybody, as if saying, "we are all Christ." And yet, if we can see Adam, the first man, in all of us, according to sameness, then we should learn to recognize Christ, the Second Adam and last man, in all of us, according to otherness. Isn't this the principle of Incarnation, namely, "that God became a human so that we, humans, become gods"? Of course, such a statement should be taken as an open invitation, and not as a fact (a fait accompli) already effected by the Incarnation. If we pay attention to the "so that . . ." of the sentence above, we will understand the Incarnation as the opening of a *possibility*. We have been given our Adamic body by means of our birth in the World; we strive for our Christic body by means of our rebirth in the Church. Christ's humanity opens the way (and shows us the way) to man's divinity (the *theosis*, of which so often speak the mystical Fathers). "Each one of you is a son of God because of your faith in Christ Jesus. All of you who have been baptized into Christ have clothed yourselves with him" (Gal. 3:26–27). What is expressed by Paul, in this passage and throughout his Letters, is succinctly stated by the Fathers: *Christianus alter Christus* — the Christian is another Christ.

For von Balthasar, then, as well as for Cusanus, the face of God cannot be anything else but this one: Christ's. However, by entering into this face-to-face relationship with Christ, every face reflects His face:

> When, therefore, I consider how this face is the truth and the most adequate measure of all faces, I am numbed with astonishment. For this face, which is the truth of all faces, is not a face of quantity . . . Thus, O Lord, I comprehend that your face precedes every formable face, that it is the exemplar and truth of all faces and that *all are images of your face* . . . Every face, therefore, which can behold your face sees nothing that is other or different from itself, because it sees there its own truth. (vi, 18)[42]

We are the icons of the truth of this face, the true icon (*vera icona*) of His face, as the archetypal and *acheiropoietos* icon of Veronica, on which Dante meditates in his *Paradiso,* and prompts Jorge Luis Borges to say the following:

> Mankind has lost a face, an irretrievable face. At one time everyone wanted to be the pilgrim who was dreamed up in the Empyrean under the sign of

the Rose, the one who sees the Veronica in Rome and fervently mutters: "Jesus Christ, my God, truly God: so this is what your face was like?" . . . These features have been lost to us the way a kaleidoscope design is lost forever, or a magic number composed of everyday figures. We can be looking at them and still not know them. The profile of a Jewish man in the subway may well be the same as Christ's; the hands that give us some change at the ticket window could be identical to the hands that soldiers one day nailed to the cross. Some features of the crucified face may lurk in every mirror. Maybe the face died and faded away so that God could become all. (*Paradiso* XXXI, 108)[43]

As we have already seen, the icon embodies this turn (about which Nicholas of Cusa so eloquently speaks) from the point of *seeing* to that of *being seen* in a unique way. Like its philosophical synonym, the *prosopon* — the icon is also intrinsically *relational*. One of the defenders of the icons during the second phase of the iconoclastic controversy,[44] Patriarch Nicephorus, does not hesitate to use even Aristotelian terminology in order to define the icon as purely relational. He notes that an icon is always the image of something (πρός τι), and therefore, it denotes relation (as defined by Aristotle in his *Categories*).[45] It is telling that the πρός by way of which we inquire into the proper status of the icon also happens to be the first element, the πρός, of the *prosopon*. The relational character of the icon, however, is not exhausted in such minor points of etymology. It is primarily manifested in its theology. For the icon makes apparent, literally at a glance, all the intricacies of Trinitarian and Christological dogma — better yet, as Cardinal Schönborn has shown, the icon is made possible by the very truths pronounced by Christian doctrine. For how else could we justify that paradox that every icon claims to be, namely, that it is the visible image of the invisible God? The answer to this crucial question is relevant for our discussion only insofar as it demonstrates the relational (and, thus, *prosopic*) character of the icon.

The depiction (or "circumscription" as the ancient texts have it) of God's form becomes possible with the Incarnation of the Second Person of the Trinity in Jesus. It is Christ and only Him that an icon can depict by virtue of His incarnation (therefore, the Father and the Holy Spirit are never to be represented). The christological foundation here is evident: in Christ two radically different natures are united without confusion but also without separation (as the Fourth Ecumenical Council of Chalcedon formulated it): the invisible and thus unrepresentable divine nature and the visible and thus depictable human one. Thanks to the union with the latter, the former, as well, became circumscribed not only in the time of history but also in the space of artistic representation. On a first level, then, the icon shows us the *relation* of the two natures in Christ's person.[46]

The question that arises next makes things a bit more complicated. What is the particular characteristic (i.e., the *hypostasis*) of Christ's divine nature that allows it to become united with the human nature? This question brings us to the core of the Trinitarian mystery as what we are asking for can be found only in the relationship of the three Persons with each other. Maximus the Confessor shows that what *distinguishes* the Father from the Son (the Son's begotten-ness) is also that very thing that *unites* Him with our flesh.[47] What distinguishes the Father from the Son is nothing else than His "sonship" (by being the Son of the Father, He is also said to be the consubstantial *icon* of the Father's *prosopon*). The "sonship" of the Son describes precisely His relation to the Father. It is this relation, then (that denotes at once the *perichoretic* identity of *ousia* and the difference of *hypostasis*) that unites Him, in Jesus' person, with our humanity. On a second level, then, the icon also shows us the *relation* of the Persons in the Trinity.

On a third and final level, the icon relates the historic moment of the Incarnation (which has happened in the past) with the eschatological promise of a future yet to come. It is easy to understand how the iconic depiction of Christ is based, as we have just seen, on the event of the Incarnation: in this sense, the icon shows us Christ as He was. To the extent, however, that we give some credibility to the testimony of the angels on the day of the Ascension (Acts 1:11: "Men of Galilee, what stand ye beholding into heaven? This Jesus, who is taken up from you into heaven, shall come *in the same way*"), the icon also shows us Christ as He will be. For the Incarnation, as von Balthasar so aptly put it in the passage cited above, *is the eschaton*. Every depiction of Christ, the Virgin Mary, and the Saints — enabled as it is by the Incarnation — is at the same time eschatological. In the icon we do not see (to the extent that we see at all) the biological or historical self of the saints but their eschatological self, transformed and deified: "It is this transfigured 'resurrection body,' resplendent with the light of the Holy Spirit, that the icon painter attempts symbolically to depict."[48]

The icon, therefore, is essentially relational; in each of the three cases discussed above the icon always "relates" to a point beyond itself: Christ's human nature points toward His divinity, the Son refers to the Father, the Incarnation promises the *eschaton*.

* * *

By way of a conclusion, a brief word on the technique of icons is in order. *De Visione Dei* was written in 1453. As Nicholas writes his text — which is nothing else than a mystical meditation on the art of icons — great changes in the artistic universe are happening around him. Some thirty years earlier (approximately in 1425), Masaccio had painted one of his Madonnas (*Madonna con Bambino e sant' Anna*, Uffizi, Florence), a work that moves between two worlds — the Middle Ages and Renaissance — and thus marks the passage from the one to the other. Masaccio is employing here the groundbreaking technique of chiaroscuro, developed earlier by Giotto. Lighting and shadowing, used appropriately, can convey the false impression of depth on the two-dimensional surface of the canvas. Thus, perspective is, at last, achieved. In Masaccio's *Madonna con Bambino* we still see an *icon* (the austere and some-how "stiff" style of Byzantine technique), perhaps for the very last time. At the same time, something entirely new is to be seen here, a *painting* (the naturalness and aliveness of a Renaissance work). After Masaccio, Western art will use perspective ad nauseam for more than five centuries. By which time, with the illusions of perspective long exhausted, the arrogance (or naiveté) of the artist who struggles to represent nature, as faithfully as possible, is finally satisfied; in fact, it is more than satisfied, it is satiated, for one detects a certain feeling of grossness in the need to move to the other extreme, that of icono-clasm, as it has been so vividly represented by abstractionist art. With this his-torical background in mind, it becomes interesting, I think, to read Cusanus's text as a praise of icons, these fading works of art that seem to lack any sense of perspective and, next to the masterpieces of the Renaissance, are made to look (as at least some modern art historians have read them) like little more than a series of primitive caricatures. The year 1453, however, is not only a year of artistic changes. It is the same year that Constantinople falls, and with it the more than a millennium-old Byzantine Empire that gave rise to and nour-ished the spirituality of the icons. Writing *De Visione Dei* is Cusanus's way to bid a solemn farewell to a civilization that he profoundly admired and to a city that he himself got to know, albeit in its twilight colors.

It would seem that with the Fall of Byzantium icons became a thing of an irrevocably lost past. Eventually we forgot how to look at them — a forget-fulness that is, in recent years, completed by making icons *en vogue* again, but only as that which they were never meant to be, that is, *objects* of a by-gone art.[49] It was precisely this objectification that characteristics of iconog-raphy, such as the inverse perspective, have resisted. In modern times, Rus-sian apophaticism — especially Malevitch's suprematism — made a strong case against the "epoch of the savage" in Western art — its desire to reproduce by means of representation and its tendency to objectify what was thus repre-sented. The "eclipse of objects" hailed by abstractionist manifestos was rather a forceful declaration against objectification. It is no accident that modern Russian art (I am thinking of the work of Kandinsky and Malevitch) displays such an affinity with its liturgical past. Yannis Ziogas has decisively shown the influence of icons on Malevitch's work, in particular his famous *Black Square*, in a study entitled *The Byzantine Malevitch*.[50] Ziogas begins by reminding us that the process of making an icon substantially differs from other paintings as it follows a strict procedure of placing precise layers of shape and color in a prearranged order. The first layer is the so-called "field" (κάμπος) of the icon, that is, the dark surface of the prepared wood. On that first layer the iconographer will first contour the outline of the depicted figure (layer 2), and then he will place the leaves of gold that make the icon's golden back-ground (layer 3). Three layers of coloring and shadowing follow next (layers 4–6), that are completed with the inscription of naming above or next to the depicted persons (layer 7). The icon is finished with the last layer (layer 8), that delineates the icon's frame. These consecutive layers function as a series of veils, the one superimposed over the other, that conceal themselves, and, by concealing each other, they reveal the finished icon. Already, then, in its structural elements, the icon becomes a symbol of the entire cosmos (as Dionysius, for example, would have understood it); for it is only through that manifold veil that this world is that the divine ray can radiate and reveal Itself (οὐδὲ δυνατόν ἑτέρως ἡμῖν ἐπιλάμψαι τὴν θεαρχικὴν ἀκτίνα μὴ τῇ ποικιλίᾳ τῶν ἱερῶν παραπετασμάτων, CH I, 121B). Should the veil of the world ever be removed, by a hyperbolic doubt or a radical reduction, it would reveal *nothing* (that very nothing of creation's ex nihilo). As the diaphanous veils of color and shape, once superimposed over each other, reveal the icon to us, so too the theophanous creation manifests its Creator:

> We ought not to understand God and the creature as two things distinct from one another, but as one and the same. For the creature is subsisting in God; and God, manifesting Himself, in a marvelous and ineffable manner is created in the creature, the invisible making Himself visible and the incomprehensible comprehensible, and the hidden revealed . . . and creating all things He is created in all things and making all things is made in all things . . . and He becomes all things in all things.[51]

It was necessary to take this brief detour in the technical making of an icon in order to be able to see how Malevitch's *Black Square*, far from being the pinnacle of iconoclasm, as it is generally regarded, is rather an icon in itself. Ziogas argues that in the *Black Square* Malevitch deliberately chooses only two layers of those that make up an icon (the first and the last). His technique, therefore, is not that of abstraction but rather that of negation (something that will make the *Black Square* the visual analogue of negative theology), especially as, by keeping only the first and last layers of an icon, he has omitted the intermediary steps of form (layers 2–3), color (layers 4–6), and language (layer 7). There is, of course, further evidence that supports the iconic interpretation of the *Black Square*: during its first public exhibition (St. Petersburg, 1915) "Malevitch took care to hang his *Black Square* high in a corner of the exhibition hall, which, for every Russian, meant he had placed it in the 'red corner,' the place reserved for holy icons."[52] Twenty years later, the *Black Square* assumed for one last time its iconic place by being hung over the coffin of its dead creator.

This square (which is not an exact square) surrounded by a frame (which is not really a frame) makes its own title the title of something it is *not*. As Ziogas puts it, the *Black Square* "depicts more what it is not"[53] rather than what it actually is. Even its function as an icon makes it the icon of an icon that is *not* here or yet. It represents an icon *in expectation*. The apophaticism of the Black Square reserves the place of an icon *until* the icon takes place. Thus, it marks a caesura in the beat of time between figuration (in the Incarnation) and transfiguration (in the *Eschaton*). Far from being the eclipse of Form, the *Black Square* — the dark "field" of an icon in the making — is Form's silent promise.

* * *

This chapter has described the difficulty that awaits us in our attempt to articulate philosophically an experience of God, a difficulty that oscillates between the either/or of the following metaphysical dilemma: either an unknowable, imperceptible, wholly other God, or a conceptual, and therefore equally fleshless, Idol; either *Gott* or *Götze*. In the modern past, metaphysics was content with the latter, that is, with the *idea* of God (see, for example, Descartes's *Third Meditation*). It is that contentment that has been called ontotheology. Phenomenology, on the other hand, all too often rushes toward the former, mesmerized by the lure of the otherness of the Other like a butterfly bedazzled by fire. Between the two positions, a third one is opened up in the paradox of the Pauline "icon of the invisible God." That icon is par excellence Christ, "begotten in our image and likeness" but, by extension, every person "created in the image and likeness" of God. It was an iconic feature, namely, that of inverted perspective, that helped us to sketch out a phenomenological analysis of inverted intentionality, of a "vision," in other words, that does not objectify God but allows Him to give Himself in the experience of myself as seen. Alongside our filled intentions (of presence and perception) and empty intentionality (of absence and imagination), a third kind of intention needs to be recognized. That third kind is the inverted intentionality of reflexive sensibility (and, as we shall see in the third part of this work, all sensibility is reflexive), where the intuition "yielded" is precisely *me*, that is, the self-experience of myself as experienced. Strictly speaking, in the "experience of God," as given through the inverted intentionality, the phenomenon is not God but rather me (*my* inability to comprehend God, *my* lack of knowledge or intuition that becomes knowledge and intuition, etc).

The second half of this chapter addressed the phenomenological merit of *prosopon*, the Greek definition of the person as being-in-front-of-another, that is, as fundamentally a relational being. In the chapter that follows, we shall examine whether the prosopic understanding of myself and others, as well as the inverse intentionality through which such an understanding is gained, supplements the phenomenological reductions to the things themselves (Husserl), to being (Heidegger), and to givenness (Marion), and by doing so, whether it safeguards the person's particularity.

two
The Existential Chiasm

Soon afterward, Jesus went to a town called Nain, and his disciples and a
large crowd went along with him. As he approached the town gate, a dead
man was being carried out — the only son of his mother, and she was a
widow. And a large crowd from the town was with her. When the Lord saw
her, his heart went out to her and he said, "Don't cry." Then he went up and
touched the coffin, and those carrying it stood still. He said,
  "Young man, I say to you, arise!"
  The dead man sat up and began to talk, and Jesus gave him back to his
mother.

— Luke 7:10–15

This is how the story has come down to us: we are in the middle of a
funeral procession in a small town; the dead body is being carried outside
the city, where the cemetery is customarily located, to be buried. The only
relative of the dead follows the coffin. There are no siblings for he was the
only son. There is no father for she is a widow. The evangelist makes sure
to mention this small but important piece of information: for immediately
we know that this mother buries the only son she would ever have. There is
always something irrevocable about the death of any person — even more so,
however, when the possibility to "replace" it, insofar as any person can be replaced, is lost.

In another town, Thebes, a similar funeral procession takes place: this
time it is a young girl, Antigone, who leads herself to the place where she
would be buried alive. On her way there, she explains the crime for which she
is being punished with so cruel a death:

Had it been a husband dead
I might have wed another, and have borne

> Another child, to take the dead child's place.
> But, now my sire and mother both are dead,
> No second brother can be born for me.[1]

Both episodes tell us something about the uniqueness of the person lost: the widow's son, Antigone's brother. What makes these persons so irreplaceable and unique is nothing to be found isolated *in them*, a quality, let's say, or a capability; it is rather the place they occupy *in their relationship* with their relatives, with other persons.

Now they are dead. One could assume, then, that the relation itself, the relation that bound them to their beloved, is also gone. In fact, someone with a good training in metaphysics might argue that since relation is only an accident of being (and among the accidents predicated of being the least important, for whereas other accidents such as quality and quantity are predicated directly of being, relation is an accident predicated only of two accidents), then together with being, relation too is gone. One might argue even further that, once the person is dead, what constituted it as this particular person (in the language of metaphysics, its form and matter) has undergone a substantial change, and, therefore, the dead person is not the same person anymore — in fact, it is not a person at all.

In the famous graveyard scene from Shakespeare's *Hamlet*, the gravedigger maintains a similar argument:

Hamlet: What man dost thou dig it for?

Clown: For no man, sir.

Hamlet: What woman then?

Clown: For none neither.

Hamlet: Who is to be buried in't?

Clown: One that was a woman, sir; but, rest her soul, she's dead.

Hamlet: How absolute the knave is! We must speak by the card, or equivocation will undo us.[2]

The gravedigger corrects Hamlet, who attributes the categories "man" and "woman" to a dead body — indeed, Hamlet becomes immediately aware of his mistake: equivocation. For he has used the words "man" and "woman," words that are predicated univocally of persons, to characterize something that is neither.

It is most intriguing, then, that this Stranger visiting the town of Nain would stop and address a dead body in a similar manner to that heard in *Hamlet's* graveyard with no fears of committing a metaphysical solecism. Even more, He would address it *as if* he was a person: *"Young man, I say to you, arise!"* To whom, then, is this call addressed? And who is there (after the subject is dead or after the death of the subject) to receive it?

Incarnation and Individuation

The preceding analysis of personhood in the first chapter has set in front of our eyes a new image: that of a "consubstantial" humanity. Its community, its common ground, so to speak, is not the abstraction of a common essence but rather that of the common way in which each human being comes to be and *is*, namely, as a person. The reciprocity deeply embedded in the term *prosopon* implied that the Other (in front of whom I stand) is also a *pros-opon*; in fact, he or she is "made" a person by the very same "gaze" that constitutes me. *Prosopon* is a relational being, and there is no such thing as a one-way relation.

Having defined the person as being-in-relation, we have moved away from the classic definition of a person as given by Boethius: *naturae rationalis individua substantia*. In the person we did not see the fragmented *(individua)* self-subsisting whatness *(substantia)*, but the hypostatization of a relational *ekstasis* occasioned by the face of the Other and moving toward the Other *(pros-opon)*. Therefore, the criterion, so to speak, that defines a person is not the *naturae rationalis* but rather the *naturae relationalis*. Our implicit claim in the first chapter was that it is precisely this relational structure of the person as *prosopon* that grants us an experience of God. Personhood is nothing else but the formal condition or the possibility for such experience. A step further we might say: personhood *is* that experience, insofar as God is a person par excellence — in focusing, then, on the prosopic mode of our existence we cannot but get a glimpse, *kat'analogian*, of the divine mode of existence.

Such a glimpse has often been described as an epiphany — the fleeting shine of the eternal in the ephemeral. It is this ephemeral that will preoccupy us in this chapter. We set out, then, to reach the same conclusion as in the previous chapter — the shining upon the ephemeral hides a showing of the eternal — only this time we have to begin from the opposite direction, that is, instead of taking personhood as that common *how* that describes our coming to being, we will venture to describe personhood as what particularizes each human being as that he or she is — a unique, irreducible thisness *(haecceitas)*.

We are proceeding thus in the opposite direction than the one followed by the Metropolitan of Pergamon John (Zizioulas), who begins from a theological understanding of personhood and then tries to flesh out the implications for an anthropology of personhood. The present analysis of person and personhood is, no doubt, deeply indebted to his pivotal work.[3] However, it is pertinent, I think, to mention in the beginning of this chapter that has as its main concern the particularity of the person that Zizioulas's theology could potentially undermine otherness because of an overemphasizing of (ecclesial) communion. As Miroslav Volf several times has pointed out,[4] Zizioulas's theology leaves the particularity of the person ungrounded (to ground it on the relationship of the Son to the Father runs the risk of turning every person into a "human clone" of Christ).[5] Although this is not the place for an in-depth analysis of this most interesting discussion, I would have suggested as a reply to this criticism a theology that takes into consideration the otherness that is represented by the saints, who, in being *alter Christus*, have not sacrificed their particularity — indeed, if they became saints it is not in spite of their particularity but because of it, and thus, they are far from being merely spiritual clones of Christ. It might be the case, then, that the filial relationship of the Son with the Father, although uniform *sub species aeternitatis*, becomes manifold *sub species temporis*, like a single ray of light that, once it hits the prism, is diffracted into a multiplicity of unique and different colors. History would be that prism that reflects a spectrum of different ways in which the person becomes a Christ of its own.

The question, therefore, that we need to address is that of the specificity of the human person — how is it, in other words, that each one of us is, not a person, but *this* person? As we shall see, the two questions are in reality one and the same: to be a person (relationality) always implies being *this* particular person (particularity).

Perhaps there is no other problem more puzzling for philosophy than the problem of individuation — of how, in other words, to account for the particular and the unique. It is much easier to speak of such abstractions — as philosophers have always done — as essences and ideas, genera and species, the "I think" and the "I am" categories that are deduced from reality but not found in it. In reality we never meet the genus "animal" or the species of "humanity"; interaction in our lives is with particular persons — each and every one absolutely unique to such an extent that one would be right to consider each person a species in itself. And yet, we know not how to account for such sheer particularity. In a sense, we do not know how to explain it because we *cannot* explain it — that is, philosophical language by its very constitution cannot take into consideration the individual; it has a "built-in" tendency for the universal.[6] It would be quite accurate to imagine the work of the philosopher as that of a lexicographer who catalogs the definitions of various words: in a dictionary you could find the definition of "man" and of "human being," but you won't find anywhere the definition of *me*. Strictly speaking, after all, I am neither "human being" nor *a* "human being" — I am first and foremost *myself*. If philosophy can provide neither a definition nor a description of what is of utmost concern to me, that is, myself, then doesn't philosophy become an irrelevant intellectual endeavor to me? Shouldn't its most lofty and comprehensive system, its most brilliant ideas, leave me utterly indifferent?

Individuation has brought an unspoken embarrassment upon philosophy: Aristotle tackled the question (*Metaphysics*, Z 1038b 14; Λ 1071ᵃ 27–29; Λ 1072ᵃ 31–34; etc.) but left it unanswered, underscoring that "individuals are indefinable; if they have an essence it is at least inexpressible."[7] St. Thomas Aquinas attributed it to qualified matter, but his answer was contested by other schoolmen, most notably Henry of Ghent and John Duns Scotus. The latter left us an interesting theory supporting the view that what makes this thing *this* thing is simply its thisness *(haecceitas)*. Modernity ultimately dispenses with the reality of individuation, beginning with Spinoza's substance and culminating in Kant's epistemology (individuality is only the effect of the pure intuitions of space and time; as the latter do not exist apart from the human subject, neither does the former).

The urgency for particularity, however, was forced upon philosophy by an event that lay entirely outside its proper scope. As a number of studies, both old and new, have shown, the thought of the classical World lacked the notion of the uniqueness of the human person.[8] The cruel Spartan law which demanded that every baby born with some physical or mental defect be discarded at the outskirts of the city[9] was consistent with the classical mentality of the person's expendability. To the Greek mind only the universal and the ideal mattered. Aristotle's pronouncement of the higher status of poetry, the vehicle of universality, over the particularity of history is only an indication of that mentality.[10] The classical worldview was turned upside down in the wake of the Incarnation. The Christian dogma of the "Word made flesh" bestowed upon any person an infinite value — or rather, the value of the infinite.[11] As Kierkegaard never tires of repeating, it is the individual now that stands higher than the universal.[12] Hegel too must have sensed these implications of the Incarnation — especially when in his *Aesthetics* he demonstrates how classical art, exemplified by sculpture, was limited in depicting only the ideal (think here of the statues of Greek gods) bereft of any particularity — a limitation that was overcome by Romantic (i.e., Christian) art, exemplified by painting, which, in loosing the spatiality of three-dimensionality, freed itself from the constraints of universality:

> The free subjective individual allows independent existence to the entire range of things in nature and all sphere of human activity but, on the other hand, he can enter into every *particular* thing and make it into material for inner contemplation; indeed, only in this involvement with *concrete* reality does he prove himself in his own eyes to be concrete and living. Therefore it is possible for the painter to bring within the sphere of his productions a wealth of things that remain inaccessible to sculpture. The whole range of religious topics, ideas of Heaven and Hell, the story of Christ, the Apostles, the saints, etc., the realm of nature outside us, human life down to the most *fleeting* aspects of situations and characters — each and everything of this can win a place in painting. For to subjectivity there also belongs what is *particular, arbitrary*, and *contingent* in human interests and needs, and these therefore equally press for treatment in art.[13]

Thus the artist, Hegel concludes, is now free to capture in art and thus make eternal the most mundane and humble scenes of everyday life, such as those that one finds in Dutch painting (peasant festivals and still lifes), but also the momentary shining of things, the fleeting light arrested in the brush stroke of the impressionists.[14] For in every humble scene portrayed, in every representation of the quaint, the simple, and the commonplace, in every such instance of the ephemeral-made-eternal, art is transformed into a celebration of and a testimony to the eternal-made-ephemeral God.

This brief sketch of the history of the problem of individuation was necessary in order to take us to a consideration of the problem from a phenomenological point of view. Such is, indeed, the phenomenology of givenness outlined by Jean-Luc Marion. Marion's effort to push, so to speak, the phenomenological reduction further than Husserl (intended *eidos*) and Heidegger (being) to unconditional givenness, and thus to locate there a "subject" without subjectivity *(l'interloqué, l'adonné)*, comes as a result of the formal objections that he raises against both the transcendental and empirical I (that is, any form of subjectivity). Among these objections, the most serious perhaps is that "the transcendental I, the 'I think' accomplishes *no individuation*."[15] Indeed, the subsequent pages in Marion's exposition of the phenomenology of givenness strive to preserve the particularity of "the gifted" against the risks of any subjectivistic abstraction (the empty "I" of the "I think" but also of the "I am") and ground its singularity to its capacity to receive.[16]

Hereby commences Marion's critique of Husserl's transcendental as well as Heidegger's ontological reductions that constitute a large part of Book V in *Being Given*.[17] Where Marion finds the phenomenologies of his predecessors lacking is with regard to a deficiency in their "subjectivism" insofar as the "I" of the intending consciousness or the "Da" of the Dasein could be anyone and thus really no one.[18] Phenomenology for Marion has remained, since its very inception, captive to its Cartesian and Kantian legacy from which one derives "neither personality nor simplicity (nor individuality either)."[19] A third reduction is, then, necessary, a reduction to givenness from which one receives oneself *(l'adonné)*. The work on such a third reduction began with *Reduction and Givenness*, it progressed through a rigorous treatment in *Being Given*, and it now reaches completion in the saturated phenomena of *In Excess*.

It is through what was described in the preceding chapter as inverse intentionality that the third reduction is effected and the "gifted" *(l'adonné)* is born. Inverse intentionality, exemplified by the call, summons me to myself. It summons me, neither to a diluted subjectivity where no taste of particularity can be detected, nor to the ontological uniformity of one-size-fits-all, but rather *to myself*, that is, to the irreducible, irreplaceable specificity of my thisness. "The passage from the nominative [of the subject] to the objective cases (accusative, dative)," Marion notes, "inverts the hierarchy of the metaphysical categories."[20] But how? And what may be the implications of such an inversion? Is the project of Marion's third reduction based only on a grammatical whim? Certainly not. What is at stake here is by far more radical than any Copernican revolution. Marion explains it in what might be the most far-reaching claim of his phenomenology: "Individualized essence *(ousia prote)* no longer precedes relation *(pros ti)* and no longer excludes it from its ontic perfection. In contrast, relation here precedes individuality," and, as he adds a few sentences later, it results from it.[21]

We should notice how Marion alludes to Aristotle by giving us within parentheses Aristotle's terminology (*ousia prote* from the *Metaphysics, pros it* from the *Categories*). This is an indication that what is said by this claim is to be understood within the realm of metaphysics proper and, perhaps, in contradistinction to its Greek beginnings. The third reduction seems to cut through centuries of tradition in order to take us back to premetaphysical understanding of ourselves.

We are back, therefore, to the problem of individuation, of Aristotle's *tode ti*, but this time we are given an answer as to what may account for the particular instantiation of a species or an essence, an answer that seems radically different from what the metaphysical tradition has given us so far: *relation*. "Toward something" (the *pros ti*), Marion says, the most frivolous of all categories in Aristotle's list, takes precedence over the highest instance of being (*ousia prote*); indeed, the latter is the result of the former. The confrontation with Aristotelian metaphysics is necessary if phenomenology is to be rescued from her own metaphysical burden: the failure of intentionality to account for particularity—the fact that, as Marion puts it in an earlier treatment of the same problem, "consciousness is intentionally every thing"[22]—is nothing more than the rephrasing of Aristotle's assertion of proto-intentionality: "the soul somehow is all the beings" (*De Anima*, 431b 21). Twenty-four centuries' worth of philosophy amount only to modifying this "somehow" as intentionality.

Even a cursory reading of Marion's claim should be able to detect this logical anachronism: the existence of the "gifted" is said to come after relation and as a result of it (against the causalistic view that would have made relation the result of a subject-cause that almost "mechanically" produces it). Secondly, by exclusively determining the existence of the "gifted" on the basis of relation (a relation that predates him or her), Marion seems to suggest that *l'adonné* is what we call a *prosopon*. Indeed, after consistently retaining the double possibility of the receiver as "to whom/which" throughout the pages of *Being Given*, at the end we are told that "only 'to whom' (and never a 'to which') can assume the full role of receiver—presenting what gives itself in such a way that it shows itself in the world."[23] A "to whom," furthermore, that is to be envisioned as the other *person*: "He [i.e., *l'adonné*] . . . exposes a face, which one will have to look in the face as a personal other."[24]

Marion's phenomenology confronts the problem of individuation and demands a solution by giving priority to relation over nature, consciousness, being, and existence. Indeed, the gifted (*l'adonné*) is called to existence as a response to a call (*l'interloqué*) that calls it to being: "*Young man, I say to you, arise!*" "Thus is born the gifted," writes Marion, "whom the call makes the successor to the 'subject,' as what receives itself entirely from what it receives."[25] The summon of the call, the resulting surprise, the call itself and its facticity—this fourfold of the phenomenology of givenness—imply a self given to oneself by an origin that precedes and predates it, and at the same time the paradox of a self who, in receiving itself, precedes also and predates itself. For this phenomenological account, therefore, the *principium individu-ationis* is the Other, the personal Other who, in relating with me, gives me to myself, a relational selfhood, in other words, a *prosopon.* "Accordingly, my sole individuation or selfhood is found only in the facticity imposed on me by the word originally heard from the call, not pronounced by *myself.*"[26]

The question, however, remains: how are we to understand the ontological priority of relation over existence, since for Marion, to put it bluntly, the *adonné* first relates and then comes to be?

The inconsequence in Marion's logic cannot but become even starker should we continue to adhere to an understanding of personhood or selfhood based on substance (Boethius), consciousness (from Locke to Husserl), will (Schopenhauer and Nietzsche), or even being (Heidegger) and existence (Sartre). All of these definitions fall short on two counts: (a) they presuppose the logical priority of an agent or a subject *(sub-jectum)*, a something in other words, that consequently "endures" the action of subsisting, willing, being, and being conscious, and (b) they cannot account for the specificity of *this* particular person but can speak only of persons in general. However, every difficulty with Marion's claim vanishes if we redefine the person, as Marion himself suggests, on the grounds of relation.

It may be easier to understand the shortcomings of the various understandings of personhood if we just name some of the ethical dilemmas that have come as a result of the association of personhood with either consciousness or being (understood as biological existence). The identification of personhood with consciousness should raise the question (as indeed it has raised a legal debate today) whether to grant the status of person and all the rights entailed therein to infants, unborn babies, people in comas, or those with severe mental disabilities. The same holds true with respect to the identification of personhood with being or existence. Are the dead persons? Should a corpse be treated with dignity reserved for persons? (Current law seems to answer these questions in the affirmative as it extends personal rights to the dead, e.g., protection against defamation, etc.) Genetics today, having reduced the person to his or her genome, puzzles over such cases where a person has more than one set of genetic material (chimerism). According to the standards of biology's own understanding of a person, each "chimeric" person should be more than one.[27]

Only the grounding of personhood on relation solves these ethical dilemmas. The unborn baby *is* a person because it is the baby *of* its mother — that is, even before birth, the baby is part of a nexus of relationships that bestow on it the status of a person. The lost son or the mother who passed away continues to be a person because their relationship with the persons who survived them is unaffected by their deaths (we need only to remind the reader of the passage from Luke that opens this chapter). We can see that a bit more clearly in a pair of spouses when one of them dies — the other is never "free" of the relationship that their marriage has established. Indeed, one does not become a bachelor again, but a widower. It remains to emphasize that the relation that binds persons together even before their birth and after their death is not a *sociological* or *political* phenomenon (as unfortunately understood by most thinkers today) but an *ontological* one. It affects the core of their being for it was relation in the first place that grounded that being.

For the sake of our discussion, however, we have to leave whatever ethical or other implications these observations might have and limit ourselves to an examination of the relational structure of the person from a phenomenological point of view. Is phenomenology supporting the understanding of the person as being constituted by relation and moreover by a relation that precedes it? Can phenomenology resolve or explain the riddle — necessary as we believe it is — of relation's priority over existence in a way that logic and metaphysics cannot? And what might be the import of such a phenomenology toward a theological aesthetic of the experience of God?

Marion's phenomenological trilogy (*Reduction and Givenness, Being Given*, and *In Excess*) has laid the groundwork for a phenomenology of the *prosopon* in the wake of his phenomenology of givenness. I have tried elsewhere to provide a sketch of such a phenomenology under the rubric of a "fourth reduction."[28] A *fourth* reduction, it should immediately be noted, cannot but presuppose the third and build upon it.[29] It draws its justification by standing to the third reduction in a way similar to the relationship of the second reduction to the first. But how is it distinguished from the third? Why, in other words, do we need yet another reduction? Aren't the three reductions enough already? No, provided that, as the third reduction has shown us, Husserl's as well as Heidegger's phenomenologies never quite succeed in breaking free from the chains of subjectivism. The third reduction indeed shows us both the necessity of doing so and the way that we need to follow, but that too needs to be implemented by a "fourth reduction" that will remove a last lurking danger of Platonism in phenomenology, that is, of seeing the gift of the "gifted" as somehow his or her "quality," superfluous to his or her particularity — as the physical world for Plato is beautiful and luminous but with a beauty and light bestowed upon it by a reality that remains extrinsic to it. Perhaps the reader could get a better sense of the difference in emphasis between Marion's work and the present one by the following example: whereas Marion acknowledges that the person in its flesh radiates the paradox[30] of an intuition incommensurable with any concept (the "banality" of the saturated phenomenon)[31] *in spite of* its foibles and faults (and, in doing so, he has already undertaken the movement of transcendence), here I, on the other hand, affirm that this paradox of saturation does not take place regardless of its shortcomings but precisely *because of them* (in the confines and frailty of immanence), and that is why it is all the more a paradox.[32]

Now, it is the case that every reduction brackets out a certain characteristic or element for the sake of an unseen (as of yet) and unattended side of things (for example, in Husserl's transcendental reduction it is our natural attitude toward things that is suspended for the sake of their eidetic appearance). What could, then, be that *x* that such a prosopic reduction, central to a phenomenology of personhood, might bracket out, and for the sake of which *y*?

The *x* bracketed off by the prosopic reduction is what Kierkegaard calls (in the *Works of Love*) "worldly dissimilarity," and the *y* which thereby comes more sharply into focus is what Kierkegaard again would call "eternity's equality"[33] (that is, an eschatology).

It is worldly divisions (the worldly dissimilarity) that, after all, allow treating the other "functionally," as if he or she were serving different functions. Indeed, it is precisely those divisions that assign the different functions to each person (a waiter, a professor, a wife), who now becomes merely an instrument toward a purpose, in other words, a means to an end. By functionality, I mean the prearranged way of conduct or attitude toward other persons—a sort of Heideggerian *Ge-stell*—that presents us a waiter, for example, as a waiter, and that presentation takes place beforehand, always already decided; or, to put it differently, the "waiterness" of the waiter is given simultaneously with the person who serves my dinner.[34] How can I disentangle the one from the other? I do not intend to limit this discussion only to social, even class-related, divisions. By worldly dissimilarities, I mean every aspect of ourselves that is imposed, so to speak, by the world: social, but also ethical, cultural, as well as biological. As John Zizioulas writes, "the other is not to be identified with his or her qualities," that is, with a quiddity (even if that quiddity is not any more a metaphysical category, but sociological or political), "but by the sheer fact that he or she is, and is *himself* or *herself*."[35]

The prosopic reduction is supposed to be cutting through those divisions to what constitutes our "equality" (not, of course, in the sense of a homogeneity, or a genus), enabled by and enabling relation. Recall how each person by standing in front of the Other reveals that Other equally as a person. In the stage of actuality—to borrow Kierkegaard's metaphor[36]—one is a king and another a beggar, but when the curtain falls, both king and beggar are equally "actors"; their worldly dissimilarity vanishes, as when the curtain of the prosopic reduction falls, revealing us all equally as persons; the dissimilarity of functionalism vanishes.

"What is essentially other" in each of us and yet "common to all"[37] is "the likeness" with each other and with God. The reduction *ad personam* reminds us of the danger that always lurks behind our interaction with others (even "conceptual" interactions such as those that we establish when we "philosophize" about human beings), the danger of mistreating God in mistreating the other person, for God is a person, God is *in* the person. Personhood is the likeness we share with each other and with God. Gerard Manley Hopkins, in one of his essays that bears the suggestive title "On Personality . . . ,"[38] alludes to such a principle when he writes:

murder is a mortal sin against God because if you will murder man you may come, as Caiphas and Pilate did, to *murder the man who is God*; and in general, if only God could be put into the position: the mortal sinner would have his way with him . . . spoil him, sell him, or make away with him. Or to put it another way, if the sinner defiles God's *image* so he might God's *person*.[39]

It is telling that in this last sentence "image" stands in symmetry to "person."

What Kierkegaard calls "eternity's equality" is not any different from what we mean by eschatology — for, indeed, this likeness, the iconic reflection of the divine in each and all of us, shines more fully at the eschaton, but it has always begun to glimmer in the now. It is this glimmer that the prosopic reduction should allow us to see — in other words, what Merold Westphal refers to in one of his essays as the "halo" that we often see emanating from the faces in Van Gogh's portraits.[40] But in order to see it, we have to hold each person up, so to speak, to the light that shines from a future unknown and unseen, refusing thus to decide about the definite being and the definition of the person on the grounds of who he or she is or has been. The truth of the other person does not lie in his or her past or present but in the eschaton:[41]

In being king, beggar, rich man, poor man, male, female, etc., we are not like each other — therein we are indeed different. But in being the neighbor we are all unconditionally like each other. Dissimilarity is temporality's method of confusing that marks every human being differently, but the neighbor is eternity's mark — on every human being. Take many sheets of paper, write something different on each one; then no one will be like another. But then again take each single sheet; do not let yourself be confused by the diverse inscriptions, hold it up to the light, and you will see a common watermark on all of them. In the same way the neighbor is the common watermark, but you see it only by means of eternity's light when it shines through the dissimilarity.[42]

In the following pages, then, we will try to flesh out what the basic principles of such a prosopic reduction might be by clarifying further the definition (discussed in the previous chapter) of the *prosopon* and its pertinence for a phenomenology of the experience of God.

Relatedness

If, as shown in the first section of this chapter, the Incarnation has opened up the way to a valuation of the person and thus led us to see in the particular and the specific neither an instant of a species nor a copy of an idea but the irreplacability and irreducibility of the person, then the reverse should also be possible — namely, the passage from the specificity and particularity of the person to the Incarnation. In retracing our steps from individuality to the *principium individuationis* par excellence, that is, the event of the Incarnation, in demanding from the person to show us from where it draws its irreducible and inalienable status as a person, the person cannot but point to the other person and ultimately to the personal Other from Whom it receives itself even before its being and its existence.[43] This pointing, this indication, what we like to call, in all the polysemy of the word, the *sense* of the prosopon, is relatedness.[44] The previous chapter has shown how relation is intrinsically connected with the etymology and conceptual genealogy of *prosopon*. We will see now how the understanding of *prosopon* as a relational structure can help us in formulating a phenomenology of the experience of God.

Indeed, a phenomenological experience of God could not follow the natural understanding of experience that distinguishes between the sensible and the sentient. What, after all, is real, the fundamental experience of myself as a unity *or* the experience of the world as a multiplicity? How can I have an experience (a discursive concept) of existence (an intuition)? Or, to put it differently, how can the sameness of *my* identity as consciousness be reconciled with the otherness of *my* experience of the world? And in which pole of the spectrum does reality ultimately lie? If the foundations of my ability to know are restricted by such rules as the law of identity, where every "I" equals itself, then how am I allowed to think of the other person, of you, as another "I," not identical with me? If everything is reduced to the One in some way, how do we escape egotism? And if everything is reduced to the ever-changing manifold of the objective world (the world of experience), how does one escape reductionism? The Other and the Same, the One and the Many: such are the Scylla and the Charybdis that await the philosopher in his quest. The answers provided by the history of philosophy to this conundrum favor, at times, the one end (the subject), at other times, the other (the objective world).

Phenomenology refuses to assign fundamentality or priority to *either* the experiencing I (rationalism, idealism) *or* to the objects of its experience (realism, materialism). This refusal is its *epoche*. The experience, to which the prosopic reduction in particular hails a return, is that of relatedness. Before an experienc*er* and before an experienc*ed*, there is experienc*ing*.[45] The relation between any two given *relata* is constitutive of them (with regard to their relationship) and, therefore, more primary and originary than their subjectivity or objectivity.[46] For example, in viewing a painting, neither I (the viewer) nor the painting (the viewed) takes precedence (metaphysical, ontological, or epistemological) over the other. For it is our *relation* (the viewing) that reveals me as a viewer and the painting as viewed. Furthermore, I am a viewer *because of* the painting and *insofar as* the painting offers itself to my look; conversely, the painting is such (viewed as such, as a painting) *because of* me and *insofar as* I look at it. Strictly speaking, neither the painting itself, nor I as a viewer, "exists" outside this relation. There is an infinite number of such relations. *Existence* is this relational infinity.

This position shows an affinity with two different and diverse theoretical systems that can provide us with examples: the striking conclusions of the

Copenhagen School (Niels Bohr, David Bohm, and Max Born) in quantum physics and the theo-philosophical work of Russian theorist and scientist Pavel Florensky. The Uncertainty or Indeterminacy Principle, proposed by Werner Heisenberg in 1925, boldly asserts that an electron "behaves" in reaction to its observer. Such a statement shattered both a static view of the universe, regulated by its universal and unchangeable laws (à la Newton), and the certainty of the epistemological claims that scientists can make concerning our physical world. It was David Bohm, however, who radicalized the import of these changes toward an understanding of a de-substantialized (and consequently de-objectified) world. We read in his *Quantum Theory*:

> The properties of matter are incompletely defined and opposing potentialities that can be fully realized *only in interactions* with other elements . . . Thus, at the quantum level of accuracy, an object *does not have any "intrinsic" properties* (for instance, wave or particle) belonging to itself alone; instead it shares all its properties mutually and indivisibly with the systems with which it interacts.[47]

Florensky presents a similar insight, only articulated in a different language. In his attempt to ground truth on a certainty more foundational even than that of the law of identity, he comes across the groundless ground of antinomy (very much like his predecessor's, Nicholas of Cusa's, *coincidentia oppositorum*). For Florensky, however, the contradictory character of an antinomy does not exclude either of the two opposite poles but rather affirms each on the basis of the other. This leads him eventually to an understanding of contraries (such as sameness and otherness) as terms in relation. For Florensky, truth cannot be anything but relational, for it is defined as "the contemplation of Oneself through Another in a Third":

> If "another" moment of time does not destroy and devour "this" moment, but is both "another" moment and "this" moment at the same time, if the "new," revealed as the new, is the "old" in its eternity; if the *inner structure* of the eternal, of "this" and "the other," of the "new" and the "old" in their real unity is such that "this" must appear outside the "other" and the "old" must appear before the "new"; if the "other" and the "new" is such not through itself but through "this" and the "other" and "this" and the "old" is what it is not though itself but through the "other" and the "new"; if, finally, each element of being is only a term of a substantial relationship, a relationship-substance, then the law of identity, eternally violated, is eternally restored by its violation.[48]

What Florensky calls "a substantial relationship" is here called the *prosopon*. To understand the *prosopon* as only the person (and thus, the other human being) is a misunderstanding. *Prosopon* defines a *tropos* (that is, a way, a "how") as well as a *topos* (a place, a "who"). Person becomes indeed *prosopon*'s primary meaning, insofar as a person fulfills the description that *prosopon* signifies ("toward-the-face-of-the-Other"). A *prosopon*, therefore, is to be understood as a dyad of *topos* and *tropos* — these two meanings stand in a dialectical relationship with each other as "obverse" and "reverse" — (and thereby the problem of which one takes precedence over the other is resolved.) "All being is, by its very nature as being, *dyadic*, with an 'introverted,' or *in-itself* dimension, as substance, and an 'extroverted,' or *toward-others* dimension, as relational though action."[49] In the remaining pages, I will try to offer a few words of description for each of these two phenomena, keeping in mind that, although this analysis has to separate them and keep them apart, the one can never occur without the other.

Relationality: The Extroversion of Tropos

The phenomenology of the *prosopon* would give us indeed the totality of phenomena (every kind of phenomenon) through the prosopic relationship. The tree in front of me and the paper I am writing on, a text or a feeling, an event and a work of art, although they might radically lack a face, are still capable of appearing in a prosopic fashion. For they would never appear if they did not relate themselves somehow back to a person. If this pen is not the pen that I use to write (or not write) to you, or for you, or about you, then what is it to me? The pen *in itself* (detached from any prosopic relationship) is meaningless. One could actually pose the question if I could possibly ever see the pen as a pure object (outside of the relational nexus). Only in relation to someone (you, the *prosopon*) does the pen, or, indeed, any other object, acquire meaning. The seed of relatedness is already contained in Husserl's breakthrough of 1900, namely, the realization that, albeit in perception, imagination, or memory, consciousness is always a "consciousness of . . ." For what else is this "of" which unities the intending consciousness with its intended world if not the indication of a relation? To the extent that the consciousness is intentional it is also relational.

Heidegger's analysis of everydayness had already revealed how the World is that referential totality of relations. Only one more thing may be added to this definition: the World is the totality of relationships that eventually take us back to a person *(reductio ad personam)*, relationships with someone and toward the Other. For us, too, the World is this complex network of relations that becomes meaningful only through the presence or absence of a concrete Other *(reductio per personam)*. In other words, the World (the totality of phenomena) appears only when it is reduced to my personal rapport with the Other. The prosopic reduction reveals the things (emotions, thoughts, acts, events) that surround us and make up our World, as things-*for*-the-Other *(reductio pro persona)*. Each thing falls into place by taking its place in this multifarious chain of relational connections that leads us to the Other, as the source of all relatedness. The Other is the implicit (and sometimes hidden) core of this configuration that reveals the World to me as such. Without the Other this complex and elaborate scheme collapses. This Other, however, is not the Other in its otherness (the Other as other) but, rather, in its related-ness (the personal Other). The *prosopon* is more than *Da-sein* (the "there" of Being); it is also and fundamentally *Da-welt* and even *Da-gott*.

With these remarks we have entered the order of the Platonic *exaiphnes*: that sudden, and perhaps urgent, emergence of the *aphanes* (the unap-parent) into the "light" of phenomenality. The phenomena of the *exaiphnes* obey a different kind of logic: in the moment of the *exaiphnes* the things that surround me have to retreat, and indeed "disappear," in order to allow that-which-is-not-seen to show itself. It is as if suddenly the things around me be-came transparent; as if the World were made of a see-through cloth, behind which I can still see you. And yet I know that it is not the things that withdraw but rather you that overwhelm them.

How, or rather, what do I see when I see you? A body? Isn't it the case that I see only *you* in your body? Are you totally exhaustible by your body? Then, what is a gesture? The tone of your voice? Posture? The same questions can be asked concerning painting. What makes this painting a Van Gogh and not a Rembrandt? What is the style? It is *in* the painting without, however, *being* the painting. It is the unapparent, the *aphanes*, that somehow appears (without making itself as such visible). How does style "appear" since it is not visible? For what is visible in a painting — the colors, the shapes, the strokes of the brush — is precisely *not* the style. It is never the eye (as a physiological organ) or the ear that sees and hears but "I" — this "I," however, cannot be seen, heard, or touched.[50] That is why it (the I) can see and hear and touch what is called here the unapparent. This is not to deny embodiment and the flesh — on the contrary. The "I" does not float in the air, it is always embod-ied — incarnate — in my body (as style is in the painting), but it is not com-pletely exhausted by the body understood as a physical, measurable, that is, objectified thing. Who would dare to say that the I is a thing? (That is, who else but Descartes, Leibniz, and Spinoza?) Strangely, then, the phenomenon of the unapparent duplicates itself on both ends of the phenomenological spectrum: the *I* is as much unapparent as the *you*.

A phenomenology of personhood, then, might take the moment of the *exaiphnes* as its point of departure, when, looking at the things, we see the Other (or we become aware of ourselves as seen by the Other — for it is not so much that *we* see the Other, rather, it is the Other that shows itself through the world to *us*).

All of this is best illustrated in unique moments of one's life — as when one falls in love.[51] When I am in love the music that plays in the background of an airport's waiting lounge (otherwise unnoticeable) comes forcefully to the foreground of my attention as soon as it reminds me of you. I am inter-ested in the things that surround me only because I have been totally disinter-ested in them by being solely interested in you — however, to the extent that this world is also *your* world, the world *as yours* and only as yours, concerns me. Everything, absolutely everything, becomes transformed by this manifold signposting that points back to you; or, failing to do so (and this is the only other alternative), everything remains utterly indifferent for me.

When the dreadful news of Patroclus's death reaches Achilles, the world around him is also lost: "I have lost the desire to live, to take my stand in the world of men" (*Iliad* XVIII.90–91); without him, Greece's greatest hero is nothing more but "a useless, dead weight on the good green earth" (104). What weighs down on Achilles is the burden of an utterly indifferent world that, left unmediated by the Other, crushes him. The death of Augustine's friend, more than a millennium later, causes an equally severe break in the referential totality of his world: "My own country became a torment and my own home a grotesque abode of misery." The very things that had once defined what was most familiar to Augustine — his house, his homeland — suddenly appear strange: "I hated all the places we had known together, because he was not in them and they could no longer whisper to me 'Here he comes!' as they would have done had he been alive but absent for a while . . . I had become a puzzle to myself" (*Confessions*, IV, 4).

And yet, there is more to be said. For the *prosopon* is not only the Other, but also and equiprimordially *myself.* Here lies a key difference with Levinasian ethics, for Levinas would have upheld "the asymmetry between self and Other," while the *prosopon* suggests a reciprocity and a community.

Particularity: The Introversion of Topos

The exclusive focus on the who-question ("who am I?") made philosophy forget the correlate where-question. All the answers given to the first question describe a man who is essentially nowhere. Place is never taken into account as part of one's identity, and this implies nothing less than the exclusion of the body, for belongingness to place is proper to our bodies. Like the infamous character of Chamisso's tale, the philosopher has sold his shadow to the devil. It shouldn't surprise us, then, that he is cursed to wander the earth without being able to find peace anywhere. The shadowless man is someone who is localized nowhere, lacks embodiment and place — he doesn't "take" place, that is, someone un-real, in Plato's language "atopos." It is highly telling, I believe, that in J. M. Barrie's novel Peter Pan loses his shadow together with his ability to grow up and mature.

But wasn't the eradication of the shadow always a dream of the Western psyche? Indeed, there are two great fascinations in the "mythology" of the West: my reflection in the mirror and the shadow that my body casts. We are more often aware of the first (from the story of Narcissus to Lacan's mirror phase) than the second. But that makes the fantasy of a shadowless self all the more interesting.

Perhaps the archetypical version of this fantasy is to be found in one of philosophy's canonical myths, that of Plato's cave. The reader of the relevant passage cannot fail to notice how many times the word "shadow" (*skia*) is mentioned in the few lines of the allegory. Indeed, the world of the cave is precisely the realm of the shadows — the very world from which the philosopher strives to escape. But to where? To the luminous world of pure forms, that is, to a *shadowless* world.

If we are to believe Gombrich's analysis of the history of Western art,[52] the European artist is someone who most strongly resists descending into Plato's cave, for he prefers to paint a shadowless world. The appearance of shadows in European painting is very slow, and when shadows do appear it is only in the rudimentary form of shades regulated by perspective, that is, as characteristics of geometry but not of topology. It is the intention of the present discussion to make the human person topical again by examining how the *prosopon*, as *topos* this time, particularizes its personhood into the specificity of myself.

We begin from where Gerard Manly Hopkins begins his own examination of what he calls "the taste of myself":

> when I consider my selfbeing, my consciousness and feeling of myself, that taste of myself, of *I* and *me* above and in all things, which is more distinctive than the taste of ale or alum, more distinctive than the smell of walnut-leaf or camphor, and is incommunicable by any means to another man (as when I was a child I used to ask myself: What must it be to be someone else?). Nothing else in nature comes near this unspeakable stress of pitch, distinctiveness, and selving, this selfbeing of my own. Nothing explains it or resembles it, except so far as this, that other men to themselves have the same feeling. But this only multiplies the phenomena to be explained so far as the cases are like and do resemble. But to me there is no resemblance: searching nature I taste *self* but at one tankard, that of my own being.[53]

That stress of pitch, the taste of self, is in Hopkins what *haecceitas*,[54] the highest principle of being,[55] is in Scotus.[56] It is also the very same thing that would make some of the existentialists of the twentieth century "sick" with nausea:

> What for the Other is his *taste of himself* becomes for me the *Other's flesh*. The flesh is the pure contingency of presence. It is ordinarily hidden by clothes, make-up, the cut of the hair or beard, the expression, etc. But in the course of long acquaintance with a person there always comes an instant when all these disguises are thrown off and when I find myself in the presence of the pure *contingency of his presence*. In this case I achieve in the face or the other parts of a body the pure intuition of the flesh. This intuition is not only knowledge; it is the affective apprehension of an absolute contingency, and this apprehension is a particular type of *nausea*.[57]

The taste of myself is an irreducible phenomenon of sheer uniqueness (or prime diversity as Scotus puts it, *primo diversa*)[58] that nothing, neither essence nor substance, neither form nor matter, nor the combination of these two, can account for.[59] It remains, thus, indefinable and as such incommunicable.[60]

What matters most, however, in Scotus's thick scholastic exposition are the radical implications of his thought: since none of the classical, metaphysical categories can account for the thisness of the things, then it follows that what distinguishes this thing from all the rest and unities it with itself must be prior to all such categories. In Hopkins's language, "Self is the intrinsic oneness of a thing, which is *prior* to its being."[61] Prior to its nature too: "Now a bare self to which no nature has yet been added, which is not yet clothed in or overlaid with a nature is indeed nothing, a zero, in the score or account of existence, *but* as possible it is positive, like a positive infinitesimal, and intrinsically different from every other self."[62] This priority, of course, is an ontological priority and a logical paradox at the same time, insofar as the self *is* itself before even coming to being.[63] Only an "antinomic" logic like the one maintained by Scotus (and, as we have seen in the first section of this chapter, by Marion)[64] can uphold both the specificity of the person and its freedom, insofar as the person is free to be and to be itself, before being-as-such or before the facticity of being determines it.[65]

The ontological precedence of personhood over being and existence cannot be maintained unless through relation. We have seen how, in Marion's phenomenology of givenness, the call, addressed to a self interpolated and given, calls this very self (as *interloqué* and *adonné*) to being. Although the call is extended to every one, it is at the same time addressed specifically to each one:[66] "Young man, *I say to you*, arise!"—One could add that this call is like the good Shepherd who "calls his own sheep *by name*" (John 10:4). The proper name then will stand as a sign of oneself's particularity granted by the calling *by name*. In other words, it is the individual call ("by name") that bestows individuality ("the name"). For us, however, the specificity of the person has its origin in the ability of the person to relate and to establish relationships. The call itself is such a relation, perhaps the most originary and primary, but nevertheless a relation. In the nexus of relationships that each person establishes, each one of us comes to occupy a very unique locus — remember the widow's son, Antigone's brother — a place that no other person could inhabit since this place or locus (a *topos*) is interiorized *in* the person, or better yet, it *is* the person itself (*prosopon* as *topos*) who, therefore, remains, strictly speaking, irre-*place*able. Thus, relation overcomes the utopia (literally, the lack of *topos*) of the modern and postmodern subject by making it topical again, in its particularity and uniqueness. It finally has its shadow back.

Phenomenologically speaking, the infinitesimal phenomenon of selfhood is the corollary of an equally minimalistic phenomenology[67] — a phenomenology that underscores the chiasmic union of the phenomenality of the phenomenon with the phenomenon itself. Or, to put it differently, the form (*Gestalt*) of the phenomenon is not any different than its content (*Gehalt*). A phenomenology of personhood would make room for a certain kind of phenomena that refer to nothing else but themselves, or rather to the fact that they appear — such are the phenomena of phenomenality. The paradox here is that every phenomenon insofar as it appears is first and foremost a phenomenon of (its own) phenomenality. Although to the extent that it carries or conveys other information (more than the bare minimum information of its appearance), it registers as a phenomenon of this or that. In exceptional cases, however, *which are not other than the ordinary*, phenomena can, even if only for a moment, fully exhaust themselves in their wondrous *phainesthai*. That means that, in exceptional cases (and what is exceptional here is not the sort of phenomena we are to encounter but our attitude toward them), we can let ourselves be enthralled by the extraordinary ordinariness of the things themselves. That is, I take to be, what Kearney has in mind when he writes: "It is the divine itself manifest in the 'least of these', in the colour of their eyes, in the lines of their hands and fingers, in the tone of their voice, in all the tiny epiphanies of flesh and blood."[68] When we let ourselves take notice of the unnoticeable manifestation of the divine in everydayness, we have arrived back at the original philosophical passion of *thaumazein*.[69]

There is, however, one phenomenon that adheres most strictly to this principle of the hypostatic union between phenomenon and phenomenality. Perhaps because it is itself, as we have seen, the very ground of that principle, the archetype, the Ur-phenomenon of all subsequent phenomena: *Incarnation*.[70] What else could be behind the divine that manifests itself in the flesh and blood of a concrete human being? Incarnation exemplifies (and at the same stroke also defies) the principles of phenomenology. If I want to offer a definition of the phenomenon of Incarnation, I would have to give an account of the singularity of its epiphany. In this case, the "what" of the phenomenon *is* its "how." Its *Offenbarung* is nothing more or nothing less than its *Offenbarkeit*.[71] The "message" of the incarnation is neither an "idea" nor a "system" (that would be an oxymoron), no matter how wonderful or lovely — it *is* flesh: body and blood.

Heidegger opens his magnum opus, *Being and Time*, with a seemingly "blasphemous" statement: "The 'essence' of this being," he writes of *Dasein*, "lies in its to be. The whatness *(essentia)* of this being must be understood in terms of its being *(existentia)*." What is provocative about this statement is the astounding fact that Heidegger defines the human being *(Dasein)* by assigning to it nothing less than the very definition of God. What Heidegger apparently had in mind was St. Thomas's definition of God, according to which *only* God "is His own essence, quiddity, or nature" (*Summa Contra Gentiles*, I, 21); and again, "in God, essence or quiddity is not distinct from His existence" (*Summa Contra Gentiles*, I, 22). Of course, such a bold move was not meant as a tacit apotheosis of the human being; it was, rather, God who was sighted as its target. When we strive to redefine the person, phenomenologically as *prosopon*, namely, as this coincidence of the phenomenon (essence) with phenomenality (existence), that is, a *hypostasized ek-sistence*, I have in mind nothing else but the event of the Incarnation. *Pace* Heidegger and St. Thomas, I do not think that God's self-hypostasizing of His existence should be mutually exclusive of man's potential for transcending his nature by choosing to be (and become) who he is. If man can exist as a person (which is what Heidegger claims concerning the *Dasein*), that is because God (the person par excellence) became man. To undermine God's incarnate person directly amounts to jeopardizing my own status as a person.[72] We have witnessed this principle throughout the history of philosophy: any distortion of God's personhood reverberates in human selfhood. The event of Incarnation has to be that center toward which all phenomenological analysis gravitates and against which each phenomenon (no matter how mundane) measures itself.

By being incarnational, the prosopic reduction is also *eschatological*. For the incarnation is the *eschaton* embodied in the incarnate Other, in the voice and visage of my neighbor. For if it were otherwise, if Incarnation were not the unsurpassable *eschaton*, one would have been justified in anticipating a time when I could have a more direct, full, unmediated understanding of the Other. In anticipation of such a time, however, one begins cheapening (relativizing) one's encounter of the Other as it is given in the here and now of everydayness. Such an *eschaton* beyond incarnation would offer me the metaphysical alibi to overlook the Other in front of me, to ignore, neglect, or underestimate him or her in expectation of a more authentic encounter with another Other (perhaps, the wholly Other, *tout autre*) at the end of History, conceived as some metaphysical totality à la Hegel.

The Departure from Religion

By speaking of the *prosopon*, incarnation, and eschatology one might wonder if a phenomenology of the *prosopon* is not religion's most triumphal capture of phenomenology to date. Doesn't the fourth reduction confirm the fears of those who speak of "phenomenology's theological turn" and even "philosophy's turn to religion"? To such questions I would like to reply that, on the contrary, the *prosopon has nothing to do with religion*, if we take religion — polytheistic, monotheistic, or atheistic — to mean the sharing of a common emphasis on two things: *nature* (which is what religion tries to understand by providing a more or less mythic model of its genesis) and (as a result of that) *cosmology*. The *prosopon*,[73] on the other hand, contrary to this religious emphasis on nature and cosmology, shifts the emphasis to *history* and *eschatology*. For this reason alone the relatedness of the *prosopon* cannot be and should not be confined to the strict limits of religion. When St. Paul experienced his conversion, he didn't change his religion for another — he abandoned religion altogether in order to offer witness to the event of the Incarnation, which surpasses religion.[74] That is why the formal characteristics of religion (ritual, such as circumcision and sacrifices, observations of feast days, dietary regulations, the place of worship, etc.) lose their meaning and are not important anymore. They become "the shadow of the law" that has faded away or "the old order that has passed away" (2 Cor. 5:17). Religion, as defined above, poses as great, if not greater, risk for the ecclesial event as secularization; for in the name of faceless love and justice it sacrifices the uniqueness of the *prosopon* by exchanging it for a fleshless ideology.

In fact, the entire objection against a "religious" *mis*reading of phenomena implies an alternative, second possibility, of a nonreligious, secular reading. Therefore, such an objection reproduces the pagan (or "primitive" according to Levinas)[75] distinction between the sacred and the secular — a distinction rendered inoperative by the prosopic. To read the eschatological back into the ordinary and the everyday means to contaminate the temporal with the eternal; to blur the distinction between a secular and a sacred world; to let the separation between the holy and the unholy collapse. It is, thus, in vain to raise the question of the "citizenship," as it were, of the phenomena: is this face in front of me a phenomenon that belongs to the order of the secular (and, thus, the face of another), or is it a sacred phenomenon (and thus the face of God)? For the *prosopic* reduction — precisely in its ability to overcome such a Manichean view of the World — this is nothing but a pseudo-dilemma; the face of the Other is essentially *both*, the face of another and the face of God. Like matter in quantum physics: it can be both, either particle or wave. It depends on how I am able to receive the Other and on how the Other is able to give itself. Phenomenology should not and cannot decide a priori (i.e., prior to my relation with the Other and with the World) how to classify phenomena — as if she were an old librarian shelving books under the right call number. This chiasmus becomes the cross on which religion and secularism would have to sacrifice their logic. Religion, law, and ethics can, in the proper circumstances, play a crucial role in pointing us toward the *eschaton* of the incarnation, but they are never more than ladders that must be left behind in time.

* * *

This chapter has sought to complement the inverse intentionality of the previous chapter with a sketch of what has been called a *prosopic reduction*. The first chapter suggested the human person as the *topos* of God's epiphany, and indeed as the genuine "phenomenon" of God — it was the task of the present chapter, therefore, to show how that disclosing character of the person is intrinsically linked with its *tropos*, that is, with relatedness as its mode of phenomenality. The necessity that compels a phenomenology of God to begin its inquiry with personhood, that is, from a hypostasized ek-sistence instead of a transcendentalized essence, cannot be mistaken for a step toward anthropomorphism. There is no regression here to a pre-phenomenological worldview of humanity's separateness from the world; no distinction is here introduced between an intramental awareness ("man") standing against an external reality. On the contrary, I have outlined the features of a phenomenology of the *prosopon* against the background of phenomenological evolution (the intending consciousness, the disclosing character of Dasein, the subjectless givenness of the *adonné*) in order to emphasize phenomenologically the fundamental unity of the within with the beyond, of being and appearances. It is this ceaseless movement of the "pros-" (toward) of the *prosopon*, namely, its being always on its way toward another, beyond itself and in the world, its synonymous ability to relate and to refer, that I have chosen as our point of departure for our phenomenology of God. Indeed, the only possible beginning for phenomenology in general.

three
The Aesthetical Chiasm

It is time now to develop a fuller treatment of the *punctum caecum* of time and visibility as mentioned *in passim* in the previous two chapters. There, and at certain instances that we have identified by the Greek term *exaiphnes* (ἐξαίφνης), a moment of negativity made itself apparent: to be sure, not as a concrete phenomenon, but as a unique mode of phenomenality that gave us, always unforeseeably, a glimpse beyond the things-themselves, toward the things-to-come. In the pages that follow, we will think such a mode of eschatological phenomenality of the invisible under two related terms: the *Augenblick*, as treated by Heidegger, and the *exaiphnes*, first conceptualized by Plato. What brings these philosophical hallmarks together is, at a first level anyway, their etymology: both terms imply a structure of vision, or an act of seeing out of the invisible and the unapparent — but both terms too are supposed to name a certain form of temporality beyond time. *Der Augenblick* obviously refers to the "blink of an eye," whereas the Platonic *exaiphnes* (commonly translated as "suddenly") speaks of a passage from what is *aphanes* to phenomenality. Both terms are inscribed by the tradition within the context of an eschatological anticipation of the kingdom's advent and its *kairos*. What does appear at the moment of the *Augenblick* or the *exaiphnes*? How is time linked to the visual? How does this aesthetics of temporality pertain to the theme of theological aesthetic as discussed in these pages? We will try to answer these questions by distinguishing first between two different understandings of the temporal, as *chronos* and as *kairos*. The tension between these two temporal phenomena cannot be resolved except by an appeal to eschatology. An eschatology, however, that is liberated from the structures of messianicity and, instead, permeates everyday phenomena, such as music, creating its own particular a-chronic temporal dimension of what Hölderlin called "a time fissured with abysses."

Two Notions of Temporality: *Chronos* and *Kairos*

"All other media have *space* as their element. Only *music* occurs in *time*."[1] We owe to Kierkegaard such an acute observation. Indeed, one thinks of the space that a painting or any piece of sculpture needs to occupy — but what about theater and poetry? Isn't there much more to a theatrical performance than the space of the stage? Or to a poem than the written pages? On the other hand, doesn't music take *place* — in space, that is? Sounds, after all, have to traverse a certain space from their source to the tympanum of our ear. Regardless of these objections, and many others that one could perhaps raise, Kierkegaard's aphorism remains true: "only music occurs in time." To understand the truthfulness of his remark we need to ask to *which* time Kierkegaard is referring? The question sounds bizarre: "which time?" Isn't there, after all, only one time — the time that we measure in minutes, seconds, and hours?

Time does not exhaust temporality. The Greeks knew of two different phenomena of temporality that have come down to us as *chronos* and *kairos*. *Chronos* is time seen either as sequence or duration — invariably constituting a chronology: every minute passing by is accumulated in those layers of dead time that compile the chronicle of our lives. *Chronos* represents what Heidegger calls "the vulgar understanding of time"[2] or "inauthentic present."[3] This time is nothing more than an indefinite series of "nows": the present is the "now" that "is," the future is the "now" that one day will be but is not yet, and the past is the "now" that once was but is no more. But between that which is "*not yet*" and that which is "*no more*" there is nothing.[4] Every present "now" thus comes from nothing and rolls back to nothing. Hence the homonymy between *chronos* and *Kronos*: the Greeks saw in this chronological experience of time the mythical figure of Kronos or Saturn, the god who devours his children.[5]

Time remained a problem for philosophy since its inception. The Ionian thinkers saw time in the revolution of the celestial spheres, or in the elusive flux of a river; Plato conceived it as the moving picture of eternity, Aristotle as the measuring number of motion or change. With Plotinus begins the long process of internalizing time — eloquent indications of which one can find from Augustine's *distentio animae* up to Kant's subjective pure intuition.

The consensus of all these sources comes down to one single point: time is fundamentally linked to motion — without which we would all fail to notice time (or to have an experience of time). Motion is here understood as *kinesis*. That term covers a number of notions of change, not only or necessarily change of location (locomotion). That is why it is not time that passes and that is how we become aware of motion, but it is because there is motion that we become aware of time. In any case (and here Kant's accusation that we think time in terms of space is right), I always perceive time in terms of a *passing*, as if it were a passing from a fixed point A to another fixed point B.

Against this concept of time as *chronos* (the passing of time) stands a different understanding of temporality as *kairos*. If chronological time is seen in a horizontal way, that is, as sequence and duration, *kairos* could be represented as vertical and dis-continuous. If *chronos* is measured in seconds, minutes, hours, and years, *kairos* cannot be measured at all, since it occurs only in the Moment. What is called here "the Moment" — that is, as we will see, the *Augenblick* or the *exaiphnes* — is characterized by this dis-continuity through which, according to Heidegger, the world is dis-closed[6] and Dasein is faced with his or her de-cision. For even if it were possible to put all the kairological moments together, that still would not give us any measurable sense of *kairos*, since each moment of *kairos* (contrary to different units of time) is, in a unique way, always the same in the sense that it recurs in repetition. This is evident in how the liturgy presents events of the past (such as the birth of Christ, His crucifixion, etc.) as always taking place "today" — a survey of the hymns used in the Church will show that the liturgy knows of no other temporal category than this "today." Repetition has become a key philosophical term thanks to the acute analysis of Kierkegaard, who devotes an entire treatise to it. Kierkegaard is right to see in repetition a new temporal category — that is, to be juxtaposed over and against Platonic recollection. Recollection, he writes, allows us to "enter the eternal backwards," while repetition is decisively futural and in its futural character pushes us to "enter eternity forwards."[7] Two different senses of eternity are here contrasted: (a) a preexisting, anterior eternity, what we could call *cosmological* eternity, and (b) an eternity that lies ahead of us and keeps reaching us in the present, what we could call an *eschatological* eternity.

Eschatological Ontology and Archeological Epistemology

Nothing oppresses us more than the weight of an irrevocable past. In front of the past we are powerless: the things we have done and the things done to us assume an undeniable authority as *facts*, as the things-themselves that, furthermore, give shape to who we are. Nothing undermines our freedom more than a predetermined and given "nature," our fixed facticity. Most of us understand ourselves as who we have been — our identity is like a record where every action, every deed and thought, is written down indelibly. Think here of police records, credit records, academic transcripts, professional résumés, and medical files. In all these cases — and for each institution that they represent, the police, the academy, the market, and the medical establishment — we simply *are* our past. The past is like our *shadow* — it follows us where we go, and it is impossible to get rid of it. Against this logic eschatology retorts a new logic — the logic of the new, the *novum*, the doctrine of *de novissimis*. In Revelation (21:5) the "new things" coincide with the last things, and together they form what is known as eschatology. Against the things-themselves stand the things-to-come.

The reason for our society's obsession with the past is the fact that our epistemology is entirely archeological (preoccupied with the *arche*, the beginnings) or protological (concerned with what comes first). In other words, our knowledge is based, by necessity, on experience (one needs only to refer to the opening lines of Kant's Introduction to the *Critique of Pure Reason*), and experience is always experience of what has been and has come to pass, what, in other words, can be measured, observed, and written down in files and records like those mentioned. In everyday life we reason according to such archeological paradigms — the origin holds the truth of the thing or the person in question. It is the beginning that determines the end and not the other way around. And how could it be differently? The beginning functions as the *cause* of what has thereby its beginning — and doesn't the cause come always before its effects?

Not necessarily. The chronological and ontological primacy of the cause is challenged by a series of events, such as the creation, the Incarnation, the crucifixion, and the resurrection. These events do not fit in the protological paradigm of causality, for what would be, for example, the "cause" of the crucifixion? Does the cross makes any sense at all if seen by itself, that is, as the effect of what has preceded it in the life of Jesus? We would argue that the cross becomes the cross only once it is seen from the future, that is, from the point of view of the resurrection that follows it. Theologically, then, it is the resurrection that is the "cause" of the crucifixion. And the resurrection itself — would it make any sense to say that the resurrection is the "result" or the "effect" of Christ's passion? "In Paul's mind," John Zizioulas writes, "even the historical event of our Lord's resurrection would make no sense if there was not to be a final resurrection of all human beings in the end: 'if there is no resurrection of the dead, then not even Christ was risen' (1 Cor. 15:13)."[8] And Jean-Yves Lacoste concurs when he writes that the Hegelian understanding of History as progressing toward the future "could only be right, finally, if the resurrection of the Crucified did not have to be interpreted as a promise, and was nothing but the meaning of the last fact — of the reconciling Cross."[9] Theologically speaking, then, the cause of the things that happen and have happened lies *not* in their beginning but "in the end" — for they do come *from* the kingdom of God, for it is the kingdom that is, properly speaking, their origin. "It is not at the beginning (in the morning of consciousness and at the dawn of history) that man is truly himself."[10] For, as Heidegger would say, the beginning determines man and history only insofar as it "remains an advent."[11] "Meaning," Lacoste writes, "comes at the end."[12] In this respect, eschatology is *anarchic* through and through, for it alone can effect such a radical subversion of the *arche*: of principles and beginnings.

Eschatology, therefore, reverses the naturalistic, essentialist, and historicist models by making the seemingly improbable claim that I am not who I am, or even less, who I was and have been, but rather, like the theophanic Name of Exodus (3:14), I am who I *will* be. The example of the shadow is properly reversed (as in the Letter to the Hebrews 8:5 and 10:1; Col. 2:16): the shadow instead of following what is real now precedes what is really real; thus, in Christian typology the present condition, that is, the things-themselves, are merely the shadow, adumbrations, of the things-to-come.[13]

It is this spirit that is captured by Bonhoeffer's concept of the "penultimate." By calling History "the penultimate" and not, say, "the subsequent," Bonhoeffer underscores the shifting of emphasis through which History is seen, not anymore as the outcome of the originary or the beginning but as that which exists because of and "for the sake of the ultimate."[14] "Loss of this ultimate," Bonhoeffer warns us, "will sooner or later lead to the collapse of the penultimate" as well, unless "we succeed in claiming these penultimate things once again for the ultimate."[15]

The ultimate, however, does not remain an empty regulatory idea beyond experience, that is, beyond the penultimate, but, as Bonhoeffer makes quite clear, "it breaks ever more powerfully into earthly life and creates space for itself within it."[16] Thus, eschatology "has become real in the cross" and in the resurrection of Christ,[17] but also in the liturgy, since "liturgy implicates the eschatological in the historical."[18] Whereas Judaism and Islam have *one* eschatological center, fixed in the future (messianism), Christian eschatology unfolds as this tension between *two* eschatological nodal points: between the *already* of the Incarnation and the *not yet* of the Parousia. This tension finds expression in the formula of the Fourth Gospel: "the hour is coming and is now here" (John 4:23, 5:25). John's eschatology is *realized*[19] in the revelation of Christ, or, better yet, *inaugurated*[20] by the Word's coming to the World (the judgment takes place "now": John 12:31, or "already": John 3:18; the resurrection of the dead is also taking place in the "now": John 5:25). In that, Lacoste is right to speak of a "splitting" of the end or of the *eschaton* into two: the eschaton of the present (at the end of time) and the present of the eschaton (in the everyday).[21] It is this bifurcation of the eschatological that enables what Richard Kearney has described as a *micro-eschatology*.[22]

There is no text that speaks more eloquently of micro-eschatology, however, than the Eucharistic prayers of the two ancient liturgies that have been handed down to us under the names of St. Basil the Great and St. John the

Chrysostom (still in use today by the Orthodox Church). Both liturgies begin with a telling doxology: "Blessed is the *kingdom* of the Father and the Son and the Holy Spirit." At the very beginning of the liturgy, then, the kingdom is proclaimed as a reality and not as an expectation. It is this bold experience of the kingdom that enables the celebrant to say during the *anaphora*, that is, the consecration prayer: "Remembering thus this salvific command and everything that was done for us, namely, the cross, the tomb, the resurrection after the third day, the ascension to heavens, the sitting at the right hand of the Father, the second and glorious coming" (PG 63, 916). Here logic is violated and history is left behind. How could it be that we remember the "second and glorious coming"?

To remember the future, to have already experienced what is still to come, this is something that goes against our protological categories of thinking. The Eucharist is thus more of a *prolepsis* than an *anamnesis*, since the events that we recall lie, from the historical perspective, in the future — a future made present in the Eucharist and by the Eucharist. To grasp what is at stake here we need to implement and juxtapose *anamnesis* as recollection (essentially a Platonic concept) with *anamnesis* as repetition (as Kierkegaard understood it).

The Aesthetics of Temporality: Painting and Music

Let us return now, after this short detour into eschatology, to our initial problem. Once we have established this distinction and spelled out the characteristics of these two different notions of temporality (i.e., *chronos* and *kairos*), defining the first in terms of a passing and the second in terms of repetition, I think it becomes easier to approach again Kierkegaard's basic insight when he said, "only music occurs in time." Especially if we think this statement in contrast with what the same author expressed a few pages earlier, namely, "music has an element of time in itself but nevertheless *does not take place* in time."[23] What Kierkegaard tries to say here is that music has an element of temporality — but one that does not confine it to the passing of time. This can be simply demonstrated by two examples.

First, take the example of a viewer who stands before a painting. One cannot say that the painting is temporal, for the painting does not need time to "unfold" before our eyes. Once we stand before the painting, everything, its entirety, is given to us *at once*. There is no time lapse here; the viewer could capture the entire work in one gaze. Augustine thinks that God — being eternal — sees History in the same way: at once and in one single gaze. Painting belongs to eternity, for as in eternity time has stopped: that is the *nunc stans* of metaphysics, and every painting or sculpture is nothing else but the depiction of this still now.

Take now the example of someone sitting in a concert hall listening to Beethoven's Seventh Symphony. The symphony, or rather its performance, lasts a certain time, but no one would be so aesthetically naive as to identify the time that the symphony takes to be performed with the symphony itself. (One cannot imagine a conductor who would inform his musicians that the exposition of the first movement needs to be played at 7:15 and repeated at 7:20.) It takes some time, but it is *not* this time. Contrary to the painting, I cannot have the symphony in one take (or at one sound), all at once. I need to go through time, through its unfolding in time—a time which is essentially different from the clock-time to which our everydayness belongs. We think that music can do what is impossible for us: it can elongate or accelerate the passing of time at will.

Along similar lines, Jean-Paul Sartre offers us some fascinating remarks on the temporal character of music:

> In the degree to which I hear the symphony *it is not here*, between these walls, at the tip of the violin bows. Nor is it "in the past" as if I thought: this is the work that matured in the mind of Beethoven on such a date. It is completely beyond the real. *It has its own time*, that is, it possesses *an inner time*, which runs from the first tone of the allegro to the last tone of the finale, but this time is not a succession of a preceding time which it continues and which happened "before" the beginning of the allegro; nor is it followed by a time which will come "after" the finale. The Seventh Symphony *is in no way in time*.[24]

What Sartre does in this passage is to contrast a certain temporality that he recognizes in music ("it has its own time . . . it possesses an inner time") with chronological time, which, as we have seen, consists in the passing of a "now" that was "before" and will be "after." But Sartre clearly denies such a structure in music ("this time is not a succession of a preceding time which it continues and which happened 'before' the beginning . . . nor is it followed by a time which will come 'after'"). That is why "the Seventh Symphony is in no way in time"—precisely because it is not characterized by the passing of time.

But it possesses the temporality of repetition. To prove how essential repetition is for music, think what would have to be the equivalent of *da capo* in painting? Repetition belongs essentially to music: music emerges precisely when a series of sounds is repeated, the same, or, more importantly, differently—when a musical phrase returns again and again in a composition (think of Wagner's leitmotivs). Noise is distinguished from music on the basis of its *lack* of repetition. It is the complexity of repetition—that is, *rhythm*—that elevates sound to the status of music.

So what happens to time when music is played? It does not go away (since retrospectively I can still say that I spent an hour listening to the Seventh Symphony in the symphony hall), but it is "negated" (*néantisé*)—it is suspended: the temporality of music transforms time by opening chasms in the body of time (the body of sequence) through which we can get glimpses of the time-less.

The Time of the Timeless—
The Vision of the Invisible

Such a "glimpse of the timeless," I would like to argue, is, properly speaking, the Moment—what in the history of philosophy has been known as *exaiphnes* or *der Augenblick.*

The *exaiphnes*, as a technical philosophical term, appears almost mysteriously for a very brief time in Plato's *Parmenides* (156d–e).[25] I have resisted translating the term *exaiphnes*, and with good reason. Some of its standard translations include "the instant," "the moment," and "the sudden"—all of which, however, fail to convey those specific semantics that Plato himself explicitly refers to when he writes, "the *exaiphnes* seems to signify that *from which* something changes to something else" (τὸ γὰρ ἐξαίφνης τοιόνδε τι ἔοικε σημαίνειν, ὡς ἐξ ἐκείνου μεταβάλλον εἰς ἑκάτερον; 156d). The "from which" alludes to the preposition "ex-" ("ek-") that means "from out of . . ." Out of what? The etymology of the term informs us, "Ex-a-phanes," that is, "out of the in-visible."

The change, then, that the *exaiphnes* occasions "comes out of what is in-visible." Its coming is always unforeseeable (hence its translation as "sudden") and, in this respect, quite different, say, from the future, which is always that toward which our hopes and expectations are oriented. As "sudden," the *exaiphnes* occurs in no time (therefore, in an "instant" or in a "moment"). Finally, the very fact that it cannot be registered by time makes it also ontologically ambivalent: "it neither is nor is not, neither comes to be nor ceases to exist."

Of course, such a concept, beyond time and beyond being, could not have escaped the attention (if only perplexed) of the great hermeneuts and exegetes of the Platonic corpus. Damascius, the so-called Diadochos, the last philosopher to succeed Plato as the head of the Academy, offers us the following gloss:

> neither all-together timeless, nor in time, but both, a timeless moment in time and a moment in time and yet timeless . . . somehow that which is in time becomes eternal and becoming assumes being, and similarly the eternal is temporalized, and the being is intermingled with generation.[26]

But how can the *exaiphnes* bring about such an unprecedented *coincidentia oppositorum*, where time is eternalized and eternity temporalized? What are its powers that can cause the descent of the timeless into temporal flux and the elevation of mundane time to the eternal — with itself being neither (neither time nor eternity) and, at the same time, both? To answer this question, we need to consider the hypothesis that the *exaiphnes* is the moment in the sense that Heidegger understands *der Augenblick.*

Three Modalities: How, When, What

What is the connection between the *exaiphnes* and the *Augenblick*? First, *Augenblick* is, according to the tradition, the term that Luther introduced in the first German translation of the Bible when he chose to translate the Pauline "in the twinkling of an eye" (ἐν ῥιπῇ ὀφθαλμοῦ, 1 Cor. 15:52). "In the twinkling of an eye" is not a chronological specification but rather kairological, to the extent that Paul employs it in order to indicate the eschatological change ("and we shall be changed," 15:52) that is to take place ἐν ἐσχάτοις καιροῖς. Within the New Testament, *kairos* is always the time of the *Parousia*. We read in Mark's gospel:

> You do not know when the appointed time *(kairos)* will come. It is like a man travelling abroad. He leaves home and places his servants in charge, each with his own task; and he orders the man at the gate to watch with a sharp eye. Look around you! You do not know when the master of the house is coming, whether at dusk, at midnight, when the cock crows, or at early dawn. Do not let him come suddenly *(exaiphnes)* and catch you asleep. (Mark 13:33–36)

In the allegory of the last things, the coming of the *kairos* is happening in the mode of the *exaiphnes*. The moment of the *kairos* is the moment of the de-cision (ἀπό-φασις that appears ἀπο-φαίνεται), that is, it emergences from the invisibility into the visible *(ex-a-phanes)*.[27]

When Heidegger, during the winter semester of 1920–1921, dedicated some of his seminars to a close reading of the First and Second Letters to Thessalonians, he chose the word *Augenblick* to translate Paul's *kairos*.[28] This choice is a pointer toward the characteristics that *der Augenblick* and *exaiphnes* share. To my knowledge, Heidegger never uses the term *exaiphnes* explicitly. We know, however, that he was aware of Kierkegaard's treatment of *der Augenblick* (to which he himself alludes in the critical note from page 338 (311 in Joan Stambaugh's English translation) of *Sein und Zeit*. Kierkegaard makes at least one explicit connection between *exaiphnes* and *Augenblick*. "A blink," he writes "is therefore a designation of time, but mark well, of time in the fateful conflict when it is touched by eternity. What we call the moment *[Augenblick]* Plato calls τὸ ἐξαίφνης." And then he continues: "whatever its etymological explanation, it is related to the category of the invisible."[29]

Both terms, *exaiphnes* and *Augenblick*, are characterized by a curious and strange conflation of *temporality* (as the Moment) and *phenomenality* (the emergence of the invisible, the blink of the eye). Heidegger, in the same lectures mentioned above, makes clear that the scriptural language of *kairos* involves the question not only of the *when* but also of the *how*.[30] That is all the more true for *exaiphnes* than for the *Augenblick*. For both terms not only point toward a moment (to come) and therefore to a *when*, but also indicate *how* this moment will come. In the case of the *exaiphnes* the *how* of its coming is revealed, as we have already seen, by the very etymology of the term. In the mystical language of Christian Neoplatonism, the *exaiphnes* becomes emblematic of the sacred time of divine presence, in its tripartite manifestation: historically (in the Incarnation), personally (in visions and apparitions), and eschatologically (in the sacraments of the Church).[31] All three events share the same structure, so to speak, of the *exaiphnes*, and all three are to some extent referenced in the New Testament (although these connections continue to occur in texts well beyond the New Testament):[32] the first is Mark 13:36, that we have already quoted, which links the *exaiphnes* with the *eschaton*; Luke 2:13 relates the *exaiphnes* with the moment of Jesus' birth[33] and in particular with the so-called "celestial liturgy" of the angels; the other two occurrences of the *exaiphnes* in the New Testament are found in the book of the Acts (9:3 and 22:6), both times describing the light that blinded Paul on his way to Damascus.[34]

Dionysius in his *Third Letter* inscribes the event of the Incarnation, quite fittingly, within the temporality of the *exaiphnes*: "The *exaiphnes* is the unexpected, and that which comes out from the invisible into the manifest."[35] Plotinus takes this analysis a step further, by examining not only *how* the *exaiphnes* comes but also *what* is coming to phenomenality. He says that what appears in the *exaiphnes* is phenomenality itself and nothing more or nothing else than that. The light that strikes in the moment of the *exaiphnes* is not a light that would light up this or that object, a light that would guide us to see some-*thing* other than itself: no, the phenomenality of the *exaiphnes* is a phenomenality independent of any phenomena, a seeing without objects: "Seeing, in *exaiphnes*, without seeing how, but the vision that fills the eyes with light did not make to see something else through it, but the light itself was the vision."[36] And again, he reiterates the same point in another passage by saying: "what ought to be seen is the very thing by which one is illuminated."[37] An idea that strangely resonates with another, more familiar perhaps, passage from the book of the Acts: "As he traveled along and was approaching Damascus, a light from the sky suddenly [*exaiphnes*] flashed about him. Saul got up from the ground and although his eyes were open he saw *nothing*."[38]

That light was the light of Christ, or better yet, Christ Himself — but notice how this moment of epiphany "out of nothing" (i.e., *exaiphnes*) turns the things-themselves (the visible) into nothing — the very nothing that Paul sees. In the moment of the *exaiphnes* the things-themselves have to retreat, and indeed "disappear," in order to allow the unapparent and the unseen (that is, the things-to-come) to show themselves. Here we have the beginnings of an all-together different aesthetics — temporal aesthetics where a reversal takes place: what we usually see has to disappear (the visual together with its static objects) in order to allow us to "see," always for a "moment," in "the twinkling of an eye," what usually remains unnoticed, the nothing (οὐδέν) of visibility itself — bare and naked.

The light of the *eschaton* — of the consummation that has already begun — keeps reaching us at the present; the daybreak of that eighth day, still to dawn, sheds its light on the now, on the momentary and the fleeting, on the ephemeral and the arbitrary, and makes each and every thing visible — *while itself remaining invisible* (that is what Heidegger calls the phenomenon of the "inapparent").[39] We speak of light: it is, of course, an old metaphor but a telling one. As light that illuminates everything in a room renders things visible while it itself remains hidden — or, rather, it is we who, by seeing only what thus comes to light, remain "blind" to light itself — so our preoccupation with the things-themselves "blinds" us as to the things-to-come, although it is in this expectancy that the things-themselves assume their proper shape and character.

The future is present in the present, hidden like the mustard seed in the soil (Matt. 13:31) and, thus, already under way to its surprising transformation. The things-themselves, therefore, can be opened up so as to expose "hidden in them" the things-to-come only by means of radical *reversal* — what earlier here was called "an inverted intentionality" analogous to the inverted perspective that characterizes the Byzantine icons. The invention of perspective by late medieval thinkers and Renaissance artists gave rise to modernity, subjectivity, and the Enlightenment. This is the point made by Karsten Harries in his *Infinity and Perspective*.[40] It is this very notion of perspective that has distorted in a decisive way our understanding of eschatology. A genuine eschatology operates by surprise, in allowing a counter-movement of history, not *toward* the kingdom but rather *from* the kingdom.[41] This structure of counter-movement in the flux of history needs to be paired on the personal level with a counter-movement of perception and understanding. The from-the-kingdom movement that runs against the forward current of *pro*-gress, but also propels it by exercising an irresistible attraction toward itself, has as its aim the disarmament of our predictability, that is, our prejudice. The *eschaton* is like the new wine that cannot be contained in the old wineskins because we all know what happens then. The old wineskins are nothing else but the concepts and categories of this world, the thinking process that we are used to and familiar with — let us call it our *perspective*. Thankfully, there are moments every day when, in anticipation of God's kingdom, our perspectives are confronted and reversed. When this happens — and it does happen — then we speak of a "transformation" (like the one that is undergone by Schoenberg's *Verklärte Nacht*) or of a moment of "epiphany" (like the ones described by Joyce). When this happens, when my perspective is countered, inversed, returned to me, I am no longer the privileged subject that establishes and constitutes the objectivity of the world (the thinghood of the things), *but merely a dative*; I become this "to whom" the world, as the world-to-come, is given. For only then can there be a world given, when I make myself available as a receiver, as gifted (*l'adonné*) with the gift of givenness.

That no object could be sustained as a phenomenon in the mode of *exaiphnes* is not an accident: that very mode, after all, is, as we have already seen, a movement of negativity that negates whatever could be used as a substitute (an idol) of its epiphany. In the first chapter of this work we encountered an instance of such negativity in the episode of Elijah's failure to "see" God where he expected Him most to be (the earthquake, the strong wind, the fire). The reading of the passage from 1 Kings negates one by one Elijah's anticipations (οὐκ . . . οὐκ . . . οὐκ) until God is finally given in the paradoxical phenomenon of an unexpected whisper of the wind.

The gospel of John provides us with yet another example of a divine manifestation that comes out from a background of negativity. This time it is one of the post-paschal apparitions of Christ to his disciples (the original has ἐφανέρωσεν, which literally means "to make visible"). Was Christ invisible before and thus in need of making Himself visible to them? No. In fact, the disciples *see* and converse with Him from the very beginning of their encounter with Him, but they fail in *recognizing* Him, that is, in seeing Him for who He was. This is how that encounter is narrated by John:

> After these things Jesus showed Himself again to the disciples at the Sea of Tiberias, and in this way He showed Himself: Simon Peter, Thomas called the Twin, Nathanael of Cana in Galilee, the sons of Zebedee, and two others of His disciples were together. Simon Peter said to them, "I am going fishing." They said to him, "We are going with you also." They went out and immediately got into the boat, and that night they caught nothing. But when the morning had now come, Jesus stood on the shore; yet the disciples did not know that it was Jesus. Then Jesus said to them, "Children, have you any food?"
> They answered Him, "No."
> And He said to them, "Cast the net on the right side of the boat, and you will find some." So they cast, and now they were not able to draw it in because of the multitude of fish.
> Therefore that disciple whom Jesus loved said to Peter, "It is the Lord!" (John 21:1–7)

What has led him to that conclusion? Why did the disciples in the beginning "not know that it was Jesus" but then come to recognize Him ("It is the Lord!")? The answer lies in the long hours of work during the night, a night that yielded nothing. The evangelist says only "that night they caught nothing." He leaves it to us to imagine the frustration of the disciples as time after time they would throw their nets into the sea only to pull them back empty. We are to imagine the weariness that such futile labor has brought to their bodies, working through the night, sleepless. So when the day dawns and this stranger asks them, "Children, have you any food?" we are to take His question as hitting precisely at the core of their disappointment. Their answer — "οὔ" — weights down their shoulders for it is a confession of their failure and frustration. It is also the necessary step that would take them to a more profound confession ("It is the Lord!"). The disciples had to utter this bare and heavy "no" as Elijah had to go through a series of negations before he recognized Yahweh in his cave. The recognition of nothing ("they caught nothing") is the first step toward the recognition of the divine stranger, because the more they experience this "no" of their insufficiency the more clearly they would see the work of God in the plenitude offered by the stranger. For as soon as they admit that they have nothing, they are found to have everything: "now they were not able to draw [the net] in because of the multitude of fish." It is this sudden moment *(exaiphnes)* from nothing to everything that becomes the sign that betrays the stranger's true identity: it is the Lord!

* * *

The fecund negativity of the *exaiphnes* (the visibility of the unapparent, the hiddenness of the manifest), insofar as it remains indicative of God's manifestation, allows us to classify it as a form of a formal indication *(formale Anzeige)* for the phenomenology of God — an indication whose sense is filled out or rather fulfilled in Revelation. The phenomenon of Revelation obeys that singular logic, already described in the previous chapter, of a phenomenon fully overlapping with its phenomenality: for example, the revelation of Christ (the phenomenon) and Christ the revealer (the phenomenality) are indistinguishable ("ce qui est révélé est le révélable").[42] The "what" *(Gehaltssinn)* of the phenomenon is also its "how" *(Bezugssinn)*. That overlapping, or rather interweaving *(Verflechtung)*, between the two modes is operated by a third modality, what Heidegger in his early seminars calls *Vollzugssinn*. That third term upsets Husserl's scheme of an intentionality neatly paired with intuition and signals a breach in the theoretical detachment of phenomenology that calls for a de-cision ("It is the Lord!") and thus, for a kairological stance toward phenomena. What connects the analysis of *prosopon* as *topos* (chapter 1) with the understanding of *prosopon* as *tropos* (chapter 2) is the negativity of the *exaiphnes* (chapter 3). It is the *exaiphnes* that functions as the indicative pointing, in the way Husserl describes it in the "Essence of Indication," from the "actual knowledge" of things to a "knowledge" of a reality neither known nor seen:

> In ihnen finden wir nun als dieses Gemeinsame den Umstand, daß irgendwelche Gegenstände oder Sachverhalte, von derem Bestand jemand aktuelle Kenntnis hat, ihm den Bestand gewisser anderer Gegenstände oder Sachverhalte in dem Sinne anzeigen, daß die Überzeugung von dem Sein der einen von ihm als Motiv (und zwar als ein nichteinsichtiges Motiv) erlebt wird für die Überzeugung oder Vermutung vom Sein der anderen.[43]

It is this motivation *(Motiv)*, a motivation that lacks any foreseeability *(nichteinsichtiges)* or perspective, which allows the indication to function, that is, to traverse and bridge the distance between the indicating sign and the indicated meaning. The two are interwoven in sense: in the double sense of "sense" as the sensible that shows itself (sign) and the sense that it makes (meaning). It is important to note that two distinct philosophical movements find their inaugural moment in this passage: Derrida's infinite deferring of sense that leads him to the deconstructive *différance*[44] and Merleau-Ponty's intertwining of sense and sensible in his notion of the *flesh*.

Each of the three chapters in this first part of this work has attempted, implicitly or explicitly, to resist the either/or dilemmas around which our thinking of God is structured, by reaffirming each time the chiasms that unite — without confusion and without division — what, under a pre-phenomenological consideration, might look contrary and incompatible. Thus, the first chapter opposed the pseudonymous dead end of the metaphysical distinction between the concept and the otherness of God, by reversing the conceptualizing schema so that now the concept *(Begriff)* of God becomes the consciousness itself as grasped *(gegriffen)* by God. The second chapter faced another set of similar dichotomies: that of immanence as opposed to transcendence, of essence and existence, of the sacred and the profane. The dual character of the *prosopon* (topological and tropological) assisted us in overcoming these pairs of contraries, exposing their complicity. Finally, the last chapter of this part posed the problem of time and eternity. Its answer was the *exaiphnes*, that is, the shadow of the eternal when it is cast over time, forming thus the third and final chiasm of a realized, or rather, inaugurated eschatology.

PART TWO. HEARING

. . . And we have heard . . .
  —1 John 1

ALLEGORY 2

Keeping in mind everything already said here regarding the principle of reading Brueghel's allegories — how, in other words, the key of deciphering them lies in the paintings within the painting in question — let us note down some initial observations about the allegorical representation of the sense of hearing.

As was the case with "Sight," here too we notice that the painter has brought together every medium of the sonic spectrum. There are musical instruments (of all kinds) and musical scores, a large variety of clocks and birds. In the center of the composition, Aphrodite turns toward the viewer, holding a lute, while Eros, seated by her feet, seems to sing from an open score. In harmony with their music making, a company of musicians in action is depicted in the farthest point of the room. It is also worth noticing how Brueghel has juxtaposed music (connoted by the instruments on the one side of the room) and time (implied by the clocks on the other). Music could be said to be in a relation of discord with time — as we shall have the opportunity to see in one of the following chapters.

It is more difficult to justify the odd, as it seems, appearance of a deer in the middle of the room and next to Aphrodite and Eros. Besides being a wild animal, and therefore hardly to be encountered walking on beautiful rugs, a deer, furthermore, is an animal that does *not* produce any sound. One is tempted to make it the equivalent of the blind man in "Sight"—for the deer is precisely imperceptible to the ear. However, it is also an animal that has been associated, by a long tradition, with acute hearing. It might be said, then, that it embodies a paradigmatic receptivity to sound.

Such a paradigmatic usage of hearing is depicted in the two major (and most discernible) paintings placed on each side of the open balcony. The one on our right portrays Orpheus, the mythical musician, playing his lyre and enchanting with his song a number of wild animals that surround him. The other, on our left, is a triptych with its main panel showing the scene of Mary's Annunciation. The choice of themes could not have been more appropriate.

The Annunciation is related to the sense of hearing in a threefold way. According to the literal interpretation, the Annunciation, after all, consists of an announcement, which is pronounced by the angel, and, thus, to be *heard*. According to the allegorical interpretation, Mary conceives the Word of God through hearing (*conceptio per aurem*, or *ex auditu*), for it is only fitting to receive Him, who is the living Word, through the organ most suitable to language and sound. Finally, according to the typological reading, as Eve transgressed God's will through hearing (ἀκοή), so the Second Eve — in a beautiful counterpoint — restores humanity through obedience (lit. *ob-audire*, ὑπ-ακοή).

Orpheus served as the prototype of Christ in Christian art as early as the first symbolic drawings in the catacombs. His *kerygma* is the new song whose captivating beauty draws the entire creation toward Him. As the incarnate Word (that has united the divine and human natures in a new harmony), He himself is the music that resonates in the heavens, on earth, and even, after His Orphic descent to Hades, in the underworld.

These remarks might prove helpful in understanding the striking and total absence of speech and language from Brueghel's composition. Isn't language, after all, addressed to the ear? And yet, there is nothing in this allegory of hearing that indicates a human *logos* (the dialogue of conversation, for example, or even the silent reading of a book). Why? Could it be, perhaps, because Brueghel restricted language to another order (represented here by the two paintings), the divine, for it is from there that the call to language originates? That same call that, like the angel's message to Mary or Orpheus's song to the animals, requires from us a new listening (*audire*, ἀκοή) as obedience (*ob-audire*, ὑπ-ακοή)? A call, finally, whose beauty initiates in response not in the doubling of language, but in the responsorial (antiphonal, as Chrétien would say) music of hymn. The only *logos* properly addressed to God is doxology.

four
Prelude: Figures of Silence

The twentieth century's so-called "linguistic turn" in both the analytic and continental traditions made language the predominant concern around which most of the philosophical production on both sides of the great divide evolved and still continues to evolve. To be sure, human logos (in its numerous transformations throughout history) was often praised by ancient, medieval, and modern authorities alike. After all, it is language, in its most simple and fundamental manifestation of our sonorous capacity for speaking, and thus communicating with each other, that makes us persons (*per-sonare*). Language gives rise to our thought, and, through speech, we give expression to ourselves and to the world around us. However, language was never before elevated to this singular paradigm under which all epistemology and all ontology, indeed, the entirety of philosophical thinking, was to be subordinated.[1]

Language makes sense only thanks to difference. Each unit in any given language (a word, a color, a piece of chess) has meaning only insofar as it *differs* from the rest. Each word (even words that sound or are spelled the same) is understood by the *different* place it occupies within a syntax (a noun, a verb, etc.). A language is this set of differences, a system based on difference and generating difference. Meaning itself becomes a by-product of this play of differences. Thus, difference casts its net so far and, at the same time, envelops us so tightly that there is nothing that can be said to be "outside" or "beyond" language.[2] There is nothing *other* than language. All *otherness* is exhausted within language, as *difference*. Whatever evades language is ineffable, unthinkable, non-existent, nothing and less than nothing.

The possibility or impossibility of a language of God is raised against this very problematic of difference and otherness, according to which a "language of God" could mean two things: either (a) "God" is taken to be just another linguistic unit among the rest (a word, a concept), its meaning regulated by the set of differences within which it is inscribed — in that case, "God" is a signifier without a signified, for, as we have seen, there cannot be an other of language; or (b) if God is to be God, He is to be taken as a "different" beyond difference, or as "non-different," other than language, that is, as radically other. His otherness marks the collapse of language insofar as He is a signified without a signifier; therefore, only silence can address Him.

With regard to God, therefore, philosophy can hold two positions: either the confinement of God in the immanence of language (the cataphatic way) or the exile of God in the transcendence of silence (the apophatic way). The one, however, is not opposed to the other, as one might think, but rather they both presuppose each other. A choice between the two is a pseudo-dilemma, for choosing one unavoidably leads to or presupposes the other. What follows in this chapter is a critical presentation of both positions by reading the works of Wittgenstein (first part) and Derrida (second part). Only such critical examination can expose the philosophical premises that analytic silence and deconstructive negation share, and by doing so, it can prepare us for the step that will take us, beyond difference and otherness, toward a language not spoken but heard. This Part 2, then, will trace our discussion from the oscillation of language between system and silence (chapter 4) to their overcoming in hymn (chapter 5) and in its inverted acoustics complementary to the inverted perspective of Part 1, until we finally reach an encounter with a new "subject" of language, understood not as speaker anymore, but rather as one who is spoken to and called (chapter 6).

Language and Difference

"Don't think," Wittgenstein exhorts us, "but look" (*PI*, 66):[3] such was his view of philosophy that it has been argued that his philosophical methodology consisted more of a "showing" than (as for the rest of the tradition) of a "saying." That is why, perhaps, "God" — impossible as such a "thing" is to show — had to be excluded early on from the proper field of philosophical thinking with the now classic dismissal: "Whereof we cannot speak, thereof we must remain silent" (*Tractatus*, 7). There were moments, however, where his silence breaks sufficiently to allow for the following two statements to be made:

> Grammar tells what kind of object anything is. (Theology as grammar) (*PI*, 373)—How words are understood is not told by words alone. (Theology) (*Zettel*, 144)

In what follows we will try to untangle these statements and their references (albeit parenthetical) to theology. What does it mean to say that theology is "as grammar"? What kind of word is "God"? How is the word "God" used? What can possibly be the meaning of such a word, and how does it mean?

It should be made clear, however, that what is at stake here is only the *language of* God (i.e., a theo-*logy*) and how such a language (with God as its "object") can be meaningful; Wittgenstein's concern about God could never have been extra-linguistic. For he knew, by remaining faithful to Kant, that the phenomenon of God could never be addressed as such but only described: a description limited to the apparatuses (most notably, language) through which one is aware of it:

> We feel as if we had to *penetrate* phenomena: Our investigation, however, is directed not towards phenomena, but, as one might say, towards the "*possibilities*" of phenomena. We remind ourselves, that is to say, of the *kind of statement* that we make about phenomena . . . Our investigation is therefore a grammatical one. (*PI*, 90)

In the Beginning: Two Stories about Language

I would like to begin this discussion by reading the opening sections of Wittgenstein's *Philosophical Investigations*, since it is there that the concept of language as *Sprachspiel* emerges. The voice that opens the book is not, strangely enough, that of Wittgenstein, but the voice of a child who, as he informs us, has just learned how to speak:

> From infancy I came to boyhood, or rather it came to me. Yet infancy did not go away: for where was it to go? Simply it was no longer there. For now I was not an infant, without speech, but a boy, speaking. So I began to reflect that [my elders] would make some particular sound, and as they made it would point at or move towards some particular thing: and from this I came to realize that the thing was called by the sound they made when they wished to draw my attention to it. That they wished this was clear from the motions of their body, by a kind of natural language common to all races which consists in facial expressions, glances of the eye, gestures, and the tones by which the voice indicates the mind's state—for example whether things are to be sought, kept, thrown away, or avoided. So, as I heard the same words again and again properly used in different phrases, I came gradually to grasp what things they signified; and forcing my mouth to the same sounds, I began to use them to express my own wishes. Thus I learned to signal what I meant to those about me; and so took another long

> step along the stormy way of human life in society, while I was still subject
> to the authority of my parents and at the beck and call of my elders.[4]

Wittgenstein's gesture in opening his *Philosophical Investigations* with a quotation taken from the fourth-century Christian bishop's autobiographical memoir has drawn the uneasy attention of his commentators and has provoked some interesting comments.[5] Augustine's story of his passage from infancy to boyhood — that is, from speechlessness to language — marks the transition from the silence before the opening of the *Philosophical Investigations* (the silence in which the *Tractatus* solemnly concludes) to the language opened up by the *Philosophical Investigations*. Wittgenstein is interested in Augustine's personal account of language acquisition because, according to him, it gives us "a particular picture of the essence of human language" (*PI*, 1). More specifically:

> It is this: the individual words in language name objects — sentences are combinations of such names. — In this picture of language we find the roots of the following idea: Every word has a meaning. The meaning is correlated with the word. It is the object for which the word stands. (*PI*, 1)

Augustine's picture of language could be stated by means of the following, simplified, motto: "All words are names." What such a view implies, then, is the isomorphic adequation between language and things: you say the word, you point at the object.[6] It doesn't take long, however, before we realize that, although such a view might seem to work for words like "stone," "table," "book," etc., it appears to be something more than problematic when it comes to words like "red," "pain," and, perhaps, "God"; not to mention, of course, such categories of words that we are using constantly although we are totally unable to point at them, like verbs and adverbs. In short, Wittgenstein's criticism of Augustine's language picture consists in the failure of the latter to distinguish between different *kinds* of words or, better yet, *differences* (in language and its usages). If Augustine's voice, however, was given a preeminent place in the very beginning of Wittgenstein's book, it was not because the latter was really interested in refuting an old theory of language that, as we suspect from other moments in the *Confessions*, even Augustine himself was not so naive as to believe, but rather, it served a twofold purpose: first, to raise a criticism against Wittgenstein's own Tractarian view of language,[7] and second, to introduce a new understanding of language based on the metaphor of language as game. His self-criticism is to be found in the acknowledgment that Augustine's picture has served as the ground on which "the following idea" has taken root: "Every word has a meaning. The meaning is correlated with the word. It is the object for which the word stands." It is not hard to discern behind these words Wittgenstein's own view, as it was exposed in the *Tractatus*, that it is the *referent* of language that constitutes also its *meaning*.[8] According to this view, it would have been meaningless to speak of anything whose referent was not apodictically evident (i.e., present).

To Augustine's recollection, then, Wittgenstein juxtaposes his own story:

> Now think of the following use of language: I send someone shopping.
> I give him a slip marked "five red apples." He takes the slip to the shop-
> keeper, who opens the drawer marked "apples"; then he looks up the word
> "red" in a table and finds a colour sample opposite it; then he says the
> series of cardinal numbers—I assume that he knows them by heart—up to
> the word "five" and for each number he takes an apple of the same colour
> as the sample out of the drawer. It is in this and similar ways that one oper-
> ates with words. (*PI*, 1)

Wittgenstein's story immediately strikes us as an odd one. It is not only the
grotesque exaggeration of our everydayness that we recognize (or fail to recognize) in its narration: one wonders, indeed, if in Wittgenstein's Vienna the
shopkeepers keep the groceries in drawers and consult their color samples
before handing them out. Moreover, what we have here is the oddity of a story
about language from which every form of speech has been eclipsed. This is a
voiceless story. In stark contrast with Augustine's account and its predominant
voice, Wittgenstein's favors the silence of the *written* sign: from the first person
to the one who runs the errand to the shopkeeper, all communication takes
place in *silence*. Wittgenstein wishes to disassociate language from speech as,
perhaps, Ferdinand de Saussure had some years earlier undertaken the famous bifurcation that distinguished between language *(la langue)* and speech
(la parole).[9] Only once this distinction has been made can we then see in
language that homogeneous system of signs that includes but by far exceeds
speech. "Language, once its boundaries have been marked off . . . can be classified among human phenomena, whereas speech cannot" (*CGL*, 15).

Inside Language: The Meaning

What makes a word or a sentence meaningful as opposed to nonsensical?
How does language mean, even prior to *what* it means? There is no easy answer to these questions. However, some insights, taken from both Wittgenstein
and Saussure, are in order. For both thinkers meaning depends on a number
of parameters: of *who* is speaking, *how* one is speaking, and *from where* one
speaks. Let's take again the example of Augustine. Wittgenstein makes the following comment:

> Augustine, we might say, does describe a system of communication; only
> not everything that we call language is this system . . . It is as if someone
> were to say: "A game consists in moving objects about on a surface ac-
> cording to certain rules . . ."—and we replied: You seem to be thinking of
> board games, but there are others. You can make your definition correct by
> expressly restricting it to those games. (*PI*, 3)

Here, for the first time, the analogy between language and games is established. Several more instances will follow where a language (or what will soon
be called *the language game*) is compared with a game of chess—the exact

same analogy, interestingly, that Saussure frequently employs in his lectures.[10] What differentiates the concept of language game from mere speech is that the former informs the *grammar* of the "game," within which its moves become meaningful. Language game is that *whole* — the unity of the rules and the practice of the game, "the language and the actions into which it is woven" (*PI*, 7) — and, ultimately, the community that carries out these actions. These three factors that determine the language game — grammar (how), practice (where from), community (who) — are also to be found in Saussure's description of *la langue*, where language is said to be a treasury filled

> by the members of a given *community* through their *active use* of speaking, a *grammatical* structure that has a potential existence in each brain, or, more specifically, in the brains of a group of individuals. For language is not complete in any speaker; it exists perfectly only within a *collectivity*. (*CGL*, 13–14; my emphasis)

One speaks the language (*die Sprache sprechen*) as one plays the game (*das Spiel spielen*); this implies a few more mutual characteristics that I can mention here only in brief: both obey certain rules (a grammar), which cannot be changed by the players (synchronic immutability) but could be altered in time (diachronic mutability); in both, meaning is autonomous, that is, it refers to no other (reality or authority) than itself;[11] and it is arbitrary.[12]

Grammar

To remain with the analogy of language game and chess game, words assume meaning depending on their function within language, as precisely each piece of chess is meaningful only when it is placed on the chessboard:

> Take a knight, for instance. By itself is it an element in the game? Certainly not, for by its material make-up — outside its square and the other conditions of the game — it means nothing to the player; it becomes a real, concrete element only when endowed with value and wedded to it. (*CGL*, 110)

Or:

> When one shows someone the king in chess and says: "This is the king," this does not tell him the use of this piece — unless he already knows the rules of the game up to this last point: the shape of the king. You could imagine his having learnt the rules of the game without ever having been shown an actual piece. The shape of the chessman corresponds here to the sound or shape of a word. (*PI*, 31)

The meaning, thus, of a word, or of any other sign, is in no way innate in it but rather constituted by the variants of its position within the system, by its juxtaposition and comparison with other words and other signs; finally, a word is meaningful only to the extent that it is *different*. Language is the "sum" (inexhaustible and not total) of this multiplicity of differences. Wittgenstein for some time even speculated about introducing his book with a motto taken from Shakespeare's *King Lear*: "I will teach you differences."[13]

To the extent that all possible differences of and between words are organized into a whole, and, more importantly, to the extent that a place is given where these differences can occur, language discloses the function of a grammar. That is how *grammar* is understood: as the possibility of a structure that allows the interplay between words, differentiates between *kinds* of words and *kinds* of usages, and acknowledges these *differences*.

The word "God" could not be an exception. For this word too becomes meaningful only in its usage according to a certain grammar by a certain community. Taken on its lexicographical value, "God" is an impossible word — impossible and meaningless — for there is nothing there to be shown.[14] A word insofar as it remains *lexis* claims to be nothing else but a *mimesis*; it represents some-*thing*; it is a representation of a *factual* reality (a lexical word is said, thus, to be the production of a duplicate, the reproduction of the *thing* only in a different order, that of phonetic and graphic signs). But there is no-*thing* that the word "God" stands for. For "God" cannot be the name of a "thing" (that would be idolatrous for religion and senseless for philosophy), and whether it is a noun or a proper name cannot be decided unless it is put in use. To have "God" without the language where it belongs is like having a "knight" with neither the chessboard nor the rules of chess: *we simply don't know what to do with it.* Wittgenstein acknowledges that much when he cites Luther and, in agreement with him, says: "theology is the grammar of the word 'God.'"[15]

But grammar operates solely on the vertical axis, that is, synchronically, and thus runs the risk of stripping language from its historical, or diachronical, dimension, reducing it to just that: a structure.

Practice and Community

What can rescue language from an a-historic reduction is its *praxis*, that is, its practical embodiment by the community's usage. As Wittgenstein emphasizes: "Here the term 'language-*game*' [Sprach-*spiel*] is meant to bring into prominence the fact that the speaking of language is part of an *activity*, or of *a form of life*" (*PI*, 23). And again: "[T]o imagine a language means to imagine *a form of life*" (*PI*, 19). There is a twofold understanding in the relation of practice to language: one that gives priority to linguistic practice over meaning, and one that returns the currency of meaning to its linguistic circulation. "The meaning of a word is its use in the language" (*PI*, 43). Meaningless is only that word which no use has yet been ascribed to, or its usage has been forgotten, and it now stands only as either the fetish of an irrevocable past or as a paleontological term that is believed to possess magical powers.

Words within the language game invite us to think of their usage before determining their meaning. To understand that, to understand why usage needs to take precedence over meaning, is to come to realize the simple fact that words are not floating in a vacuum. The word "God," for example, becomes intelligible because we have heard people using it before, in this or that way. We have come, thus, to an "understanding" of what "God" means by its different usages before undertaking a formal investigation into its meaning. What people mean when they say "God . . ." (and they mean more than one thing) is not *invented* by the individuals who make these utterances, but rather, it refers back to a long history of meaning. It is precisely because of this shared history of meaning that words are recognized as meaningful. The contrary, to use a word by inventing its meaning ad hoc, would have been, literally, idiotic. We are born into language, and we live in a world where things come already with meaning. None of us had the paradisiacal privilege to assign names to things, as if it were for the first time (Gen. 2:18–20). That seems to be what Wittgenstein's image of language as an ancient city suggests:

> Our language can be seen as an ancient city: a maze of little streets and squares, of old and new houses, and of houses with additions from various periods; and this surrounded by a multiple of new boroughs with straight regular streets and uniform houses. (*PI*, 18)

As has been said, language (especially religious language) is always "consecrated by use."[16] This is what I would like to call the *liturgical* character of language, where "liturgical" emphasizes that aspect which the etymology of the term conveys: the *ergon* carried out by a certain community — its praxis and practice. For a long time now, our words have been part of this liturgy: they have been spoken, written, cried out, and whispered. They have come to express agonies, fears, and desires; they caused violence, and they brought peace. Surely, words don't come alone. And words are not *just* words.

And "amongst the earliest that we learnt,"[17] the word "God." Far from being meaningless, the long-lasting use of this word has accumulated an excess of meaning. In fact, if we do not know anymore what "God" means, that is precisely because we know *too much* of its meaning. It is that case of polysemy that Ricoeur describes as follows: "it is a process of expansion which continues to the point of a surplus charge of meaning (overload), as we see in certain words which, because they signify too many things, cease to signify anything."[18] "God" could very well be such a word where it has ceased to name *someone*, and it has just become a sign in its own right — a "sacred" sign, to be sure, that can have only the function of a holy relic: it is displayed, worshiped, and lifeless. When such a collapse of signification occurs, then the word is elevated to the status of a fetish. The fetishization of language is a symptom of the pathology of the sign (of which religious language is constantly susceptible). Roland Barthes was able to diagnose this pathology when he wrote:

> We can manipulate the signifieds of a sign or signs only by naming these signifieds, but, by this very act of nomination, we reconvert the signified into a signifier. The signified becomes a signifier in its turn . . . [T]he retreat of the signifieds is in some sense interminable; theoretically, we can

never halt a sign at a final signified; the only halt we can give a sign in its reading is a halt which comes from *practice*.[19]

Barthes speaks here of the medical signified, as in the case of a disease; when the doctor assigns a name to it (the act of nomination); the disease, from being a signified, is now reversed to a signifier. This process can repeat itself infinitely, trapping us in "the dizzying circuit of signifier and signified." The only way that we can escape this vicious circle is, for Barthes, *practice*, that is, at some point the doctor should stop being concerned with naming the disease and proceed to curing it (that marks the conversion of "the semiological system into a therapeutic problem"). The move out of the infinite chain of signifiers, even if it is only for a moment, is therapeutic by itself. It is "a venture outside meaning" where meaning is re-discovered anew in practice.[20]

Outside Language

Saussure has insisted in more than one place in his lectures on language's precedence over its speaker:[21] I am not the "master" of language, but rather in language I obey my master. In other words, language constitutes my *facticity*: I am born in language, and "the limits of my language mean the limits of my world" (*Tractatus*, 5.6). How, then, can I even conceive of something "outside" of language? What of religious language, then? Is "God" yet another word among the many? Are we to imagine God (without quotation marks) reduced by an absolute reduction to language's immanence?

When Wittgenstein is quoted in relation to religious language, this is, more often than not, within the broader discussion of the *verifiability* or (what is the other side of the same coin) the *falsification* of religious statements. If I say, "I believe in God," but I have no empirical data to verify that a God (in whom I believe) exists, then my statement makes no sense. And if I say, "I believe in God," but experience cannot put my statement to test then, again, my statement makes no sense. Both principles try to apply the methodology and the criteria of the so-called "hard sciences" to religious statements. Wittgenstein's later philosophy is then employed as a corrective intervention to remind us that we ought to distinguish between science and religion as two different language games where the modus operandi of the one cannot and should not be applied to the other. Language games are thus depicted as a series of closed systems, with their own criteria of intelligibility that are quite unintelligible when transferred from the one to the other. In short, the language of one language game (say, science) is untranslatable into the language of another (say, religion) and vice versa. This untranslatability of languages implies a qualitative difference between different language games. Emblematic of such a view, that has come to be known as Wittgensteinian fideism, is Malcolm Norman's position: "Religion is a form of life; it is language embedded in action — what Wittgenstein calls a 'language game.' Science is another. Neither stands in need of justification, the one no more than the other."[22]

I have two serious objections to such a view. First, if religious language is its own untranslatable *Sprachspiel*, then we are all divided into two opposite categories: knowers and ignorants. The former know how to play the game; they know its rules. Moreover, their *knowledge* of the game gives them the *right* to play it; the latter do not know how to play the game. They ignore its regulations. Simply put, "they don't speak the language," they have no right to it, their lack of knowledge *excludes* them from the game. The risk here is obvious: we render religion an esoteric sect, available only to that elite of initiates who are able to decipher it. Second, if religious language is its own untranslatable *Sprachspiel*, then there are only two categories of propositions that it is able to utter: (a) revealed truths and (b) nonsense.

In any case, the implied assumption is that we cannot "play" both language games at the same time. It is an assumption that obeys a logic of exclusion: either the one or the other, religion or science, belief or knowledge, either faith or reason. But, then, we would be not much different than the builders whom Wittgenstein describes in the second section of the *Philosophical Investigations*; like them we would have to speak only one language and play only one game: always the same. The fact is, however, that we are polyglots and that we pass easily from one language game to the other. Otherwise, it would mean that language games are constructive of our identities in such a way that the former cannot change without having the latter changed as well. Rather, what determines the language as a game is the *role* that we play — the *place* that we hold. Here is where we need to call upon hermeneutics and the hermeneutical question par excellence: *d'où parlez vouz?* It is that *place* implied in the "*where* do you speak from?" that makes all the difference in the language we play:

> If one says "Moses did not exist," this may mean various things. It may mean: the Israelites did not have a *single* leader when they withdrew from Egypt — or: their leader was not called Moses — or, there cannot have been anyone who accomplished all that the Bible relates of Moses — or: etc. etc. — We may say, following Russell: the name "Moses" can be defined by means of various descriptions. For example, as "the man who led the Israelites through the wilderness," "the man who lived at that time and place and was then called 'Moses,'" "the man who as a child was taken out of the Nile by Pharaoh's daughter" and so on. And according as we assume one definition or another the proposition "Moses did not exist" acquires a different sense, and so does every other proposition about Moses . . . When I make a statement about Moses, — am I always ready to substitute some one of these descriptions for "Moses"? I shall perhaps say — By "Moses" I understand the man who did what the Bible relates of Moses, or at any rate a good deal of it. But how much? Have I decided how much must be proved false for me to give up my proposition as false? Has the name "Moses" got a fixed and unequivocal use for me in all possible cases? — Is it not the case that I have, so to speak, a whole series of props in readiness,

and am ready to lean on one if another should be taken from under me and vice versa? (*PI*, 79)

What can prevent us from replacing the word "God" for "Moses" in Wittgenstein's statement? Is Moses' existence more probable or less falsifiable than God's? Does it make more sense to say "Moses exists," while if I say "God exists," then that is meaningless? I will suggest changing the proper name "Moses" with the word "God" and reading again this passage under this new light:

> If one says "[God] does not exist," this may mean various things. It may mean that *this* God does not exist (this *kind* of God) or that God does not exist any more (as in the case of Nietzsche's "death of God") or that God is beyond the category of existence altogether, etc. *We may say, following Russell: the name* ["God"] *can be defined by means of various descriptions.* For example: as "the God who led the Israelites through the wilderness," "the God who spoke to the prophets," "the God whom Jesus called 'Father,'" and so on. *And according as we assume one definition or another the proposition* "[God] *did not exist" acquires a different sense, and so does every other proposition about* [God] . . . *When I make a statement about* [God],—*am I always ready to substitute some one of these descriptions for* "[God]"? *I shall perhaps say*—*By* "[God]" *I understand the* [being] *who did what the Bible relates of* [God], *or at any rate a good deal of it. But how much? Have I decided how much must be proved false for me to give up my proposition as false? Has the name* "[God]" *got a fixed and unequivocal use for me in all possible cases?*—*Is it not the case that I have, so to speak, a whole series of props in readiness, and am ready to lean on one if another should be taken from under me and vice versa?*

The meaning of "God"—neither fixed, nor unequivocal—is, for Wittgenstein, disclosed in descriptions preserved in our scriptural (i.e., textual and narrative) memory. That could imply, first of all, a preference for descriptions' pluralism over and against definition's monism. Our scriptural narratives, to which the meaning appeals, do not define *what* "God" is, but rather describe *who* this "God" is.[23] Secondly, these descriptions, by just being that, resist the conceptualization of "God," and thus, all the talk about its truth or falsity. Description is not an absolute, but practice.

The meaning of "God" implies also a certain *memory*. "I am the God of Abraham, Isaac, and Jacob" places the speaking voice within a certain history, in the Abrahamic story, the memory of which helps us in recognizing the name of "God" as referring to the biblical God. The name, qua sign, becomes such only in repetition, that is, only "the second time around." There are no virgin phenomena, for they could not be recognized (and thus identified) as anything. The revelation of sign, the name of "God," requires always two parameters: its "incarnation" into some sensory element, for fleshless signs are not signs at all; and a "Second Coming" that establishes that first as such, by authenticating the revelation. If there must be a sort of verification for religious statements, that could only be a verification *à venir:* to come, at the end — *an eschatological verification.*

Religious statements are, thus, suspended in this "time difference": between the First and the Second Comings, the synchronic of the now that seeks its validity from the diachronic memory of a revelation that occurred in the past and the expectation for a revelation to occur in the future. To the extent, however, that we commemorate the Second Coming *as if* it had already happened — as the Eucharistic prayer explicitly reminds us — or, even more, as happening every time that the Eucharist takes place, diachrony crisscrosses synchrony in a moment that Benjamin calls the *Jetztzeit* and Paul defines as *kairos.* When, in liturgical time, the memory of the immemorial *occurs,* then the statement "Christ is the Lord"[24] is uttered not only with meaning but also with *certainty.*

"Grammar tells what kind of object anything is. (Theology as grammar)" (*PI*, 373). Grammar is that interplay between words that allows different *kinds* of words or *differences* in words to be registered and thus to become meaningful. We have seen how a kind of thinking inattentive to this understanding of grammar can result in a theology that conflates its objects by taking God to be an *object* and failing to see the difference in *kind.* One could read Wittgenstein's phrase as follows: "Grammar tells what kind of *object* anything is"; I believe it should be read as "Grammar tells what *kind* of object anything is." Perhaps a small difference in reading but a telling one. "How words are understood is not told by words alone. (Theology)" (*Zettel,* 144). It is also told by practice and by the community. Words assume meaning once they are put in use. That is what was called above the *liturgical* character of language; perhaps theology (parenthesized here by Wittgenstein) could be said to be an exemplary case of the dependence of lexical signification upon the meaning bestowed by praxis. Religious statements, when uprooted from their practice, run the risk of becoming irrelevant and thus meaningless. To put it another way: theology (literally speaking, the *logos* about God) would fail to become a *logos* and would remain nothing more than a cluster of meaningless *lexes* unless it is put in use, that is, unless it addresses God. Augustine, after all, seems to have been aware of this small but important difference in trope: the *logos* of the *Confessions* does not speak *of* God; it is, instead, spoken *to* Him.

Language and Otherness

In the second part of this chapter, I endeavor an exploration of deconstructive negation, as a representative sample of which I take Derrida's much-discussed reading[25] of the Platonic *khora.*

Khora, in the Platonic work, corresponds to the second programmatic statement made by Timaeus in the beginning of the dialogue: τὶ τὸ γιγνόμενον μὲν ἀεί, ὄν δε οὐδέποτε ("what is this that is always becoming, without ever being?"; 27d28a). *Khora* is introduced as a "conceptual" device that would support the world of Ideas. She, thus, becomes Plato's answer to his critics, for it is the *khora* alone that can explain the workings of that world. For there are two risks in the theory of the Ideas (or Forms) that Plato needed to avoid: (1) the notion of "participation" (μετοχή or μέθεξις) of the sensible world to the intelligible could imply a form of "contact" and thus a "mingling" between the two—a highly improbable scenario for Plato—(but then, one still needs to demonstrate *how* the sensible world is a mimesis of the intelligible); and (2) if the sensible world is taken to be completely alienated from the Ideas, then things around us lack ontological ground, and, therefore, nothing can account for their existence. The introduction of *khora*, that is to say, of something that is neither intelligible nor sensible, avoids both risks. *Khora* is to be understood as a kind of mirror: on her immeasurable surface the eternal Ideas are reflected without mixing with (their own) reflections. The reflection does not really exist. The "real reality" is only that of the reflected Idea. These two never "touch" upon each other. The process of reflecting, however, provides the reflection (that is, the sensible thing) with a kind of existence, albeit temporary and conditional. The mirror itself (the *khora*) "suffers" nothing. It "is" nothing. As long as the Idea is reflected, it "gives place" to the reflection; once the process of reflection ceases, the "mirror" returns to what has always been: an anonymous, amorphous, indifferent surface with no attributes whatsoever. *Khora*, then, as this intermediate or the ontological "third" between being and becoming, prevents and even prohibits a coincidence between what really is (the Ideas) and what is not (their sensible reflections). By virtue of this function *khora* makes language possible. *Khora* herself cannot be subject to language, granted, but without *khora* language itself would have been impossible. How can we possibly speak, Plato asks, of that which is in perpetual flux? How can we name it? Isn't it slipping through our fingers without waiting for us to attach names to it (49b–e)? What we name, Plato says, when we speak is nothing else but the "impressions" (τυποθέντα, ἐντυπώσεις) that the Ideas leave on the amorphous receptacle (ὑποδοχήν), that is, *khora*. It is she, therefore, the only thing that language can name, and by naming it, language rises to existence. It is *khora* that we point at every time we say, "this is . . ." As Plato advises us, an "accurate" use of language will never say "*this* is fire," but rather "that which is always *like* this is fire" (μηδὲ τοῦτο ἀλλὰ τὸ τοιοῦτον ἀεί, 49d). *Khora* becomes the ultimate reference of language, the exclusive and unique object of our speech. If Plato, then, walks down the *via negativa* of *khora*, this is only as far as it is necessary for him to return back to the world of affirmation and language with greater confidence. His detour into the dark and ineffable apophasis of *khora* is for the sake of a more emphatic cataphasis of the luminous Ideas.[26]

Although, as Derrida acknowledges, it is the Platonic corpus itself that has provided the foundation for both structures of opposing apophaticism, he, nevertheless, introduces *khora* as a paradigm of deconstructive negation prior, if not superior, to but certainly different from its Christian equivalent or epigone of "negative theology." The first example is that of the "Good beyond Being" of the *Republic* (τὸ ἀγαθόν ἐπέκεινα τῆς οὐσίας), which institutes the Neoplatonic and Christian apophatic movements,[27] while the other—for which Derrida does not hide his preference—is that of *khora*. So, from the very beginning, *khora* is set up as the one pole in a bipolar antithesis: "In the Platonic text and the tradition it marks, it seems to me that one must distinguish between two movements or two tropics of negativity. These two structures are radically heterogeneous."[28] Is Christian negation, however, as different from its deconstructive twin as Derrida would have us believe? Are they not both insisting on the impossibility of naming or knowing God? Do they not both refuse to privilege any name, image, or concept that would come to represent God? At the end, is "God" *qua* a signifier-without-signified that much different from the mirror image of "God" *qua* a signified-without-signifier?

According to Derrida, Christian apophatic theology—especially the apophaticism of Dionysius the Aeropagite—is simply a pseudo-one, since it pretends to get rid of metaphysics by transcending language and essence only so that metaphysics can return "through the window," so to speak, by being re-posited as "hyper-essence" and "hyper-presence" at a higher level: "'negative theology' seems to reserve, beyond all positive predication, beyond all negation, even beyond Being, some hyperessentiality, a being beyond Being."[29] We will discuss in a moment the accuracy of this assessment. But, first, it is necessary to point out that initially Derrida formulated the argument of hyperessentiality in an effort to distinguish his *own* project of *différance* (and not Plato's *khora*) from Christian apophaticism:

> Already we had to delineate that *différance is not*, does not exist, is not a present-being *(on)* in any form; and we will be led to delineate also everything *that it is not*, that is, *everything* and consequently that it has neither existence nor essence. It derives from no category of being, whether present or absent. And yet those aspects of *différance* which are thereby delineated are not theological, not even in the order of the most negative of negative theologies, which are always concerned with disengaging a super-essentiality beyond the finite categories of essence and existence, that is of presence, and always hastening to recall that God is refused the predicate of existence, only in order to acknowledge his superior, inconceivable, and ineffable mode of being.[30]

The connection between Platonic *khora* and deconstructive *différance*, as we will see, remains implicit in Derrida's texts but has been stated more explicitly by his commentators.[31] Thus *khora*

> has nothing to do with negative theology; there is reference neither to an event nor to a giving, neither to an order nor to a promise, even if, as I have just underscored, the absence of promise or of order—the barren, radically nonhuman, and atheological character of this "place"—obliges

us to speak and to refer to it in a certain and unique manner, as to the wholly-other who is neither transcendent, absolutely distanced, nor imma-nent and close.[32]

This makes *khora* a sort of proto-*différance*, as they both share the character-istics of radical heterogeneity and otherness, on the basis of which they are opposed to negative theology—the latter being, according to Derrida's accu-sation, too weak an apophaticism, for "beyond being" is defined over against being, and thus it is reinscribed within the language of ontotheology.

Things, however, are more complex with Christian apophaticism than this line of argumentation assumes, as will be shown at greater length in the next two chapters, when our discussion turns to the texts of Gregory of Nyssa and Dionysius the Aeropagite. Then it will become clear that the apophati-cism inherited through the Neoplatonists and modified by the Christian authors does not allow any measure of comparison—not even a hyperbolic one—between God and being, but rather insists on their radical incommen-surability thanks to a more consistent and daring understanding of negation than any deconstructive method would have ever been able to imagine.

For the moment, however, one wonders how the very same charge of hyperessentiality, of which deconstruction accuses such thinkers as Diony-sius, Meister Eckhart, and Nicholas of Cusa, does not apply—turned upside down—to deconstruction itself. Isn't, say, the "hypoessential" negativity of *khora* defined over against the *agathon* and thus reinscribed within the meta-physics of Plato's language?

Indeed, *khora*, in Derrida's exposition, lies at the antipodes of *agathon*, the Good beyond being, with which she forms a strange couple. She is pre-sented as the irruption of the very binary opposition within which she is a pri-ori inscribed. She is the "other" of another (of *agathon*), the one limb of a pair of oppositions, a thesis always antithetical to its opposite.

Neither *khora*'s much-emphasized otherness nor *différance*'s radical dif-ference, however, can effectively secure or achieve that level of transcendence that deconstruction proudly claims for itself. Indeed, deconstructive transcen-dence is doomed to remain incomplete precisely because of its hold on other-ness and difference. Both terms are relational, that is, they have meaning only in relation to something else in comparison to which they are predicated: if *khora* is "the other of the name,"[33] "wholly-other," and "irreducibly other,"[34] its very otherness will always place it within a system of relations (to the good, God, or being).

On the other hand, Christian apophaticism, by denying even otherness as an attribute of God, undertakes the truly radical step toward transcendence.[35] It was Plotinus's mediations on the One that became the cornerstone of Chris-tian apophatic theology. To Plotinus, and, indeed, to his Christian epigones, Derrida's unfortunate remark ("hyperessentiality is precisely that, a supreme Being who remains incommensurate") would have sounded rather ludicrous:

"supreme being" is a contradiction in terms, for no being, on account of its very beingness, could ever be supreme.[36] In the Plotinian metaphysics, only the One can occupy this place exactly on account of His transcending beyond being. But the One can indeed transcend being (and beings) thanks to His lack of otherness:

> For bodies [i.e., the sensibles] block bodies from communicating with one another, but bodiless [i.e., the intelligible] things are not separated by bodies; accordingly they are not cut off from one another by place [τόπῳ, a key term in the topologies of *khora*], but rather by *otherness* and *difference* [ἑτερότητι δὲ καὶ διαφορᾷ]. So whenever there is no otherness, those things that are not other are present to one another. That One, then, *having no otherness* is always present.[37]

Deconstructive negation, by being unable to move beyond otherness and difference, is left behind, in the realm of the intelligible (for these are the "bodiless things" in Plotinus's passage), which is precisely the world of Being and of the Ideas. Indeed, predicative language and conceptual thought — the scarecrows of metaphysics — were always based on the categories of otherness and difference — the hallmarks of deconstruction. However, the overcoming of the former is never achieved without the abandonment of the latter. The deconstructionists' fear of immanence costs them the loss of transcendence, for a "transcendence which is not immanence is not true transcendence, but mere otherness."[38] God is nothing in anything because He is "all thing in all things" (1 Cor. 15:28), and "although He is nowhere, there is nowhere that He is not" (*Enneads* V, 5, 8: 24–25), or in Dionysius's words, the apophatic movement (God's anonymity) is never completed without its cataphatic counterpart (God's polyonymity) (*DN*, VII, 3, 872A).

Contrary to what one might fear, the complementary relation suggested here between negation and affirmation, anonymity and polyonymity, transcendence and immanence does not lapse back into metaphysical dialectics. Their relationship is governed by the paradoxical (and, thus, nonmetaphysical) formula of Chalcedon: "indivisibly, unchangeably, unconfused, inseparably." Any imbalance in the hypostatic union of the contraries — in other words, if the contraries are taken as such, if, for instance, apophatic silence is seen as incompatible with cataphatic language and transcendence as irreconcilable with immanence — is bound to deny the Incarnation of the Unnameable and Indescribable in language and history.

Even a prudent and acute reading of Christian apophaticism, like Merold Westphal's recent treatment of Dionysius, can fall prey to the simplification of seeing in "negative theology" only a movement of transcendence.[39] Westphal's discussion of Augustine, Dionysius, and Aquinas invokes the specter of Kant time and again.[40] The reason for that, as he himself asserts more than once, is a simple one: Christian apophasis is, according to him, a lesson in "epistemic humility" very much like Kant's Copernican revolution ("There is something wonderfully Kantian about all this. When it comes to God we do not know the 'thing in itself'" [137]). This is, to some extent, true: Kant, very much like the Church Fathers, did show that our reason cannot step outside or go beyond its createdness and that each of our concepts unavoidably bears the stamp of our mind's creatureliness on it.[41] Such a statement, however, inevitably puts the emphasis only on the one side of the chiasmus (on the transcendent, ecstatic nature of God), and thus it undermines the hypostatic union of the Christic phenomenon. With regard to Dionysius in particular, the very language of hymn and liturgical celebration (as we will see in the next two chapters) is enabled precisely by a "Kantian" gesture *against* Kant. For Dionysius's *hymnein* presupposes and, at the same time, effects the overturning of Kant's *Transcendental* Aesthetic for the sake of a *Theological* Aesthetic as the one we are exploring in this work, that is, *by the possibility of sensory experience of God* — an experience endlessly occasioned by Christ's Incarnation. Could, for Kant, the noumenon ever *become* the phenomenon?

Deconstruction's often-attested preference for a one-dimensional *ekstasis* that refuses even the minimum of *hypostasis* — evidenced again and again under a variety of rubrics, be it the *infinite* Other, *absolute* justice, *unconditional* hospitality, or *pure* gift — exemplifies a trait occurring with an alarming frequency in contemporary theories, namely, their phobia of anything incarnational. It is precisely the Incarnation that Derrida picks up in a later essay[42] in order to emphasize Christianity's break with the other two monotheistic religions (a break with considerable philosophical, and not only theological, implications). In this essay it becomes more and more evident that Derrida seems to show a preference for the *transcendence* of the voice over the *immanence* of the image. This kind of preference justifies placing Derrida in that tradition of transcendence that goes, via Levinas and Husserl, back to Kant.[43]

On the other hand, the immanentism of certain post-modern thinkers, such as Deleuze or Foucault as well as their intellectual forefather, Spinoza, reduces the incarnational flesh into the asphyxiating body of a history bereft of spirit. This polarity, once again (between a Hellenic — *hypostatic* — and a Hebraic — *ecstatic* — way of thinking, culminating in the pseudo-dilemma between an either *sur*-real or *sub*-real God), can be overcome by a third term that will be neither an *ekstasis* without *hypostasis* (deconstruction) nor a *hypostasis* without *ekstasis* (ontotheology), but rather the chiasmic (and Christic) crossroads of the two. A sojourn neither to Jerusalem nor to Athens, but, perhaps, to Chalcedon. This third term will be a *hyphen*[44] that links the *hyper* of the apophatic theology with the *hypo* of the deconstructive atheology; in other words, we need to follow, what I would like to call, a *hermeneutics of hyphenation*. Finally, it is by means of such a hyphen that *khora* is allowed to acquire a face, as in certain iconographical and hymnological depictions.

I have in mind the mosaics of the Chora Monastery,[45] whose extraordinary frescoes and mosaics that date back to the fourteenth century explain its unusual eponymy. Its iconographic program includes depictions of both the

Virgin Mary and Christ that bear the same inscription: "ἡ χῶρα" (the *khora*). In particular, the Virgin Mary is depicted as ἡ χῶρα τοῦ ἀχωρήτου (the *khora*, i.e., "container," of the uncontainable). The iconic representation of Mary as *khora* is suggestive of her role as the instrument of the Incarnation. During the Incarnation, Mary, like the Platonic *khora*, serves as the intermediate, the *triton genos* (*Timaeus* 52a) between the human and the divine; she is the point of contact between the two poles of all dualisms (Greek or Jewish), the hymen that hyphenates them. Like the receptive *khora*, Mary receives the entire deity within her body without appropriating it into herself. Thus, she becomes a paradox, an antinomy, the *khora* of the *a-khoron*, a topos that sustains what is a-topos: the receptacle of the un-receivable, the container of the uncontainable. The epithet *khora* was attributed to Mary by the unknown poet of the famous *Akathistos Hymnos* (a fifth/sixth-century hymn in twenty-four stanzas arranged in abecedary form, still in use as an Office of Lent in the Eastern Church); in the fifteenth stanza, beginning with the letter omicron, we read: Χαῖρε, Θεοῦ ἀχωρήτου χῶρα ("Hail, the container [*khora*] of the uncontainable God"). Christ is depicted as ἡ χῶρα τῶν ζώντων (the *khora* of the living). Christ is par excellence the *khora* that receives both humanity and creation in their entirety, but with no confusion, in His incarnate person. The Incarnate Christ bears the same characteristics that characterized His hyphenated birth: neither exclusively God nor only Human, but both God and Human; neither just the Word nor only Flesh, but the Word who became Flesh.

five
Interlude: Language beyond Difference and Otherness

Our study turns now to an exploration of Christian apophaticism, represented here by two Eastern Fathers, Gregory of Nyssa and Dionysius the Aeropagite. The choice of these two authors is rather obvious: they both have exercised a long and lasting influence on the theological and philosophical production of the West, through a number of distinguished translators and commentators, such as John Scotus Eriugena, Albert the Great, Thomas Aquinas, and Nicholas of Cusa. But also, each of them has experienced a sort of revival in the writings of contemporary thinkers, such as Jacques Derrida, Jean-Luc Marion, and John Milbank. To set the tone of what is to follow, let me begin by quoting (at some length) what I believe to be a crucial passage from Gregory's *Commentary on the Song of Songs*, where the problematic of knowing and naming God — the very problematic that outlines Christian apophasis — is raised. The Scriptural lines in question are the following:

All night long on my bed
I looked for the one my soul loves;

> I looked for him but found him not.
> I called him but he didn't listen.
> I will rise now and go about the city,
> through its markets and squares;
> I will search for my beloved.
> So I looked for him but found him not.
> The watchmen found me
> as they made their rounds in the city.
> "Have you not seen the one my soul loves?"
> Scarcely had I passed them
> when I found the one my soul loves.[1]

And here is Gregory's exegesis:

> All night long, I would look for Him on my bed, so as to know what is His essence, where is His origin from, in what does He aim, what sort of thing does His existence consist of — but, I would not find Him. I called Him by names, as much as it is possible to find names for the Unnameable, but it was not the meaning of a name that could reach what I sought. How is it possible to find Him, who is beyond all names, by naming? . . . That is why she [i.e., the bride] rises again, and, by means of her mind, she wanders about the intelligible and transcendent nature (which is what she means when she speaks of the "city"), in which the principalities and the dominions and the thrones appointed to the powers as well as the celestial assembly (which is referred to as the "markets") and the multitude, incalculable by number (indicated by "the squares") are located — in hopes that she would find among them her beloved . . . And she asks them: have you not seen Him, the beloved of my soul? To such a question they fell silent, and by their silence demonstrated that what she is looking for is also beyond their own capacity. However, having gone through that celestial city by the futile restlessness of her intellect and having failed to find among the intelligible and bodiless beings Him whom she desires, she abandons everything that can be found and thus she comes to know Him, the One she was searching for, Him, who becomes known solely by His incomprehensibility. Every attribute that comes from understanding is turned into an obstacle in our search to find Him. For that reason, she says, "scarcely had I passed them" — meaning that, once she left behind all creation and moved away from everything that can be thought, abandoning even every attempt to reason, she finds her beloved by faith. (*Cant*, 181–183)

The searching (ζήτησις) for God, or the beloved of *The Song of Songs*, is destined to fail insofar as it limits itself to a knowing (γνῶσις). The reasons for this failure are not to be blamed on the inability or the incapacity of the knower but rather in the "unknowability" (ἀγνωσία) of God. His "unknowability" is primarily indicated by the insufficiency of language *to name* God. Gregory (citing Phil. 2:9) states the paradox as follows: "how is it possible to find Him, who is beyond all names, by naming?" Language breaks down because the beloved does not belong in that order where language can properly function. Using the metaphors of the text under his interpretation, Gregory succeeds in showing how the bride's intellect searches the entire spectrum of intelligible things (τὴν νοητήν τε καὶ ὑπερκόσμιον φύσιν) without being able to find Him. She then turns to the angels, asking them whether they have seen (a synonym for "knowing") Him, but they remain silent. Their silence here should not be taken as the lack of an answer, but on the contrary, as the only answer. He, whom she looks for, is "spoken of" only through silence. Silence also marks the limit of language, the border which language is not allowed to trespass. Silence demarcates the distinction between a created (and thus subject to language) and uncreated (and thus ineffable) order. The latter becomes by far a more fundamental distinction than the classical dualism between the sensible and intelligible spheres. The bride has to leave behind her the whole of the created order (which includes *both* sensible *and* intelligent things) in order to find Him. More precisely, she abandons "everything that can be found" (καταλιποῦσα πᾶν τό εὑρισκόμενον), and *thus* she finds Him. What "can be found" stands here for "what can be named" (τὸ ὀνομαζόμενον) and also for that "which can be thought" (τό σκεπτόμενον). Gregory is clear: "every attribute that comes from understanding is turned into an obstacle in our search to find Him." It is important to notice at this point that instead of the senses, which are traditionally branded as insufficient to comprehend what lies beyond them, it is precisely the comprehending mind that becomes an obstacle in "thinking" God. God's very incomprehensibility serves as a "definition": "solely by [our] inability to capture [or, comprehend] '*what* He is' is He known *that* He is." Such a definition seems to have the function of a "proof" of the existence of God, similar to those given by Anselm and Descartes. If that were the case, then for Gregory, God's unknowability would be more fundamental than His perfection or infinity. In a similar tone, he adds elsewhere that the divinity "offers no signs of its nature, but is known [or recognized] solely by the impossible of [its] comprehension" (σημεῖα δὲ τῆς ἰδίας φύσεως οὐ παρεχομένη, ἀλλ᾽ ἐν μόνῳ τῷ μὴ δύνασθαι καταληφθῆναι γινωσκομένη) [*CE* I, GNO I, 137]. God's radical unknowability, doubled, as one would expect, with an equally radical ineffability, sows the seeds of what is to become a major theme and concept in Gregory's thought. God is known by the fact that He cannot be known, and that is the only "sign" of His nature. What we have here is the demarcation of a limit (of human knowledge)—but there is nothing novel about that so far; it assumes, however, tremendous importance once the next step is undertaken: the *recognition* of this very limit constitutes, at the same time, the highest point of our knowledge of God. In other words, in our falling short in knowing God, at the moment of reason's failure, knowledge is given. We get to know what we are looking for once we are forced to the painful and humbling realization of our inadequacy to know. Like the bride, we get to have what we desire by giving up on it (καταλιποῦσα).[2] What kind of an epistemology or ontology necessitates such a strange logic? The answer should be sought in Gregory's signature-concept: *diastema*.

Diastema: "The Verdurous Wall of Paradise"

Before I discuss what *diastema* means and how it functions in Gregory's understanding of theological language, we need to examine briefly the historical and theoretical background of its appearance. It was in the context of the Eunomian controversy that Gregory's philosophy of language found its fullest development. Eunomius was a second-generation Arian (of the Anomean sort), whose argument against the Son's divinity was based on an essentialistic understanding of language, namely, that *de dicto* meanings are necessarily *de re* truths. According to this necessary connection between "name" and the "essence" of the thing named, one simply needs to decide which of the divine names characterizes Godhead properly in order to have access to divine essence itself. Eunomius, following Arius, took the "ingenerate" (τὸ ἀγέννητον) of the Father to be the exclusive characteristic of divinity; that meant that the Son (as begotten) and the Holy Spirit (as proceeded) could not share the same name as God the Father, and, therefore, they have no share of the divine essence either (as Gregory puts it, "τοῦτο γὰρ εἶναι τὴν θείαν φύσιν, ὅπερ σημαίνει τὸ τῆς ἀγεννησίας ὄνομα"; *CE* II, p. 243). Necessarily, then, Gregory's criticism of Eunomius's heresy was to become at the same time a critique of Eunomius's philosophy of language. This critique unfolds in two main principles: (a) a *hermeneutical* (as opposed to an essentialist) understanding of language in general and about God in particular, and (b) the introduction of the notion of *diastema* (between created and uncreated order) and the function of the language of God in relation to this distinction.

Concerning the hermeneutical understanding of language (especially in naming the divine), Gregory had to advance a theory of language that would convincingly avoid the popular (for the Mediterranean world of Late Antiquity) theory of naturalism without reverting to sophistic conventionalism.[3] The debate whether names, and language in general, are according to nature (φύσει) or by convention (θέσει or συνθήκη) dates back to classical Athens (Plato's *Cratylus* is a lively record of such debate). For Gregory, however, what was at stake was much more than a mere philosophical curiosity. His answer to the problem is summarized in the following passage:

> Many believe that the name of the divinity is properly given according to [its] nature (κατὰ τῆς φύσεως) and that, as it is the case with the sky or the sun or any other element of the world which by their proper name connote the meaning of their substances, similarly — they are telling us — the name that indicates the divinity is applied to the supreme and divine nature as if it were some proper name (κύριον ὄνομα). We, however, following the Scripture, have learned that it is unnameable and ineffable; and we think that every name about the divine nature, be it by human custom or by scriptural tradition, is hermeneutical (ἑρμηνευτικὸν), without containing the meaning of the nature itself. (*Abl.*, GNO III, 42–43)

Gregory's hermeneutical understanding of language cannot be maintained apart from the characteristically Christian distinction between divine nature (or essence) in itself and its effects (energies). The different names we attribute to God (such as "being," "good," "truth," "eternal," etc.) name only His providential "effects" as perceived by us and not His own essence as it is in itself (the latter remains unfathomable and unnameable). This principle is eloquently expressed in a long passage from Gregory's commentary on the Beatitudes; there, in his effort to reconcile two seemingly opposed traditions on the vision of God,[4] Gregory articulates with clarity the *ousia/energeia* distinction. He begins by reaffirming the position that God's nature in itself (αὐτὴ καθ' αὑτὴν) is "beyond every apprehending thought" (πάσης ὑπέρκειται καταληπτικῆς ἐπινοίας).[5] After he has established the standard position of God's unknowability, however, he adds a surprising statement: "being such according to His nature, He who is beyond all nature, He is nevertheless both seen and comprehended by means of an other discourse (ἄλλῳ λόγῳ)." This "other discourse," like an alternative road, leads us not to one but to a multiplicity of ways in understanding God (πολλοὶ δὲ οἱ τῆς τοιαύτης κατανοήσεως τρόποι). He offers us two examples. As when we are admiring a great painting we somehow "see" the painter's skill and style (but not his essence) in it and, in this way, we have come to know something about the artist as he "appears" in his work, so with God's creation, we can know something about God (His "style") by looking at the world around us. In a similar way, when we come to think of our own existence — how it is not the result of any necessity but the outcome of God's goodness — by that thought too we are learning something about God. In each case, we cannot turn our gaze directly upon God as He is in Himself (without properties), for, in doing so, we would be like those who gaze at the sun (to use Socrates' famous metaphor from the *Phaedo*): the intensity of its light would blind us. It would be more prudent if, like Socrates, we "take refuge in the *logoi*" (99e5) and their hermeneutical reflections. When we contemplate, then, God as He has and still is appearing to us (through His sustaining providence), then "the invisible by [His] nature becomes visible by [His] effects" (ὁ γὰρ τῇ φύσει ἀόρατος ὁρατὸς ταῖς ἐνεργείαις γίνεται).[6] For Gregory, then, theologians are hermeneuts par excellence, and theological language progresses only by the "second sailing" (99d) of hermeneutics, in its movement both of suspension (that allows it to traverse God's radical otherness without reverting to deconstructive negation) and of suspicion (that guards it from making absolute claims about God and thus collapsing into ideology).[7]

In Gregory's work, *diastema* governs three fundamental principles:

a. The absence of *diastema* pertains only to God

b. *Diastema* pertains to the creation *as such*, that is, in its creatural finitude, and

c. *Diastema* is the insurmountable distance that separates the uncreated God and creation.

These three statements say the same thing, only each time it is viewed from a different angle. The common ground that supports them is Christianity's break away from the classical (mainly Platonic and Neoplatonic) view of the cosmos as a continuum unfolding between God and matter. Such a view allowed for communication and interaction between the uncreated God and the created cosmos (for example, the Neoplatonic notions of *proodos* and *epistrophe* — with theurgy being the most extreme example of this worldview). With Christianity a new picture emerges, one that emphasizes the qualitatively infinite abyss that separates God and His creation. The difference between man and God in the classical world is a difference of degree (in perfection); in Christian eyes, however, it is a radical difference of kind.

The first two senses of *diastema* appear to be common ground for both classical and Christian sources.[8] For Plotinus, as for the bishop of Nyssa, *diastema* is a sine qua non condition of the creation (be it ex nihilo, as a result of the Creator's will, or by emanation, through the hierarchy of beings), and the negative ἀ-διάστατος is reserved only for the divine.[9] The reasons for this distinction are quite apparent: one of the primary meanings of *diastema* is "dimension," in the sense we use this term today to speak of the four dimensions of our universe. *Diastema* presupposes and requires a dimensional world (i.e., a material and temporal world) where things have length, height, depth, and duration.[10] *Diastema*, thus understood, is translated as *interval* (in both spatial and temporal senses). For Gregory, *diastema* is also the very "space" circumscribed between two terms (πέρας): a beginning and an end; this is in particular the case of the creation. *Diastema*, then, in respect to its end, underlines the finitude (περατότητα) of our world, while, in respect to its beginning, it invites us to think of the creation as something that was not always here (as granted), but that was offered to us (as gift).

It is the third sense of *diastema*, as the insurmountable distance that separates the uncreated God from creation, which is of more interest for our purposes in this chapter. If we were to translate Gregory's *diastema* into the philosophical terminology of our days, we would have to choose "distance" as its closest, if not synonymous, analogue. "Distance" is here understood in the way that Jean-Luc Marion has used it in his work (*The Idol and Distance*, 1977) as that distinction which separates as it is "by that very fact, uniting all the more," as that incommensurability between God and man which "makes intimacy possible" (*ID*, 198). According to this strange logic of distance (that distinguishes it from both the ontological difference and the deconstructive *différance*) God approaches us by withdrawing, and in the absence occasioned by His withdrawal, His approach is felt all the more: "the intimacy of man with the divine grows with the gap that distinguishes them, far from diminishing it. The withdrawal of the divine would perhaps constitute its ultimate form of revelation. This is what we attempt to delineate under the name of distance" (*ID*, 80).

For Gregory, too, *diastema* is that gaping space open by the incommensurability between creation in its creatureliness and the uncreated God. What the di-stance (the standing apart) of the two safeguards is their radical inequality. Nevertheless, it is precisely this gap, the abyss, that challenges and confronts any language of God. The *diastema*, understood in this sense, should make it impossible for this "of" to ever unite "language" (*diastemic* par excellence) and "God" (*a-diastemic* par excellence):

> For the created essence and the uncreated nature are fenced off by a great and impenetrable wall (διατετείχισται); the one is limited, the other does not have limit (πέρας); this one is circumscribed by its proper limits according to the decision of the wise creator, the other has as its measure infinity (ἀπειρία); this one is stretched out within a certain dimensional extension (διαστηματικῇ τινι παρατάσει), enclosed by time and space, that one transcends all notion of dimension (διαστήματος) . . . In this life we apprehend a beginning and an end for all being, but the blessedness which is above creation admits neither beginning nor end but is beyond all that is connoted by either, being ever the same, firmly established but itself, without passing from one point to another by a distension (διαστηματικῶς) of its life. (*CE* II, GNO I, 246)[11]

The imagery employed by Gregory in this passage is quite significant for the understanding of the third meaning that *diastema* carries in his thought. Already from the very beginning the emphasis falls on the distance that separates the two orders in question, the "created *ousia*" and the uncreated "*physis*." This is not any distance, however. Gregory is speaking of "a great and impenetrable wall" that fences off what is created from what is uncreated. The image of the wall provides the exposition of his argument with the structure around which Gregory is building an energetic counterpoint. The juxtaposition of their differences is consistently cast in terms of limits (πεπεράτωται, πέρας, ἀπειρία), measures (μέτροις, μέτρον), enclosures (ἐμπεριείληπται, συμπαρεκτείνεται), and circumscribed spaces (περιειργομένη). *Diastema* figures twice, in the middle of this composition, defining creation and, antithetically, divinity. Once read with an attention to these details, this passage says more than providing us with a full inventory of the differences between worldly and divine attributes. It speaks the metaphorical language of the Scripture, invoking the image of "the verdurous wall of Paradise"[12] from which man was once expelled (Gen. 3:23–24) and for which he is still longing. In this passage, *diastema* becomes the conceptual equivalent of an ontological wall that keeps creation and Creator apart.

Such a separation, however, has far-reaching consequences for language and for the language about God in particular. The limits of the *diastema* that circumscribes creation are also the limits of our knowledge and language ("the limits of my language are the limits of my world," as Wittgenstein famously said).[13] God beyond *diastema* lies also beyond our capacity for comprehension and articulation. Gregory depicts a rather gloomy picture of our mind's failing attempts to "leap" over the *diastemic* wall. No matter how many times, he says, creation tries "to violate" (βιάζεται) this barrier of *diastema* in her attempt to "go beyond itself" (ἔξω ἑαυτῆς γενέσθαι) by means of comprehension (διὰ τῆς καταληπτικῆς θεωρίας), she can never succeed; the wall of *diastema* forces her to "stay always within herself" (ἐν ἑαυτῇ μένει ἀεὶ), and thus no matter where she turns her gaze, it is herself she looks at (ὅπερ ἂν ἴδῃ, ἑαυτὴν βλέπει).[14] This amounts to a very humbling experience for our theologies, and, thus, it might prove to be a good antidote against the dangers of doctrinal rigidity and confessional triumphalism. Our language of God, Gregory seems to say, is more *our* language than it is God's. But, given the impenetrability of the diastemic barrier, is such a language about God possible at all?

Gregory, of course, knows that there is a language of God, a theology he himself professes, which would mean that the abyss is bridged and the gap is traversed every time we speak of (or, as we will soon see, praise) God. How does this happen?

So far Gregory's apophaticism could have been that of Wittgenstein's or Plato's; neither Wittgenstein nor Plato, however, could have gone beyond maintaining this distinction between a world, about which we can speak, and what lies beyond it or beneath it, that remains unspoken (*das Mystische*, the *epekeina tes ousias, khora*). Their thought knows of no chiasmus between the two sides of the ontological wall that could unite them "without confusion or change" and distinguish them "without division or separation." To speak of such intertwining would require a language of Incarnation, and such is the language that Gregory employs famously in the following passage:

> For as air (πνεῦμα) is not retained in water (ἐν ὕδατι) when it is dragged down by some weighty body and left in the depth of the water, but rises quickly to its kindred element, while the water is often raised up together with the air in its upward rush, being molded by the circle of air in a convex shape with a slight and membrane-like (ὑμενώδει) surface (ἐπιφανείᾳ), so too, when the true Life that underlay the flesh sped up, after the Passion, to Itself, the flesh also was raised up with it, being forced upwards from corruption to incorruptibility by the divine immortality. (*CE* III, GNO II, 131–132)[15]

With the first two nouns in this passage — πνεῦμα and ὕδατι — two different and distinct orders are brought to the foreground: πνεῦμα is invisible and represents the world "from above," while ὕδωρ is perceived by our senses and belongs to the material world. Thus, the opposition of the two elements serves as a reminder of the *diastemic* distinction. Πνεῦμα and ὕδωρ are also the two elements of baptism (an allusion that would have been immediately noticed by Gregory's Christian readers); thus we are invited to think of the duality between the two orders in a sacramental way.[16] The rest of the passage accommodates its reading as a baptismal formula: Gregory does speak here of an immersion into the βάθος τοῦ ὕδατος. But there is more than that. The immersion into the water is a symbol itself of a different "going under," that is, of dying.[17] Gregory moves on to speak of the πάθος, the suffering and death of the "true Life." Between the first descent (into the water) and the second descent (in the underworld) the passage structures itself around the key term "ἐπιφανεία"—a term that can mean a "surface" (as its primary meaning is here in the context of this metaphor) but also, and more importantly, epiphany. It is the epiphany on the "thin and membrane-like surface" of the flesh that constitutes the third descent (into Mary's womb) that precedes and makes possible the other two, completing thus the entire spectrum of Christ's Incarnation. It is through this metaphorical recapitulation of the events of the Incarnation that we reach the crescendo of the conclusion: ἀπὸ τῆς φθορᾶς συναναωσθεῖσα ἐπὶ τὸ ἄφθαρτον. The corruptible (read "created") is "forced upwards" by the incorruptible (read "uncreated") and united with it. Thanks to the Incarnation (τῇ ἐπιφανείᾳ), the insurmountable, impenetrable wall of *diastema* has now become "a thin membrane-like surface" *(hymen).*[18]

Thus, the hymen that unites *diastematic* "water" with *adiastemic* "air" (but also keeps them apart) makes language possible. What sort of language is at stake? I believe that the *hymen* in Gregory's metaphor should be taken as the allegorical equivalent of *hymn*.[19] The language that the Incarnation makes possible—and for that reason, as I shall attempt to show in the remaining part of this chapter, the *only* proper language with respect to God—is that of the hymn. The language about God (theology) is better understood as a language of praise for God (hymnology).

Hymn: The Language of the Kingdom

If the uncircumscribed can be described and the unrepresentable depicted in iconic representation in virtue of the flesh of the Incarnate One (as the discussion has shown in Part 1), what, then, prohibits us from advancing a similar hypothesis with respect to language, namely, that, thanks to the Word-made-flesh, created flesh can now utter the unnameable and ineffable Word? And if the icon was revealed to be the proper model, so to speak, of exemplifying this new, incarnational paradigm of vision, could not hymn serve as an example of "iconic" language?[20]

To find the answer we need to return for one last time to the image of the wall. For the wall, as limit and border, not only separates what lies on either side but, by the very act of separating, brings those which it divides into proximity with each other. For each opposite side "shares" the wall of *diastema*, which becomes a sort of common ground, a point of contact where the opposites meet. This coincidence of opposites "is the wall of paradise," Nicholas of Cusa writes, addressing God on the other side of the wall, "and it is there in paradise that you reside."[21] Herein lies the impossibility of speaking of Him, as language operates on the basis of distinction, separation, and classification (e.g., grammar and syntax). But God's "there," as Nicholas understands, is quite different from our "here." "Thus, it is on the other side *(ultra)* of the coincidence of contradictories that you will be able to be seen and no-where on this side *(citra)."*[22] For the human mind to reach God an impossible task is prescribed: one would need to go through the wall of the *coinciden-tia oppositorum*, which, like the fiery revolving sword of the cherubim (Gen. 3:24), guards the gates of Paradise. To penetrate this wall of fire, however, amounts to the death of reason and predicative language (two of logic's most cherished principles, noncontradiction and identity, should be violated) — it means that language has to abandon itself altogether on the hither side. But for the bishop of Nyssa as well as for the cardinal from Cusa, thought can have a glimpse of the mysteries that lie on the *ultra* side of Paradise by finding itself at the very threshold of language *(in ostio coincidentiae oppositorum).*[23] Greg-ory never ceases reminding us that "ἐν μόνῳ τῷ μὴ δύνασθαι καταληφθῆναι γινωσκομένη," that is, God is known solely by the impossibility to compre-hend Him. This epistemological paradox — where the farthermost point of our knowledge of God coincides not simply with lack, but with the very im-possibility of such knowledge — is complemented by an equally paradoxical language: *hymnology.*

What does it mean, to stand at the threshold of the coincidence of oppo-sites? And what sort of language does one speak from there, if one is capable of speaking at all? What is the difference between a language that predicates and a language that praises? As in every threshold, the distinction between an inside and an outside becomes blurred. Firstly, the epistemological distinc-tion between the senses and the mind, or between the sensible and the intelli-gible, is abolished ("for you are there where speaking, seeing, hearing, tasting, touching, reasoning, knowing, and understanding are the same"). Secondly, the distinction between the subject and the object is undermined ("where seeing coincides with being seen, hearing with being heard, tasting with being tasted, touching with being touched").[24] As the principles on which predica-tion is grounded are one by one eliminated, another kind of language slowly emerges, a language without reason and without ground. Like the rose of An-gelus Silesius, this groundless "language" is "without why." "It blooms be-cause it blooms."[25] Language, on the other hand, as we know it through our everyday acts of speech, always serves a purpose: it communicates, it demands, it informs, it prohibits, it explains, it describes, and so on. It is with a language as *tool* that one can "do things with words" (to borrow Austin's title). Standing, however, on the fiery doorsteps of the coincidence of opposites, where most of the distinctions that necessitate such a language collapse, one needs to learn how to speak a new language, the "language of Paradise":

> And suddenly, he realized that all his life he had done nothing but talk,
> write, lecture, concoct sentences, search for formulations and amend
> them, so in the end no words were precise, their meanings were obliter-
> ated, their content lost, they turned into trash, chaff, dust, sand; prowling
> through his brain, tearing at his head, they were his insomnia, his illness.
> And what he yearned for at that moment, vaguely but with all his might,

was unbounded music, absolute sound . . . to engulf, once and for all, the pain, the futility, the vanity of words. Music was the negation of sentences, music was the anti-word![26]

This anti-word quality of music is to be understood as its radical anti-conceptualism — music fundamentally is a language that resists its confinement within the limits of an idea or a concept.[27] Even when we are speaking of the "ideas" of heroism, joy, or tragedy as expressed by this or that composition, we improperly transpose a term of our ordinary language to that of music. A phenomenological listening to music can identify three characteristics that account for music's freedom from the bondage of conceptual thinking and distinguish music from language: (a) music's lack of reference (there is no "reality" beyond music itself that is signified by music), (b) music's lack of intention (the language of music is indeterminable and on that indeterminacy is based its often-cited universality, that is, its independence from translation), and (c) music's lack of reflection (the language of music is immediate).[28] Immediacy, indeterminacy, and semantic autonomy make music a far more proper language to address God and a more appropriate channel for God to address us: "The language of music . . . contains a theological dimension. What it has to say is simultaneously revealed and concealed. Its Idea is the divine Name which has been given shape . . . It is the human attempt, doomed as ever, to name the Name, not to communicate meanings."[29] Indeed, as Denys Turner has suggested in a recent paper, music "is the nearest you can get to a sort of spontaneous and demotic 'natural theology,' to a sort of pre-theological anticipation of theology."[30] As Turner rightly observes, "ancients did not think, as we do now, of some music as sacred and some secular. They thought music was sacred as such." He concludes: "perhaps that is why music is the most commonly experienced form of what the medievals called an *excessus*, or in Greek, *ekstasis*, or in English, 'taking leave of your senses': but in music, by the most sensual, most bodily, of means."[31]

The very literary trope employed in *De Visione Dei* exemplifies such an ecstatic movement. For in this treatise Nicholas (as Augustine before him in his *Confessions*, or Dionysius in his *Mystical Theology*) does not speak *of* God but *to* God. This turn of speech (trope) that turns its speaker toward Him who is spoken of, is, at the same time, a turn away *from* speech, *toward* hymn.

It is important to make the difference between hymnody and homily as clear as possible. It would be a mistake to regard hymn as if it were another form of speech ("sung speech"); hymnody properly belongs to music (music with words, i.e., song). To speak and to sing are two distinct capabilities of a human person, and the one is not reducible to the other. By speaking we use language (or language finds its expression in our act of speaking); by singing, on the other hand, we create music.[32] In this case, our body becomes an instrument, and song is its sound.[33]

For Gregory, the entire universe rings and resounds in a magnificent harmony whose music is the symphony of the multiplicity of beings.[34] Of that "music of the spheres" (or as Gregory puts it, "the celestial hymnody"),[35] the mind becomes not only its listener but also its participant. Man, after all, is a microcosmos—a small-scale image of the entire universe—and as such, he couldn't but participate in this sacred music making. Gregory finds evidence for this in the human body itself, which seems to have been made especially for musical purposes. So in a beautiful passage where anatomical and musical terms come together in order to form this body-instrument, he writes: "this is also shown by the construction of our body as organism, designed as it is by nature for the creation of music. Do you see the flute of the artery, the bridge of the palate, and how the tongue plays with the cheeks in the mouth as if it were harp-playing with plectrum and chords?"[36] Viewed under such a prism, man's authentic existence (with regard to himself and to his position in the world) consists in adding his voice to the incessant singing of this cosmic *Magnificat*. Heidegger credits someone like Mozart with such an honor for making himself "The Lute Piece of God."[37]

Liturgical Language

> And He hath put a new song in my mouth,
> A song of praise unto our God.
>
> —Ps. 40:3

When Kierkegaard rightly said, "in the world of time God and I cannot talk with each other, we have no language in common,"[38] he used a pleonasm. The world *is* the world of time and space (the *diastemic* world), and the lack of a common language between man and God is to be credited precisely to time. Language unfolds in time. Each of my sentences "takes" time; the words are uttered one by one in a sequence that is essentially duration. Language is subordinated to the temporality of this world, outside of which it would cease to exist. Insofar as language (interiorized in thought) governs reflection, time becomes an intrinsic part of our thought process (one needs only to refer to Kant's Transcendental Aesthetic to find ample evidence for that). This observation poses anew the problem of the difference between the *diastemic* (i.e., time-bound) language of man and the *adiastemic* (i.e., time-less) "language" of God. Language and thought are *chronic*—the "language" of God, on the other hand, follows an entirely different temporality, that of *kairos*.

The distinction between kairological and chronological temporalities—already discussed in chapter 3—has helped us to elucidate the modalities of the *Augenblick* and the *exaiphnes*. It is telling that, although at that point of the discussion our interest was only on the visual character of these phenomena, that is, on their distinct mode of phenomenality, yet the example we were compelled to use was auditory: music was shown to be the only art among the arts that unfolds *in time*, and yet does not belong to time, but reveals another temporality, not chronological but kairological. Furthermore, we have seen, with evidence drawn from relevant texts, that both terms, *kairos* and the *exaiphnes*, belong to a discourse that is at once eschatological, mystical, and liturgical.[39] However, it is only now, after a rather long exposition, that we can bring these two observations together. If music is a fissure in the continuum of chronology, through which we can catch a glimpse (an *Augenblick*) of the temporality of the *exaiphnes*, and if the latter is itself that single radiance which envelops the triptych of mystical, eschatological, and liturgical time, then doesn't one have to conclude that music, more than any other human activity, occasions, in ways that we will still have to think out, what Goethe's *chorus mysticus* confesses in rapture — namely, that *das Unbeschreibliche, hier ist's gethan?*[40] Doesn't one have to conclude that, as Adorno already and quite explicitly has said, music strives to utter the Divine Name?

This is all the more so, when we consider that kind of music that is liturgical par excellence, namely, hymn. "I will declare thy name unto my brethren, in the midst of the congregation will I praise thee,"[41] says one of the Psalms (22:22), to which the Epistle to the Hebrews gives a new meaning by quoting it within a Christological context (2:12). The two clauses of this verse ("I will declare thy name . . . I will praise thee") constitute one and the same act, expressed, as it is, by a hendiadys. It is in the liturgical hymning that the Divine Name is "declared." Nowhere is this insight more vividly and widely attested than in Dionysius's *Divine Names*. Dionysius, throughout this treatise (the longest in his corpus), consistently replaces the verb "to say" (λέγειν) and its derivatives with the verb "to hymn" (ὑμνεῖν) when the direct or indirect object of the clause is God.[42] Such an extensive tactic is quite difficult to carry out and maintain in all its occurrences throughout the text without good reason, and merely a whimsical choice of words on the part of its author would be hard to justify it. Dionysius's text offers us two ways of making sense of the central place given to liturgical language: a methodological point of view, that links hymnology with apophaticism, and a theoretical exposition, that focuses on the function of hymn itself (as opposed to language).

The phenomenon of hymnic proliferation in Dionysius's work both defines and solves the paradox of naming God. How does one go about writing a (lengthy) treatise on the divine names, sustaining all along the thesis that the divine can neither be spoken of nor thought about (οὔτε εἰπεῖν οὔτε ἐννοῆσαι δυνατόν; DN, I, 593B)?[43] The longer the list of such apophatic assertions grows,[44] the more frequent the usage of hymn-language becomes, until one realizes that the one is in direct proportion to (and a result of) the other. *Contra* Wittgenstein and Derrida, Dionysius's apophaticism does not result in silence (as if that were the only other alternative to predicative language and speech), but is transformed into a fecundity of hymns. Silence is indeed only hymn's prelude:

> When we honor what is ineffable by a temperate silence, then we are lifted up to the bright light which wholly illumines us in the sacred writings. They guide us in their light toward the thearchic hymns; we are outworldly illuminated by them and formed toward the sacred hymnologies. Thus, we turn toward seeing the thearchic light which is commensurately given to us by them, and toward offering hymns to the good-giving source of every sacred manifestation of light. (*DN*, I, 589B)[45]

"What cannot be said," as Marion says, "must not be silenced" (*ID*, 185) but celebrated and praised in the music of liturgy. Hymn, thus, becomes the methodological *via tertia* of the Aeropagite, a middle way between the extremities of cataphatic language and apophatic silence.

By taking into consideration some classical examples of hymnology, coming from both the Judaic and Christian traditions, we cannot but notice that in the hymn the subject ceases to speak with the authority, certitude, or arrogance of the I. It keeps speaking, nevertheless, but another voice emerges here, a voice that prays, begs, wishes, promises, hopes, and even demands. Here is an example from Psalm 51:

> 1 Have mercy *on me*, O God . . .
> 2 *Wash me* from my iniquity
> and *cleanse me* from my sin . . .
> 8 *Let me* hear joy and gladness;
> let the bones you have crushed rejoice . . .
> 10 Create *in me* a pure heart, O God,
> and renew a steadfast spirit *within me*.
> 11 Do not cast *me* from your presence
> or take your Holy Spirit *from me*.
> 12 Restore *to me* the joy of your salvation
> and grant *me* a willing spirit, to sustain *me* . . .
> 14 *Save me* from bloodguilt, O God,
> the God who *saves me*,
> and my tongue will sing of your righteousness.

We immediately note that in the verses cited above the psalmist never once speaks by means of an I. When speech is addressed to this Other, as wholly other (God), then the voice of the I is silenced. In front of God I am turned, with violence perhaps, into the accusative *me*. As I speak to Him, I become *me*.

This becomes all the more a paradox once we realize that the hymn, strictly speaking, is never mine. The hymn, its words and its music, does not belong to me as my speech does. Hymns, like icons, do not bear signatures. They are artistic creations free from a restricted authorship that would assign them to a single individual. Rather, hymns are the creations of a community united by communion. It is only our modern perversion that seeks, by all means, to attribute every hymn to an individual without recognizing in their "composer" the mere spokesman of his or her community. Therefore, in repeating the old words of a hymn and singing its ancient melodies, *I* speak not. Like the actor who lends his or her voice to Shakespeare, I give (my) voice to the community of saints. The psalmist, for example, never utters a word of his own — his song is always given to him by Him whom he praises: "a new song He hath put in my mouth" (40:3); "open my lips, O Lord, and my mouth will declare your praise" (51:15). In hymn, another language is spoken through me: language's other. In hymn, I barely speak a language, for hymn is "in" language but not "of" language.

The effects of liturgical language, however, do not concern solely its speaker but have some bearing on the speaker's interlocutor as well. What do prayer and praise reveal to us about God? Who is this God that the accusative *me* addresses in hymns and songs? Let us take another example of liturgical language, that of the Latin *Gloria: Laudamus te, benedicimus te, adoramus te, glorificamus te, gratias agimus tibi propter magnam gloriam tuam.* To the accusative "me" corresponds a vocative "you" (*te*). This "you," however, remains unqualified.[46] Certainly, it can be predicated by a series of conditions (e.g., *qui tollis peccata mundi* or *qui sedes ad dextram Patris*, etc.), but its capacity to receive every name indicates the insufficiency of all names to name what remains without proper name. Here we return to the perennial thesis of apophaticism, that polyonymity amounts to anonymity. "The theologians knew this," Dionysius says, "and so their hymns have praised [the Thearchy] both as anonymous and as fitting of all names" (*DN*, I, 596A). When it comes to God, either all or nothing, or better yet, *both* all *and* nothing applies.

Through hymn the impenetrable wall of paradise is overcome (insofar as we can name the Unnameable) and yet retained and respected (insofar as the naming of God does not result in a panentheistic knowledge that confuses the distinction between God and creation). Hymn can approach the distant God in a striking proximity. On the other hand, we come now to understand that the very distance of God's withdrawal, absence, or silence is what gives rise to the music of hymn — a music loud enough to bring down walls:

> You, neighbor God, when I disturb with heavy raps
> Your quiet during a lonely night,
> It is because I rarely hear you breathe,
> Though know: You're in your room alone.
> And while in need, there's no one there to bring
> Your groping hand a drink. But I
> Am listening. Just give me a sign.
> I am close by.
>
> Only a thin wall is between us,
> Mere happenstance; so there is a chance
> That a call from your or my mouth
> Might break it down
> Without sound.[47]

Rilke's voice brings us, full circle, back to the beginning. To the bride's empty bed and to her agonized search for her absent beloved in the long, nuptial night of the *Song of Songs*. The poet speaks to a lonely and silent God, a "neighbor" God whose breath he can hear from the other side of a separating wall. But this is far from being the formidable wall of paradise, the boundary of all creation, the cosmic border of *diastema* that nothing and no one could ever trespass. This has been transformed into "only a thin wall," so thin, in fact, "that a call from your or my mouth might break it down." We are left to ponder what this "call" could actually be if it is not the quiet call of prayer. For He whom the bride seeks and the poet awaits is always only a step or a call away.

six
Postlude:
The Interrupted Self

Hear, O daughter, and see
And incline thine ear . . .

—Ps. 45:10

Turning to Speak
Turning to Hear
Open the Kingdom

—*Philip Glass*, Liquid Days, *Part II*

If we wish to understand what Adorno says when he admits that music attempts "to name the Name" and in doing so it is "simultaneously revealed and concealed," we will need to turn to one of the most famous — and for our discussion, crucial — passages of Dionysius's text:

> As you know, once we and many of our holy brethren, as well as James, the brother of God, and Peter, the highest and eldest summit of the *theologians*, were gathered together to view the God-receiving and life-giving body. At that time it was determined to have all the hierarchs offer *hymns* to the unlimited power of goodness of the thearchic weakness, according to the ability of each, after having seen the body. Hierotheus, who was also among our divine hierarchs, excelled all the other sacred initiates among the *theologians* (πάντων ἐκράτει μετὰ τοὺς θεολόγους), as wholly outside himself (ὅλος ἐκδημῶν), wholly ecstatic (ὅλος ἐξιστάμενος ἑαυτοῦ) by "suffering" a communion with what was *hymned* (τὴν πρὸς τὰ ὑμνούμενα κοινωνίαν πάσχων). He was considered to be a divine and God-receptive *hymnologist* by all those who had seen, heard, and known him and, yet, did not know him. What am I to say about what was there *theologised?* For

> I know—unless I do not know myself—that you have often heard some
> parts of their divinely inspired *hymnodies*. (*DN*, III, 681D–684A)[1]

This passage constitutes a diversion in the narrative that takes us back to an
occasion that, according to Dionysius, was none other than the dormition of
the Virgin Mary (referred to in the passage cited above as the "God-receiving
and life-giving body").[2] It is not clear whether Dionysius claims to have been
present at the historical event that took place in the first century or is simply
describing the liturgical celebration of the feast of the Assumption (which, in
accordance with the temporality of the *kairos*, "re-*presents*" the events that are
celebrated as occurring always "today"). Given the recent emphasis on the
liturgical understanding of his theology,[3] I think it would be safe to assume
the latter.

Regardless of the nature of the event that it describes, this passage provides us with the most eloquent evidence yet of the relation between theology and hymnology. Indeed, a first reading seems to prove that the two terms
are interchangeable. Hierotheus is said to have offered hymns (ὑμνῆσαι) to
God, and in doing so, he stands out among the other theologians (μετὰ τοὺς
θεολόγους): we should immediately note that he is compared to the other
theologians not on account of his theological ability but because of his hymnological capacity. So far the analogy between the two terms is established,
although not yet determined. However, Hierotheus's excellence, in comparison to the rest of the hierarchs, did not consist of his eloquence or skill in
performing the hymns but rather in the fact that he "suffered" them in his person (πρὸς τὰ ὑμνούμενα κοινωνίαν πάσχων). This is a statement that might
surprise us. What does it mean, after all, to "suffer" the hymns? It is about the
same Hierotheus that Dionysius had said earlier, "not only had he learned
the divine things but he had also suffered them" (οὐ μόνον μαθὼν ἀλλὰ καὶ
παθὼν τὰ θεῖα; *DN*, II, 648B).

Through hymn, or in the celebration of hymnody, Hierotheus is not
speaking anymore about God, that is, "theologizing," but experiencing God
in the pathos of ecstasy (ὅλος ἐξιστάμενος ἑαυτοῦ). As a consequence of
this, he is not considered to be a theologian any longer but a hymnologist
(θεόληπτος εἶναι καὶ θεῖος ὑμνολόγος κρινόμενος). So much did Hierotheus
come out of himself (ὅλος ἐκδημῶν), and so much did the One praised manifest Himself to him who praised Him, that those who had seen and heard and
knew Hierotheus did not know him anymore (ὧν ἠκούετο καὶ ἑωρᾶτο καὶ
ἐγιγνώσκετο καὶ οὐκ ἐγιγνώσκετο). Thus, hymnology, at the end of Dionysius's narrative, ranks higher than theology.[4] If theology can give us at best a
speculative knowledge of God, hymnology can give us infinitely more: not a
knowledge or a language about God, but communion (κοινωνίαν) with God.

One still needs, however, to demonstrate how hymnology can attain such
a communion. What are the special characteristics, endemic to hymn but
lacking from speech, that enable hymnology to succeed where theology fails?

Dionysius's narration about Hierotheus offers us a sort of dramatization of hymn's effects, and there, in this tableau, we find that the answers we are looking for are painted with bright colors and intense strokes. The state of ecstasy and trance that befalls Hierotheus as he is praising God, the fact that he now appears in a strange way to those who knew him, and, more importantly, the fact that the things he is praising God about (τὰ ὑμνούμενα) are reflected or happening to him: all are indications of the iconic experience of language in the hymn, an experience analogous to iconic vision as we have discussed it in the first two chapters of this work.

We witness here too a similar splitting of the subject between an "I" that speaks and a "me" that listens. Hierotheus "suffers" the hymns: that means he is not the subject giving a praising discourse, but, somehow, the hymn envelops him, turns back on him, and turns him into its recipient. Dionysius suggests that much when he calls Hierotheus "θεόληπτος"—God has received his praise, and he has received God. He becomes thus unknown to those who knew him, for the unknowable God has cast His light on him. He was also "wholly outside himself," for he has left himself (that is, his "I") behind him. As in front of the icon, I can see Him by being seen by Him (inverse intentionality), and in being seen by Him I see myself as seen, that is, as "me" (and not as an I), so too in the iconic language of hymn, I experience myself as already spoken to, as addressed by Him, as being given Him. There is also an erotic element in Hierotheus's praising manifested in his ecstasy: "for divine love is ecstatic," Dionysius writes a few paragraphs later, "such that does not let the lovers belong to themselves but to their beloved" (DN, IV, 13, 712A). As he explains in another chapter of his work, the "union" (ἕνωσις) with God presupposes the ecstatic "transcending" of oneself (ὅλους ἑαυτοὺς ὅλων ἑαυτῶν ἐξισταμένους—note the similarity with the language used to describe Hierotheus's ecstasy) for the sake of becoming totally God's (ὅλους θεοῦ γιγνομένους), "for it is better to belong to God than to ourselves" (κρεῖττον γὰρ εἶναι θεοῦ καὶ μὴ ἑαυτῶν).[5]

The crucial difference, however, does not lie in the content of any given hymn but in the hymn's singing. As emphasized in the last chapter, the language of the hymn is essentially music. What distinguishes a hymn from everyday language and common speech is precisely the fact—self-evident as it may be, but significant—that a hymn is sung and not spoken. In fact, nothing in liturgy is supposed to be read (as one reads a paper), but everything (even the text of the scripture, or especially the text of the scripture) ought to be sung, or intoned. Reading and speaking belong to the created order—when I read something I seek to *comprehend* it. Language in the created order communicates meaning and serves a didactic purpose (it seeks to inform or educate, to explain or demonstrate). The liturgy, on the other hand, reflects the *eschaton*, where there is no need for didactic language.[6] In the *eschaton*, language is doxological, that is, hymnology. When reading, the words are captured and comprehended by our reason; in doxological singing, however, the words are amplified or dilated so that *they* surround and comprehend us. As Paul writes to the Philippians, "I follow after so that I will comprehend that for which Christ has apprehended me" (3:12).[7] Paul cannot *understand* Christ—he lacks all concept of Him but one: that he has been captured by Him; being "grasped" *(gegriffen)* by Christ is the only concept *(Begriff)* available to us. Thus, Paul has reversed Descartes's principle a few centuries earlier than the famous declaration of the latter: it is He who thinks me, and, therefore, I am *(cogitor, ergo sum)*.

The reading of the Dormition episode in Dionysius's text, and the interpretation that it has compelled us to develop in understanding the hymnological "subject" as the recipient of the hymn's effects (eloquently suggested by Hierotheus's "suffering" the hymns) have necessitated a shift in emphasis from speaking, that is, the predominant paradigm of language, to hearing. Philosophy has dealt rather awkwardly with hearing, for her dominion was that of the eye. From the assertion on the primacy of sight made by Aristotle at the beginning of his *Metaphysics* to the vocabulary employed in Husserl's phenomenology, the history of philosophy has been held hostage to the splendor of vision. When philosophy speaks, even today, even in English, she speaks of ideas and *eidos*, theory and wisdom, insights and speculations—all of which, etymologically and metaphorically, imply vision, for "to see" after all is "to know." The blind ear, therefore, and the invisible sound that addresses it have for long evaded philosophy's attention, being, as they were, her blind spot. Similarly with speaking. Philosophy was always so much preoccupied with human *logos*—our ability to speak language that sets us apart from the rest of animals—that she almost forgot that man can also listen.[8]

It is through the ear, however, that I remain constantly open to the word of the World. The utterances of the things keep coming, continuously, like waves, on the shore of my ears. Sounds arrive to this great receptacle by day or night, while sleeping or awake. Even if I were to eliminate every sound from my surroundings, one after another, from the louder to the most imperceptible ones, at the end I would be surprised at becoming suddenly aware of the sounds of my own body: the constant rhythm of breathing and my heart beating. The gates of the ear never close—"it is in the highest degree symbolic that only our eyes, not our ears, have lids."[9] In that hymen, known as the acoustic tympanum, the inside of my body meets the exteriority of the world—a world that is translated into buzzing signals, bits and pulsations, sonic waves in which I am endlessly immersed and drawn. Indeed, if blindness damages my link to things, deafness breaks up my relation to people.

A phenomenology of listening and hearing—if the term "phenomenology" is still applicable—could offer us fascinating descriptions of a whole variety of auditory "phenomena" (or, as it has been suggested, *akoumena*),[10] providing us with further evidence that would confirm the preceding analysis of the hymn.

In order to see an object our eyes have to turn toward it—sight demands that the phenomenon of an object is given together with the object itself. We couldn't see, say, the reflection of this red book without, at the same time, looking at the book itself. All the characteristics through which the book becomes visible — its redness, its shape, the place it occupies on the desk, etc. — cannot be perceived apart from looking to the place where the book actually is. Things are different, however, with sounds. Like the presence of God, which is a presence manifested in absence, the invisible sound of music surrounds me like the wind that blows: "you hear its sound but you cannot tell where it comes from or where it is going" (John 3:8). "All speaking and singing conceal at the same time the speaker and the singer," von Balthasar writes, as "an arrow speeds across and penetrates me more deeply than a look would have been able to do, but the bow from which the arrow comes does not itself come into my hand."[11] The sound does indeed reveal music by concealing its source. Let us not trivialize our discussion by suggesting that we could point to the speakers in my room or the orchestra in the concert hall. For music does not come from the instrument that vibrates in the hands of the musician — that is *how* the music comes to be. *Where* it comes from, however, one knows not, because it comes from *silence*, and to silence it returns, and silence (hermetically sealed inside itself) is precisely what one cannot know. "The horizon of sound is silence," Ihde and Slaughter write, concluding their study on the phenomenology of sound: "silence is the primordial ground" or "the unspoken background" of music.[12] The proof is simple enough: listening to music one strives for the maximum of silence — the headphones, for instance, improve our experience of music not by enhancing music itself but by enhancing the silence that accompanies music. Further evidence is provided by silence's visual analogue, namely, darkness. What compels listeners, in public or private, to close their eyes when listening to music? Is it simply the recognition that one does not need to look when one cannot see? Or is it a synesthetic effort to induce silence by closing their eyes (since they cannot close their ears)? Both silence and darkness are precursory phenomena of theophanic manifestations. From the Greek mysteries to Hebraic and Christian epiphanies, reverent silence and darkness demarcate the space and the time of the divine apparition. Places of worship today retain something of that aesthetic memory when they purposefully appear silent and dark. In Ihde's words, "phenomenologically, the dark, the vague or the blind may be the visual background for the presentation of God in sound."[13]

In hearing I always find myself on the receiving end. Auditory perception is a passive affair, and it reveals a vulnerable "subject." My sight, like Medusa's gaze, turns everything into objects — it captures, at once, what it seeks. In hearing, however, it is I who am captured by the "thing" that emits the sound — a "thing," moreover, that I cannot turn into the object of my perception as I don't necessarily see it and even less "know" it. For example, I am alone in my study working when suddenly I hear a voice in the next room or a shout coming from the street. Three things deserve to be mentioned regarding such an ordinary experience: (a) the sound (the voice or the shout) arrives always *suddenly* — there is nothing to prepare me for it, no anticipation, as it happens neither at my initiative nor at my will; it is the sound that invades my perception and not the latter that turns to it; (b) I have no "power" over the sound (as I have with the object presented in my gaze) — as soon as I hear it, it is gone, there is nothing that I can do to retain it in my perception; and (c) I cannot know what might be its cause — if I wanted to know whose voice was in the next room or who was shouting in the street, I would have to go there and *look*. In other words, the sound alone is always an intuition asymmetrical to and independent of my intention: it catches my intention by surprise (in hearing, consciousness is always a consciousness "in response to . . ." instead of a "consciousness of . . .": more of a *responsorial* consciousness than an intentional one); it gives as much or as little as it pleases, not as I need or demand; and finally, it is an intuition that resists objectification by turning the objectifying intentionality of consciousness against itself (inverse intentionality).[14] Let me rehearse again the hypothetical example I have been using here: I am alone in my study working, when suddenly I hear a voice — what is my reaction? I stop typing on the computer, I leave the books open on the desk, I neither speak nor move, all of my attention is turned toward the sound by which I have been summoned. It is this kind of reaction, demonstrated in being "captured" or "interrupted," that illustrates the effects of the auditory inverse intentionality on consciousness:

> it is not we ourselves who determine on our part what is heard and place it before us as object in order to turn our attention to it when it pleases us; that which is heard *comes upon us*, without our being informed in advance, and *it lays hold of us* without our being asked. We cannot look out in advance and take up our distance . . . we know instinctively, when a noise comes to our ear, that what we hear is basically already "over" and have no more power over it.[15]

This *inter*ruption of the self through the ear is prior and more originary than the *ir*ruption of the self which the phenomenology of the look envisages: selfhood irrupts once the self has been interrupted from being absorbed in itself (as if it had to be forcefully separated from itself, from its non-thetic identification with itself). Had the call of the sound not interrupted it, my being would have remained a being among beings *(interesse)* — always preoccupied with itself and always unbeknown to itself. But now the call that comes from nowhere has brought this "nowhere" into the here and now of my perception. The voice has struck at the core of my very being (i.e., the "absorption" of myself in myself, my self-preoccupation), and it has created an empty space where the Other can now come, enter, and dwell. The penetration of one's self by listening results in a self impregnated with the Other — egocentrism decentered.

It is not, perhaps, an accident that Plato puts a similar metaphor in Socrates' mouth when the latter is about to speak about eros, but he needs to explain how he knows what he knows, given his famous ignorance: "I know well that what I know comes not from me, for I am aware of my own ignorance; but it would seem that I was filled with the knowledge through the ears, like water fills a vessel" (ὅτι μὲν οὖν παρά γε ἐμαυτοῦ οὐδὲν αὐτῶν ἐννενόηκα, εὖ οἶδα, συνειδὼς ἐμαυτῷ ἀμαθίαν· λείπεται δὴ ἐξ ἀλλοτρίων ποθὲν ναμάτων διὰ τῆς ἀκοῆς πεπληρῶσθαὶ μεν δίκην ἀγγείου; *Phaedrus*, 235c6–235d1). Loving and hearing are placed in juxtaposition: as sound invades my ears independently of my will, so does love.

The *per* of the person is not quite the same as the *pros* of the *prosopon* — it does not imply a direction, it does not point toward the Other with whom the *prosopon* is in relation. The *per* of the *persona* suggests a hollow space *within* (an interiority, a hidden depth that finds its physiological representation in the auditory tube and the helix of the cochlea) through which the sound (per-*sonare*) resonates. This is the force of this *per* that permeates with sonority the perforated self. The sound, however, itself does not belong to the person but comes from beyond, from an external source — thus, it is indicative of an exteriority *within* me, an exteriority that has invaded me without becoming interiorized: it is the Other in myself.

An exemplary case of this function of listening is illustrated by Mary and, in particular, her conception "through the sense of hearing" *(conceptio per aurem)*. Nicholas Constas, in his study on *The Cult of the Virgin in Late Antiquity*, has amassed a great wealth of sources and information about the homiletic, dogmatic, and cultural developments of Mary's impregnation of and by the Word.[16] It would be, however, impossible to provide a complete picture of the subtle imagery associated with the scriptural readings, patristic commentaries, and Byzantine iconographies discussed in Constas's work; this discussion will limit itself, therefore, to drawing only a sketch of this fascinating idea. Mary's virginal conception became one of the first Christian beliefs to be harshly contested (and some times even ridiculed) by Christianity's old and new enemies.

In their attempt to supplement Mary's virginal birth with the explanation that neither Scripture nor tradition provided them, the Church Fathers, in putting Luke's Annunciation passage under their relentless hermeneutical scrutiny, unearthed the aural imagery that lay therein. For once, it made sense to take the ear as the very medium through which the Word entered the virginal body ("for the sense of hearing is the natural channel of words").[17] As Proclus has Mary explain, "I heard a Word, I conceived a Word, I delivered a Word."[18] The complementary character of spoken (annunciation) and heard word (conception), and the underlining dialectics of sound and silence offered the great preachers of the fifth and sixth centuries a seemingly inexhaustible source of rhetoric that sustained anything from the longest to the shortest homily. (A personal favorite is the — Christmas? — homily of Cyrus of Panopolis, which in its entirety reads as follows: "Brethren, let the birth of God our Savior Jesus Christ be honoured with silence, because the Word of God was conceived in the holy Virgin through hearing alone. To him be glory for ever. Amen.")[19] What lit bonfires in the imaginations of the Fathers, however, was the typology entailed in the momentous encounter of Gabriel with Mary. The passage in Luke became the contrapuntal text to Genesis: as Eve in her disobedience (παρακοή) had "given birth" to death, so Mary, the second Eve, through hearing (ἀκοή) gave birth to Life. Whereas Eve obeys (ὑπακούειν) the serpent, Mary listens to (ἀκούειν) the salutation of the angel. To God's creation of man (Adam), humanity responded with the re-creation of man in the New Adam (Christ). Although both creation and Incarnation are the deeds of the Father's love, Christ's birth could not have happened without Mary's response. That's why Mary's *fiat mihi* in "let it be done to me according to your word" (Luke 1:38) repeats and completes God's *fiat* as in "let us make man" (Gen. 1:26).[20] Both creational formulas share the same paradox: as God creates the world through a self-contraction, that is, a self-limitation of His will, so Mary assents to God's plan of the Incarnation by will-fully abandoning her will; "let it be done to me."

In our everyday affairs, we enact a similar paradox when we pause in order to let the Other speak, when we hold our tongue in order to lend the Other an ear. When we listen to another person *(hören)*, we undertake a will-ful surrender to the Other, who, in claiming our attention, lays also a claim over ourselves. We do not only hear the Other; for as long as we listen to him or her we belong *(gehören)* not to ourselves but to another. We, thus, demon-strate an obedience *(Gehorsam)* similar to Mary's submission to the angel's message. And similarly, every heedful listening creates the space for some-thing new to be born:

> Hearing is a very special mode of perception. Sounds cannot be handled or pushed away. We can close our eyes, hold our noses, withdraw from touch, and refuse to taste. And though we can partly muffle our ears, we cannot close them. If the "eye is the lamp of the body" (Mt. 6:22) casting its light on the objects it sees, the ear is a tympanum that is struck, a shell for the thunderous heaves of the ocean. In the experience of sound, we are "struck" by something, by someone else. Through sound we experi-ence the distant as proximate, the other as near, and hearing is a process in which we become the other, and let the other become part of us. Hearing seeks selflessness rather than self-expression. Even in a dialogue of equal partners, the one who at the moment happens to be hearing is in the posi-tion of humbly receiving. While the word resounds, the ear belongs to the other. For that brief moment, we suspend our own identities, after which we return to ourselves and either accept or reject what has been said. But in that fleeting moment of self-evanescence, something new is born.[21]

PART THREE. TOUCHING

And our hands have touched . . .
  —*1 John 1*

ALLEGORY 3

If the enigma of the first allegory was unlocked by means of an anagogy and the mysteries of the second were revealed thanks to connotation and typology, the third allegory is organized by the rules of a threefold antithesis. It is an antithesis that vertically splits the painting into two opposing halves.

The first contrast we notice is that between the possibility of touching (suggested by the naked and exposed bodies of Aphrodite and Eros on the right part of the painting) and the lack — one could even say the prohibition — of touch indicated by the pile of body armors and armory that dominates the left part of Brueghel's painting. The soft, ruddy flesh of Aphrodite's body invites touch — an invitation already fulfilled in her embracing and kissing of the young Eros. In sheer opposition to this scene, the coldness and stiffness of the iron armor plates, next to it, obliterate even the slightest possibility of touching. It is not an accident that Brueghel inscribes these two contraries within the sphere of two equally contradictory worlds: on the one hand the world of War, and on the other that of Love.

War demands physical strength, production, and a reserve of expendable "matter" (in both forms of commodity and manpower) — all of these are represented on the left side of the painting, by the labor of the men who work the iron on the anvil to produce more armor, in spite of what already lies in waste in the forefront of the painting. Behind the workers, the scene opens up onto a green landscape. That is nature, but nature understood only as that vast supply of matter that has made itself available to be spent in human production. In the world of Love, on the other hand, nature is represented only by a bouquet of flowers in a vase (that is, in its aesthetic dimension). Such a view of nature serves no purpose and is, in its superior character, useless. Human work too is represented only by the paintings that hang behind the kissing couple. It is as if Brueghel were saying that man can be enslaved by his work, but he can also be the master of his creation.

As it was the case with *Sight* and *Hearing*, here, too, Aphrodite and Eros are engaged in the very sense that the painting has set to illustrate: they embrace and kiss each other. Brueghel seems to have made a choice by deciding which aspect of touch to depict, for touching is not homologous to kissing; indeed, there is a whole variety of qualities or activities that fall under the sense of touch: holding and feeling with one's hand, grasping, distinguishing roughness from smoothness, warmth from cold, feeling an object's weight, etc. The choice to make the kiss the representative paradigm of touch is certainly a telling one. In kissing, one's lips do touch another's, but one cannot kiss another's lips without being kissed back. It is this reciprocity exemplified by the union of the lips that makes the kiss the most characteristic case of touching, for touch in each of its manifestations remains essentially reciprocal.

The kiss is also a sign of passion — in this case, the passion of love. Both touch and passion share a locus: the body. If sight has the eye as its organ and hearing works through the ear, the sensorium of touch is none other than our flesh. For the flesh that burns with such a passion, it is not enough to see or hear the beloved — it begs the beloved's touch, in touching and in being touched. Our body, however, is more than simply the organ of contact; it is the register that more acutely *suffers* the entire scope of the beloved's impact on us. It is the flesh that palpitates in expectation, trembles in anguish, blazes with arousal, and is caught in rapture.

On the next level, the armor — prohibiting the Other's touch — could also be taken not as the antithetical but rather as the reverse view of the inventing flesh. When the two contradictory paradigms conflate and their antithesis collapses, a new antithesis emerges: the armor is an allegory of the skin — of the epidermis of the body — or of the body itself, which, by allowing one to touch it, at the same time, protects its intangible interiority. In touch the intangible makes itself all the more evident — for what you touch is never the Other, but only the Other's skin, the Other's body, the natural armor of flesh, the impenetrable veil of the Other's penetralia, inside which the Other remains untouched and untouchable. Could it, then, be the case that I can never touch the Other — or even be touched?

The first painting within the painting (the place where Brueghel hides the key to his allegories, as we have seen) depicts the flagellation of Christ. The theme's relevance to the sense of touch is apparent: the impassible God suffered by means of His body. Touch is not only the carrier of pleasure but of its twin as well, that is, pain. But what do these obvious observations mean? What else than that by Christ's Incarnation it is the Intangible par excellence that makes Himself corporeal and contingent? That it is the very veil of the flesh in which the intangible is touched? In the Incarnation it is the Creator who creates Himself anew in the creature's fashion — if in the Creation God gave the first man spirit, in the Incarnation man gives Him a body. It is the Incarnation that complements and completes the Creation.

Each sense in the polysemy of "touched" applies: the affection of kenosis that revealed a Person so much touched by our affairs that He was driven out of Himself; a Person that comes in contact with our human nature, so that He can be physically as well as emotionally touched by each one of us and so that He can touch us back.

seven
Touch Me, Touch Me Not

Pone me sicut signaculum in corde tuo,
Sicut signaculum in brachiis tuis.

—*Cant, VIII, 6*

"There is nothing that man fears more than the touch of the unknown."
With these words Nobel laureate Elias Canetti opens his phenomenological
study of social behavior. His observations on the fear of being touched are so
revealing and pertinent to our following discussion that I shall quote from
them at some length:

> There is nothing that man fears more than the touch of the unknown. He
> wants to *see* what is reaching towards him, and to be able to recognize or at
> least classify it. Man always tends to avoid physical contact with anything
> strange. In the dark, the fear of an unexpected touch can mount to panic.
> Even clothes give insufficient security: it is easy to tear them and pierce
> through to the naked, smooth, defenseless flesh of the victim.
>
> All the distances which men create round themselves are dictated by
> this fear. They shut themselves in houses which no-one may enter, and
> only there feel some measure of security. The fear of burglars is not only
> the fear of being robbed, but also the fear of a sudden and unexpected
> clutch out of the darkness.

> The repugnance to being touched remains with us when we go about among people; the way we move in a busy street, in restaurants, trains or buses, is governed by it. Even when we are standing next to them and are able to watch and examine them closely, we avoid actual contact if we can.[1]

For Canetti, a large part of the functions and customs of our civilized society, if not civilization itself, stem from the fear of all fears, the fear of being touched. Even our appreciation of the beautiful, in its basic traits of symmetry and proportion, would seem to have originated as defense mechanisms against the fear of being touched: "Symmetry, which is so striking a feature of many ancient civilizations, derives in part from man's attempt to create uniform distances all round himself."[2]

What sort of irrational instinct, however, or immemorial trauma fuels such an entrenched fear? Canetti alludes to the answer when he adds that these and many more examples of such phobic behavior prove "that we are dealing here with a human propensity as deep-seated as it is alert and insidious; something which never leaves a man when he has once established *the boundaries of his personality*."[3]

The fear of the Other's touch is the fear triggered by the violation of the established boundaries of one's personality. It is my subjectivity itself, the awareness of a distinctiveness demarcated by my body, which the proximity of another body threatens. How ironic, then, to realize that the very gesture that I now perceive as a threatening breach of the space that defines me as an "I" was the same as the original act that had earlier established my subjectivity over and against the Other. For it is by virtue of the violence of the hand (its grasping, seizing, and killing the Other) that I first became aware of myself as a separate and distinct self.

The Birth of Subjectivity: *Grasping*

The first Other, against which I defined myself, was — and in some sense, still remains — the animal. In my ability to turn the animal into the victim of my hunt and my hand (the two words are, in fact, related), I become non-animal. The very activity of hunting has distinguished the hunter from the prey. Even before the hand throws the fatal stone, it is the hand, having prepared the tool suitable for killing, that has separated me from my prey. The man who makes the first tool is not anymore an animal. The man who hunts and eats his kill with his own hands is not anymore an animal. In eating the animal, the animal becomes part of me — it becomes incorporated into me, and thus I become *more* than an animal. I become a human. Other humans, however, have no indemnity against being treated as animals. The other human, once fallen to my *hands*, loses its human status and assumes that of an animal. I may have ceased long ago from eating other humans, but new ways have been invented to help me appropriate the Other. Wars imitate tribal huntings and reenact the game of killing. Slaves were counted together with other animals as part of one's livestock, and they were to be treated as such. Arrest and imprisonment are institutions that spring from the practices of catching and caging wild animals. The Other, whom I can manipulate according to my will and whims, has taken the place of the animal.

The origin of humanity, as both historians and anthropologists agree, is to be traced back to the invention of tools. But even before the first tool came to be, I was equipped with the hand. It was after the hand that the tool was made, as we often say, a "second" hand, only better and more effective. Thus, the hand became emancipated from being used only as a tool — it now manipulates the tools it had itself produced. With much of its duties transferred to the tools, the hand became free — it became creative. In fact, the two moments must have coincided: the creation of the first tool by the hand marks the moment when the hand ceases to be a tool. It is now recognized as that which it has always been, but only now can I become aware of it: *my body*.[4] The awareness of my body and consequently, as we shall soon see, my self-awareness as a subject have always been dependent upon this dialectical relation between the grasping hand and its tool.[5] The tool always refers back to the hand, for the one is meaningful only in relation to the other. The tool is precisely what is *graspable*: our first concept *(Begriff)*. It is not an accident that even for a sophisticated analysis of our being-in-the-world such as Heidegger's in *Being and Time* the world *is* this referential totality of "tools" that, in turn, reveal themselves according to two modes of "handiness" *(Handlichkeit)*: as ready-at-hand *(Zuhanden)* and as present-at-hand *(Vorhanden)*.

In more than one way, man was able to develop the ability to speak thanks to his hands. As he didn't have to use his mouth as a hand — in order to fetch or hold things, as most animals do — his mouth became available for speech. Moreover, "as a man watched his hands at work, the changing shapes they fashioned must gradually have impressed themselves on his mind. Without this we should probably never have learnt to form symbols for things, nor, therefore, to *speak*."[6]

Indeed, in one of his characteristically dense passages, Heidegger attempts to establish such a connection between the hand and the word:

> Man himself acts [*handelt*] through the hand [*Hand*]; for the hand is, together with the word, the essential distinction of man. Only a being which, like man, "has" the word (μῦθος, λόγος), can and must "have" "the hand." Through the hand occur both prayer and murder, greeting and thanks, oath and signal, and also the "work" of the hand, the "hand-work," and the tool. The handshake seals the covenant. The hand brings about the "work" of destruction. The hand exists as hand only where there is disclosure and concealment. No animal has a hand, and a hand never originates from a paw or a claw or talon. Even the hand of one in desperation (it least of all) is never a talon, with which a person clutches wildly. The hand sprang

> forth only out of the word and together with the word. Man does not "have" hands, but the hand holds the essence of man, because the word as the essential realm of the hand is the ground of the essence of man.[7]

Dare we say that without his hands man would have been also unable to think? That man began thinking, and still thinks, *with* his hands, that is, according to a fundamental structure implied by paradigms of touch? That "every motion of the hand in every one of its works carries itself through the element of thinking" so that "all the work of the hand is rooted in thinking"?[8] It seems that Aristotle would have agreed with this.

* * *

Thinking has always been thought in terms of sense perception. It is a paradox that becomes all the more striking in our post-Cartesian era. To think thought one needs to have a recourse to its other, the senses, as if thinking were lacking metaphors or examples of its own in order to think itself. On the other hand, metaphors derived from the senses — even when thinking is to be distinguished most emphatically from them — have become quite common in describing the thinking process in both everyday language and the terminology of various philosophical schools. Sight and its faculties were given a certain predominance among the other senses as the classical paradigm in Western civilization that illustrates the activity of the mind — to such an extent, perhaps, as to allow some to speak of a hegemony of the ocular, or an oculocentrism.[9]

One of the earliest breakings in this ocular hegemony is to be found in the very foundations of the Western tradition, that is, in Aristotle's *De Anima*. The identity of a being's *eidos* (its form) with its concrete (i.e., tangible) embodiment in matter allowed Aristotle to speak of the soul not only as seeing the ideas of things but *grasping* them as well. As he clearly states: ἡ ψυχὴ ὥσπερ ἡ χείρ ἐστιν (the soul is like the hand; 432a1).

"Despite the opening lines of *Metaphysics*," Rosen writes, "it is not sight, but touch, which is the most philosophical of the senses, because touch is prior to, more general, and more intimately related to *ta pragmata* than sight." And he continues, "we grasp the forms of the things which are, and thereby know them: touch is the differentiation of forms which is the necessary condition for knowing. Knowing is touching."[10] It is not, however, *any* kind of touching that exemplifies knowledge but *grasping*. The soul stretches out toward the things, like a hand ready to feel and hold them in its grip. One presupposes, therefore, the things-to-be-thought as things-to-be-grasped, things that, in the grasp of mental comprehension, are to be turned into "tools." Indeed, you know something once you know how to use it. Knowledge amounts to instrumentality. For things become known to us by their usage *qua* "tools." In fact, we never quite *know* a thing in itself; we know only its function, that is, its instrumentality. To know a thing is to know how to *handle* it. Lack of knowledge (τὸ ἀγνοεῖν) is defined by Aristotle elsewhere as absence of contact (μή θιγγάνειν; *Meta.*, Θ, 1051b 24).[11]

In comparing the soul to the hand, Aristotle is not merely seeking to embellish his speech with a nice metaphor. "The metaphorical exists only in metaphysics,"[12] and this metaphor takes us to the heart of Greek metaphysics. In his *Physics*—"the foundational book of Western philosophy"[13]—Aristotle reveals that central principle that organizes Greek thought in its entirety, and through the Greeks it exercises its influence over the subsequent philosophical tradition. We call it "the ergological difference" because it differentiates between those beings that are φύσει and those that are ἀπὸ τέχνης (192b, 8 and 18), that is, it thinks beings according to *manufacture*. With "manufacture" we mean the work (ἔργον, factus)[14] that is carried out by the hand (χείρ, manus). The ergological difference determines what makes a being be the kind of being it is. It questions about its *aitia* and *arche*. According to their *aitia* and *arche*, the entirety of beings falls in two categories: those "produced" by the work of the hand (that have their *aitia* "outside" themselves, namely, in the hand that produced them; thus, Aristotle calls them χειρόκμητα [493b 30]) and those that "sprang forth" (φύσει) and are the *aitia* of themselves.[15] Φύσις, what later would be rendered as *natura*, is first thought in opposition to the work of the hand *(ergon)*.[16] The latter has given rise to a series of metaphysical concepts: *energeia*[17] (that was translated as *actualitas* and thus it came to mean "actuality" but gave us also the English word "energy") and *katargesis* (used by Paul in his *Epistles* and translated by Luther as *Aufhebung*, a hallmark term in Hegel's philosophy), *synergy* and *demiurgy* (that allude to a laborious God who creates and preserves the world), *organon* (the Greek term for a "tool" but also the etymon for such words as *organic* and *organism*), and finally, our own *work*. Throughout these conceptual and lexical transformations of the word *ergon* and the metaphysical tradition that it sustains from Aristotle to Hegel and beyond, it is the hand that looms over it as its very symbol.

When, then, the soul is compared to the hand, much more is said about the soul than what, we might, at a first glance, think to be the case. For in "touching" the things it seeks to know, the soul-hand is also "touched" back by the world. As "touched," in the act of comprehending, the soul becomes aware of itself. It becomes aware of itself as a soul that "touches" the world. This self-awareness achieves the impossible—for it could be said that in some sense the soul, aware of itself as a soul, *is touching itself*. It would seem as if, in some fundamental sense, the soul becomes aware of its own thinking only insofar as an object is presented to its contemplation; and, similarly, a subject becomes aware of its perception—or better yet, of itself as a sentient subject—only insofar as it perceives. Indeed, the middle voice of αἰσθάνεσθαι aptly illustrates the double meaning of "to perceive" and "to be aware" of one's own act of perception.[18]

For Aristotle, the awareness of our sensibility is not the result of an additional special sense — that would perceive, as it were, our perception — but of our senses themselves and only insofar as they are engaged in the act of perceiving, that is, only as long as "objects" affect them. Aristotle himself, after all, raises the very question: "There is the aporia as to why there is not some sense that would perceive the senses themselves and why without the external things the senses do not perceive?" (417a 3–5). His response reminds us of his definition of the sense (τό αἰσθητικόν) as a capacity (δύναμις) that cannot sense in the absence of the sensible, as a flammable thing cannot be burnt in the absence of fire. This passage is of crucial importance as it marks one of the earliest philosophical inquiries into the nature of self-consciousness. Aristotle's reply to this aporia implies the interesting position that, although we cannot sense our senses directly (e.g., the eye cannot see itself, the ear is deaf to itself, etc.), we do sense ourselves, nevertheless, *obliquely*, in the sensing of the others. "Tactile experiencing of the other is simultaneously *self-experiencing*, since otherwise I would not be the one experiencing."[19] But without the other made available to me by my body there would have been no self-experience or self-awareness at all. "We feel only the other, and if we feel ourselves this will be only on the occasion of, and by dependence on, a feeling of the other . . . I feel myself only by a favor of the other. It is the other who gives me to myself."[20]

"Can I not see and touch my hand while it is touching?"[21] Sartre rightly asks. To touch my hand, as it touches this or that thing, would mean that I turn my hand into an object for me (and, therefore, it is not anymore *my* hand, but an objectified hand that occupies a space next to this book — once touched the hand becomes a tangible thing among things). "I can not touch my hand *as it is* touching"[22] because my hand *is* me. "In fact what I am can not on principle be an object for me inasmuch as I *am it*."[23] That body, which I am, I know not. That body, through which I know everything that I know, remains for me unknown. That is of what the privilege of touch consists: touch gives me the knowledge of my body through the body of the Other.[24] Only the body of the Other can be touched, for the Other is the Other because he or she appears as a tool for me in a way that my body cannot present itself. Therefore, I am not the Other because "his body appears to me originally as a point of view on which I can take a point of view, an *instrument* which I can utilize with other instruments . . . The Other's body is therefore the Other himself as transcendence-*instrument*."[25] The Other's accessibility or resistance to my touch (mental or sensory) furnishes me with a sense of myself *qua* myself. I *am* myself because I can grasp, hold, or seize the Other — who, precisely because of my capability to handle him or her, is not I. The notion of the I cannot come before or independently of the Other. The soul cannot touch (i.e., know) itself but in touching the Other. Self-consciousness is a by-product excreted by the process of sensing the Other.

The hand can grasp the cup because it is not a cup, and it can hold this book because it is not a book — if the hand were any of these objects, it could not touch any of them. It touches them by virtue of being none of them, but also because it is capable of becoming like every single one of them. So with the soul. It is necessary for the soul, in order to know beings, not to be a being itself. The soul is not some*thing* because then it couldn't be *any*thing, and if it couldn't be anything it, would know nothing. "The soul somehow *is* all the beings" (ἡ ψυχὴ τὰ ὄντα πώς ἐστι πάντα; 431b 21). That is perhaps the strangest and arguably the most difficult of Aristotle's statements in *De Anima*. It has been interpreted as affirming the capacity of the soul to *know* all the forms of the beings and therefore (in accordance with Aristotle's principle of the identity of the *nous* with *ta nooumena* [430a 1] and the similarity of the senses with the sensibles [418a 1]) to *be* all the beings. However, the implications of this statement are far-reaching. In order for the soul to be all beings, it itself has to be none. For if the soul was one being, it could not be other than itself and certainly not all the beings.[26] Not only the soul *is not* — insofar as it is not an *on* — but, by not being an *on*, it cannot be known or sensed — it is neither intelligible nor perceptible, first and foremost to itself. As the Freudian epode in Derrida's *Le Toucher* goes: "Psyche ist ausgedehnt, weiss nichts davon":[27]

> Not merely, then, does the *psyche* not think itself, *qua* itself, but it does not know *how* to think itself, and consequently, it does not know *whether* it ever thinks itself. For how could the *psyche*, which thinks by becoming an entity or determinate form, even know what it would be like to think pure or *indeterminate* form? Precisely then if the *psyche* is itself formally indeterminate, it cannot think itself, since to do so would be to determine the indeterminate.[28]

Therefore, the soul knows only what is other than itself. What is other than the soul is everything that the soul can grasp. Like the hand of the first man, the soul reaches out and grasps the things. In doing so, however, it grasps itself as the "thing" that can grasp, that is, as a *hand*.

The Birth of Objectivity: *The Caress*

The domestication of the grasping hand has given rise to the caress. If we wish to find the origin of the caress we should probably look at the "picking" over a primate's fur by a fellow animal. The tedious task of grooming a fellow animal's fur demands such dexterity, coordination, and patience that this habit alone would have sufficed for the classification of the animals involved in it as anthropoids.[29] Contrary to wide-held opinion, this often-observed practice among monkeys and other apes serves no practical purpose (e.g., flea-catching, as has been assumed). "This behaviour is commonly misinterpreted as an attempt to remove lice. Actually vermin are rarely found on either captive or wild monkeys."[30] Zuckerman believes that grooming has sexual overtones, as it is often combined with sexual activity.[31] Canetti, on the other hand, goes even further back, to a pure "pleasure of the fingers."[32] Whatever meaning we assign to this habit, one thing remains clear: the hand, for the first time, is engaged in an activity devoid of practical purpose.

Whereas the grasping hand sought to establish distance by affirming dominance over the Other (a subjugated human being, a hunted animal, a seized object), the caress is nothing else than the continuous annihilation of the distance that separates me from the Other. It is a curious thing that the hand should execute both these seemingly opposing gestures. In fact, however, the one contains the possibility of the other. In annihilating the traversed distance, the caress only "veils" distance as its very condition; conversely, the grasping hand, in presupposing the distance between a capturing subject and a captured object, "veils" the proximity in which it results. The caress is not the contact of flesh with flesh, but rather the *approach* of a body toward another. The approach cannot take place but in the space opened up by the interplay between distance and proximity:

> To show that touch involves a sense of proximity is to show that it involves a sense of distance. To touch is to approach or to be approached, not to apply a surface against another. Proximity forgets, through contact, what separates it from the thing that it touches. It no longer feels this distance as such, precisely because distance no longer impedes touch but instead constitutes the medium through which we feel . . . For proximity to remain proximity, it must always replenish itself with new distance.[33]

The veiling (*Verdecktheit*) of distance in the caress amounts to a forgetfulness (*Vergessenheit*) of the violence of the touch: the caressing hand is nothing else than the grasping hand that forgets or resigns from its violence. Or else: the caress is still a struggle to hold the Other, but in an effort in principle doomed to failure. Each stroke of the hand over the Other's body is a sign of a repetitive failure to touch the Other — for in "touching" the Other one touches only a thing. The Other as Other evades my grasp, he slips through my fingers; what I am left with is only the outer skin, an empty garment:

> To be sure, I can *grasp* the Other, grab hold of him, knock him down. I can, providing I have the power, compel him to perform this or that act, to say certain words. But everything happens as if I wished to get hold of a man who runs away and leaves only his coat in my hands. It is the coat, it is the outer shell which I possess.[34]

The otherness of the Other, what the caress passionately seeks, remains intangible. Hence one has always to begin again — and in vain.

The very vanity of the caress, its failure, succeeds in revealing the Other as more than a thing: the Other's body is presented as the body of a Subject, that is, as a person. In the caress the Other is not any more the Object of my grasp but the intangible Subject of my touch:

> Since I can grasp the Other only in his objective facticity, the problem is to ensnare his freedom within this facticity. It is necessary that he be "caught" in it as the cream is caught up by a person skimming milk. So the Other's For-itself must come to play on the surface of his body, and be extended all through his body; and by touching this body I should finally touch the Other's free subjectivity.[35]

Of course, the Other's free subjectivity is precisely that which cannot be touched, and in this respect we begin to understand Levinas's very problematic statement: "The caress aims at neither a person nor a thing."[36] Neither the person nor a thing could possibly be the "aim" of the caress (its *telos* in a teleological totality), for the caress is aimless and purposeless. My caress offers recognition to the Other's subjectivity, witness to the Other's transcendence, a transcendence beyond the realm of the things palpable by my hand—*for it would be meaningless for me to caress an object or a thing*. In caressing the Other, I have already recognized the Other *as Other* and not as a thing to be felt or known. Under my caress the Other is not a "tool" assigned with a given function—the purposelessness of the caress signals the suspension or de-activation *(katargesis)* of the operation of *ergon* and thus the emancipation of the Other from the sphere of "managing" manufacture. As such, the caress seeks the infinite[37] but an infinite mysteriously immanent, that is, embodied in the body of the Other. It is with regard to this last point that Levinas commits a hermeneutical faux pas of rather considerable proportions. For, in his anxiety to turn his reading of the caress against Sartre's, he radicalizes its structure to such an extent that it becomes an absolute:

> Anticipation grasps possibles; what the caress seeks is not situated in a perspective and in the light of the graspable [and thus, as Levinas writes more than once, "beyond the possible"]. The carnal, the tender par excellence correlative of the caress, the beloved, is to be identified neither with the body-thing of the physiologist, nor with the lived body of the "I can," nor with the body-expression, attendance at its own manifestation, or face. In the caress, a relation yet, in one aspect, sensible, the body already *denudes itself of its very form*, offering itself as erotic nudity. In the carnal given to tenderness, *the body quits the status of an existent.*[38]

Faceless, bodiless, and lifeless, the "body" revealed in the "darkness" of the caress is absorbed by the elemental night of the *il y a.*[39] Far from revealing the sensuous flesh of the Other, the Levinasian caress is swallowed up by the anonymous, impersonal, numinous virginity of the feminine.

However, it is the person of the Other — the Other as person — and nothing more that turns my touch into a caress. The Other's evanescence under my touch is complemented with the Other's enfleshment in the very body I caress. The soft fingertips of the hand, their sensation that causes the skin to shiver, the lingering and repetitive movement of the hand that runs up and down the Other's body, the stupor induced by the delicate stroking of the skin,

a stroking that seems to have neither end nor beginning — all these characteristics observed in the act of the caressing are part of what Sartre has aptly
called the "rituals which *incarnate* the Other."[40] The caress invokes the otherness of the Other to come and inhabit, or rather manifest itself, in the body
given to my touch. "This is because the caress is not a simple stroking; it is a
shaping. In caressing the Other I cause his flesh to be born beneath my caress,
under my fingers."[41] This act of "creation" effected by my touch presupposes
(but also results in) a movement of incarnation — in fact, "a *double reciprocal
incarnation.*"[42]

Each stroke of my hand assures the Other of my resignation from violence, of the relinquishing of my power to grasp, seize, or kill him. Each stroke
of my hand abdicates my authority as a subject to whom the Other is forced
to be subjected. In facing the Other's subjectivity, or better yet, precisely in
order to allow the Other's subjectivity to manifest itself as such, I have to re-
sign from mine. I have to undertake or undergo a self-willed *kenosis.*[43] I let
myself become an object for the Other. I make myself open and vulnerable to
the Other's touch. Sartre's analysis is quite unambiguous on this point: "I incarnate myself in order to realize the incarnation of the Other. The caress by
realizing the Other's incarnation reveals to me my own incarnation."[44] Hence
the reciprocity of the haptic phenomenon: there cannot be a touch that is not
"touched" back — to touch already means to make oneself tangible — to reveal
oneself in the condensation of one's own flesh.

It is the incarnation of myself, as at the same time both the precondition
and the aftermath of the caress, that opens up what Sartre calls the "third ontological dimension of the body": "in so far as *I am for others*, the Other is revealed to me as the subject for whom I am an object . . . I exist for myself as a
body known by the other."[45] That this third dimension — a chiasmus between
the being for-itself and for-others that would become central to Merleau-
Ponty's analysis of the touch — constitutes an exemplary instance of what we
have been discussing in the previous chapters of this work under the name
of "inverse intentionality" remains undeniable: "With the appearance of the
Other's look I experience the revelation of my being-as-object,"[46] but it is not
only the look that effects such an inversion; a few lines later Sartre adds: "I
feel myself *touched* by the Other in my factual existence" — the Other's touch
in the touch of the Other yields a self in the accusative, touched, a "me." It
is at this precise moment that *being*-a-body is abandoned and *having*-a-body
emerges. The Other's touch has caused me to *have* a body (incarnation),
which is still the body that I am, but now posited as another's. It is only once
this synthetic "vision," the coalescence of my subjectivity (the distance of
grasping — "I *am* a body") with my objectivity (the proximity of the caress — "I
have a body"), is achieved that I can see (or touch) myself: "the Other accomplishes for us a function of which we are incapable and which nevertheless is
incumbent on us: *to see ourselves as we are.*"[47]

The self-consciousness of the I, regardless of whether the I experiences it-self as a subjectivity or an objectivity, is a phenomenon always originating out-side or beyond the I, through another, or more precisely through the Other (be it another human or the sensible world). That is the invariable conclu-sion of any philosophical examination of the phenomenon of touch. There is nothing to indicate that I become aware of myself independently of the Other or without him or her. Both modalities of being (what Sartre calls the for-itself and the for-others which have been thought here under the para-digms of grasping and caressing respectively) presuppose a beyond embodied in the things of the world and incarnated in the flesh of the Other. All self-consciousness is not a touching (not even if one were to touch oneself) but a being touched. *Affectivity* is the underlying structure of all consciousness (as "consciousness of . . ." and self-consciousness):

> Incarnation is not a transcendental operation of a subject that is situated in the midst of the world it represents to itself; the sensible experience of the body is already and from the start incarnate. The sensible — maternity, vul-nerability, apprehension — binds the node of incarnation into a plot larger than the apperception of the self. In this plot I am bound to others before being tied to my body. Intentionality, the noesis which the philosophy of consciousness distinguished in sensing, and which it wanted, in a regres-sive movement, to take hold of again as the origin of the sense ascribed, the sensible intuition, is already in the mode of apprehension and obsession, assailed by the sensed which undoes its noematic appearing in order to command, with a non-thematizable alterity, the very noesis which at the origin should have given it a sense. The Gordean knot of the body, the extremities in which it begins or ends, are forever dissimulated in the knot that cannot be undone, and that commands in the ungraspable noesis its own transcendental origin.[48]

* * *

Every sensation is an affection of the soul, as Aristotle has pointed out in *De Sensu*, "the sense takes place through the body in the soul" (ἡ δ' αἴσθησις διὰ σώματος γίνεται τῇ ψυχῇ; 436b 7–8). The body serves as the sensorium that allows the world and the soul to "touch" each other. The body then be-comes the point of contact between an interiority (the soul) and an exteriority (the world) and, at the same time, their border, a limen that differentiates be-tween the two — not, as Proclus claims in his *Elements of Theology*,[49] between a corporeal reality (the world) and the incorporeal soul, but, rather, between the only corporeality of the body and the incorporeal nature of both the soul *and* the world. For the body does not perceive the things of this world as bodies similar to itself (if that were the case it could not perceive anything at all, for the same reasons that it cannot perceive itself) but only as (incorporeal) forms.[50] Thus, between the soul and the world the body stands alone as this absolute singular flesh — the in-between (τὸ μεταξύ; 423b 26) of a double touching, from its inside as well as from its outside, while remaining itself intact.

How, however, do the world and the soul touch each other? One basic principle that runs throughout the pages of the *De Anima* and governs Aristotle's conception of sensibility is the belief that the sense in sensing its object somehow *becomes* like it — better yet, no sense can perceive unless it has the capacity to become *similar* to the sensible it seeks to perceive (τὸ δ' αἰσθητικὸν δυνάμει ἐστὶν οἷον τὸ αἰσθητὸν; 418a 1). It is this very principle of Aristotelian aesthetics that Meister Eckhart employs, several centuries after Aristotle, to explain the paradoxical union between God and man:

> As I was coming here today I was wondering how I should preach to you so that it would make sense and you would understand it. Then I thought of a comparison: If you could understand that, you would understand my meaning and the basis of all my thinking in everything I have ever preached. The comparison concerns my eyes and a piece of wood. If my eye is open, it is an eye; if it is closed, it is the same eye. It is not the wood that comes and goes, but it is my vision of it. Now pay good heed to me! If it happens that my eye is in itself one and simple (Mt. 6:22), and it is opened and casts its glance upon the piece of wood, the eye and the wood remain what they are, *and yet in the act of vision they become as one*, so that we can truly say that *my eye is the wood* and *the wood is my eye*. But if the wood were immaterial, purely spiritual as is the sight of my eye, then one could truly say that in the act of vision *the wood and my eye subsisted in one being*. If this is true of physical objects, it is far truer of spiritual objects.[51]

The same term that sustains the similarity between the sentient and the sensible in Aristotle's text (οἷον) is employed once again later in the discussion in order to illustrate how this likeness is to be understood:

> With regard to all senses in general we have to accept that the sense is this capacity to receive (τὸ δεκτικόν) the sensible without its matter, like (οἷον) the wax which receives the imprint of the signet ring without its iron or its gold, it takes [the form] of the golden or bronze imprint but not *qua* gold or bronze. (424a 17–21)

In this example, the sentient is paralleled to a piece of wax capable of receiving the imprint of a signet ring, which holds the place of the sensible object. We can now question the similarity between sentient and sensible by asking in what ways is the piece of wax, after it has taken the shape of the signet, similar to the signet itself? This is an easier question, for we could, tentatively at least, answer by noticing that the wax has now taken the *form* of the signet — the seal, in coming in contact with the wax, has left its imprint on the wax, reproducing, as it were, its *form* on it. That means that, indeed, the wax and the signet ring are similar with regard to the imprint (the form), for looking at the imprint of the seal left on the wax one should easily recognize it as the impression of that particular ring. On the other hand, they do differ in terms of their matter (the impression is "made" of wax while the ring is of iron or gold). Aristotle explains how the example of the wax illustrates our sense perception:

> Similarly, each sense is affected (πάσχει) by those things that have color, or flavor or sound, but it is not understood as one of these things insofar as they are what they are but insofar as it is such (τοιονδί) and in accordance to a relation (λόγον). The primary sense organ is that in which such capacity (δύναμις) is found. The sense organ is, in one respect, the same with its capacity, but in another respect they are different: for the sense organ is an extended thing (μέγεθος), but neither sensibility nor sense are extensions, but some kind of relation and the capacity to such a relation (λόγος τις καὶ δύναμις ἐκείνου) (424a 21–28).

The effort to explain the similarity between the sentient and the sensible has prompted Aristotle to draw a distinction between the physiological organ of perception (τό αἰσθητήριον) and the sense itself (ἡ αἴσθησις) defined as a *logos* (loosely translated here as "relation") and as a *dynamis* (i.e., the capacity or possibility of such relation). Taken together, τό αἰσθητήριον and ἡ αἴσθησις constitute what Aristotle calls τό αἰσθητικόν, i.e., sensibility or the sentient faculty of man. In juxtaposing the latter with the sensible object (τὸ αἰσθητόν), we become aware of a certain symmetry that makes their similarity (established by *DA*, 418a 1) a bit more comprehensible. We could render their symmetry schematically as follows:

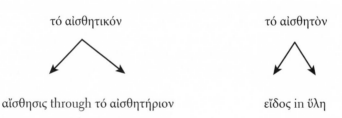

τό αἰσθητικόν   τό αἰσθητὸν

αἴσθησις through τό αἰσθητήριον   εἶδος in ὕλη

Sensibility appears now similar to the sensible object in terms of their mirroring duality: our capacity to perceive is enabled by our senses' being affected by the sensible objects—but how does this happen? The sense (being psychic—in Aristotle's terminology "not an extension"—insofar as it was defined as relation and capacity) is affected thanks to the sense organ (an "extended thing"), which is physiological and, as such, capable of coming in contact with the equally physical things. But, then, how can Aristotle say that the sense (a psychic element) not only is "affected" (πάσχει) by the sensible but also becomes similar to it? The answer lies in the duality of the sensible itself: the sensible thing, like the signet ring in Aristotle's example, has a dual property of εἶδος (i.e., form: for example, the seal of the signet) and ὕλη (i.e., matter: for example, the gold out of which the ring is made). The form, like the sense, has no extension and therefore is not a physical (we would say today "material") quality, while the second, like its counterpart, the sense organ, is.

What, then, affects the sense is not the matter of the sensible but rather its form: the wax, after all, does not receive the metal of the ring but only its form. As, however, just the form of the ring makes no ring in the end, so too there is no sensibility without the sense organ that would allow the sense to come in contact with its object. By slightly altering the previous schema we have the following sequence:

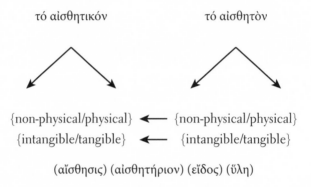

τό αἰσθητικόν   τό αἰσθητὸν

{non-physical/physical} ⟵ {non-physical/physical}
{intangible/tangible} ⟵ {intangible/tangible}

(αἴσθησις) (αἰσθητήριον) (εἶδος) (ὕλη)

This schema confronts us with a new question: even with the duality (non-physical/physical) of both sentient and sensible as given, how can the (physical) eye perceive the (non-physical) form of the sensible? How can the (non-physical) soul of the sentient perceive the sensible matter? At the precise point of contact, sensible and sentient "touch" each other with different—indeed, opposite—properties: on the one hand, the sense organ (eye, ear, tongue, nose, skin) is itself a sensible, a thing perceivable among other things; without the perceiving, sense is *blind* to the form of things. On the other hand, though, the sense can recognize the form of things but not the things themselves; without the sense organ the world of *aesthesis* is an *empty* world of phantasms and phantasies.[52]

Aristotle resolves this perplexity by understanding the interaction between the sentient and the sensible as a change (ἀλλοίωσις) "suffered" by the sense at the moment of perceiving its object: better yet, perception *is* this changing of the sense (416b 34) from being dissimilar (ἀνόμοιον) to being similar (ὅμοιον) to the object of perception (417b 20 and 418a 5). It is similar to the object insofar as it has been affected (πεπονθός) by it. Every act of perception (αἰσθάνεσθαι), therefore, is complemented by an act of affection (πάσχειν):

perception is this *pathos* undergone and undertaken by the sentient subject that finds itself immersed in a sensible world. In seeing the table in front of me, touching this paper, etc., I am in a variety of ways continuously affected by the forms of the objects that surround me. The two moments (perception/ affection) do not form a sequence (e.g., first I see the table and *then* I am affected by its form) but occur synchronically — the one because of the other. I couldn't sense anything without having been affected by it prior to my sensing it, but also I couldn't be affected without having first sensed.[53] *The subject of perception and the object of affection are one and the same.*

Beyond the Subject/Object Distinction: *The Kiss*

The mouth is the arbiter of touch. It has been often observed that as soon as babies are able to grasp their toys, they bring them to their mouth. In that gesture, the infant reenacts a "natural" move: from the hand to the mouth. The mouth or, more precisely, the possibilities of the mouth reveal the implied intentions of the hand: the grasping of an object implies biting while the caressing of the Other implies kissing. Without forgetting, of course, the connection between the hand and speech, already discussed above. The mouth provides the context within which the hand's activity becomes meaningful.

When it comes to the kiss, philosophy has very little to say. The kiss as such was never thematized in the history of philosophy, while it has been avoided even as a metaphor. It would seem that the lovers of wisdom don't know how to kiss. Perhaps there is good reason for philosophy's awkwardness toward the kiss: there is nothing "philosophical" about it. By that I mean that the kiss resists conceptualization. What concepts, paradigms, or metaphors could be employed in order to think the kiss? Is there only one kiss or more? How to distinguish or unite different types of kissing, like the maternal kiss, the erotic kiss, the kiss of betrayal, the social kiss, the ceremonial kiss or the kiss of respect, the kiss of peace, the kiss in adoration, etc.? And how can one organize the kisses of the different parts of the Other's body, like the kiss on the forehead, on the cheeks, on the mouth, on the hand, on the feet, and so on?

Despite the kiss's polysemy and ambiguity, our thought suffers primarily from the lack of concepts by which to think the kiss — for the kiss itself is a *symbol* (in the literary sense of *sym-ballein*: to put together two halves) and thus unable to be represented with anything other than itself. Plato was the first to use the term to describe the fragmentary nature of man,[54] but also the longing for union with our "other half." The metaphor comes from the ancient practice of two people breaking between them a piece of pottery, a coin, or a seal, with each keeping one fragment of it, as a reminder and future evidence of the kinship or friendship between them. When the holders of each half meet again they would put together (συμβάλλειν) the two pieces and thus affirm (or prove) their relationship with each other. For that reason, each fragment of the divided coin or seal was called a *"symbolon."* It is easy to see how the union of the lips, the two mouths brought together in kissing, stands as a symbol of this practice of *symballein.* As if my mouth were one of two matching tallies, to be "fitted" on the Other's mouth, like two pieces of a puzzle fit together. The kiss is a symbol of this symbol, a symbolism of an intimacy that affirms itself as it strives to achieve perfect unity.

What is united by the kiss? Two fragments of self-consciousness, two fragmentary views of my body. The "I am a body," yielded by the act of grasping, and the "I have a body," revealed to me through the caress. These two different ways of affirming myself cannot be dismissed as merely two different phenomena of *one* and the same reality (essence or nature), but rather as two distinct manifestations that are brought to unity by a chiastic "kiss."[55] As Michel Henry advises us:

> Phenomenology cannot advance such an illusory solution because it reduces being to its appearance, because for it there is nothing beyond phenomena, nothing behind the different manifestations which are given to us and which are all reduced to two essential types whose ontological structure we have studied. Phenomenology is not a theory of appearances, a theory which would leave behind it the real being of things. This real being, as phenomenology shows us, is entirely in the manner in which it presents itself to us, in appearances; phenomenology shows us that *being is its own revelation,* such that where two phenomena are in opposition, we must also say that we are in the presence of two beings.[56]

Here we are indeed in the presence of two phenomena in opposition, in fact, of two phenomenalities different altogether. Are we to conclude from this, and in accordance with the phenomenological reduction, that the phenomenon of the "I am a body" and the phenomenon of the "I have a body" constitute two different beings and, therefore, I am in possession of two bodies? It would seem so. ("There is a natural body and there is a spiritual body"; 1 Cor. 15:44). But even if we consent to such a seemingly absurd hypothesis for the sake of the argument, we are immediately confronted with a far more demanding difficulty: on which grounds can the "I" of the "I am a body" claim to be the same as the "I" of the "I have a body"? In other words, what allows us to unify these two phenomena by taking them to be both *mine*? How can it be that the body that I am and the body that I have are both *mine*? Isn't the mineness implied in these statements an unfounded inference?[57]

Henry rightly observes that "the duality which splits in an incomprehensible manner the unity of the being of my body and which causes this being to be given to me twice, so to speak, finds its foundation in the *ontological* structure of truth."[58] In reconsidering the differences in these two phenomenalities — that is, my experience of things (grasping) and persons (caressing) — we notice that the "I am a body" phenomenon belongs to the sphere of ontology as it describes my finding of myself among things; it "gives" me to myself in the perception of the world, as thrown in the midst of it, and yet as different from the things that I perceive (*distance* from others), for I cannot perceive myself. On the other hand, the "I have a body" phenomenon belongs to the sphere of epistemology, as in this statement the body has already become an object for me. As a consequence, a *distance* from myself ensues on the basis of which not only the objectification of my body but also my knowledge of it is made possible.

Ontology and epistemology are the "two sources of evidence" of which Maine de Biran speaks, or the twofold manifestation of corporeality for which Henry argues. Being is indeed given to us twice, and it is this duplicity that allows for experience.[59] But experience is also a unity, and this is where the difficulty arises, since for philosophy, at least from Descartes onwards, ontology is subordinated to epistemology. The two phenomena, however (and, indeed, phenomenology itself), do not admit such a distinction between the ontological and the epistemological: for phenomenology there is no ulterior reality, neither knowable nor unknown, beyond phenomena. Indeed, a closer examination of the two phenomena shows that the "ontological" phenomenon of the "I am a body" yields the knowledge that I have of the things that surround me, a knowledge that, as we have seen, precedes and grounds my self-experience, while the "epistemological" phenomenon of the "I have a body" raises the very question concerning my being. Ontology and epistemology crisscross each other in the double manifestation of my body that is united in the chiasmus of the kiss. The kiss is the "symbol" that unites the two fragments of a broken philosophy: the ontological and the epistemological. Only thanks to that unity, the "I" of the "I have" fully overlaps and is at last identified with the "I" of the "I am"; thanks to that unity, the experience of the world amounts to the experience of oneself; thanks to that unity, the immanence of subjectivity is transcended toward the transcendence of an objectivity immanent in the subject.

What else could be the "ontological structure of truth" which Henry, as we have just seen, claimed to be the foundation of my body's duality? How else could truth, an epistemological category, have an ontological structure unless it is in its unity with being?

What does this unity mean, however, if not that true knowledge is only a knowledge founded on the ontological event of *communio personarum* and not on the ontic comprehension of things? A knowledge grounded on ontology is knowledge eventuated by relation, relation between persons, that is, a knowledge grounded on relatedness. *Only a person* can know, and *only a person*. We have seen in the previous sections of this chapter how a theory of sensibility and perception is impossible unless it begins with the unity of sentient and sensible. Phenomenology posits a similar prerequisite as its starting point, when it emphasizes the intentional "of" in the "consciousness *of . . .*"

There is no consciousness that is not a consciousness *of* something, that is, an identity of the perceiving, imagining, or remembering consciousness with the phenomenon perceived, imagined, or remembered. According to such an identity, to know a thing is to become or to *be* that thing; namely, epistemology is possible only as ontology. However, a person can never become a *thing*,[60] for a person cannot become a thing *while* he or she knows. Either knowledge is altogether impossible, or a person knows only a person for only a person knows.[61] To be sure, we "know" things, but only insofar as they refer to or signify relations with persons. We can never know a thing *in itself*, not because reason cannot penetrate the world of phenomena and reach to that of noumena, but simply because there is no such world, for there can be no world outside of the referential totality of interpersonal communion within which things first appear and from which they acquire their meaning.

Unless the personal character of being and knowledge (that is, their hypostatic union in the person) is fully retrieved and recovered, then any insight on the nature of sensibility—for instance, Merleau-Ponty's understanding of the sacramental quality of perception—would remain puzzling and mystifying. We have spoken of that union as a kiss, that is, as a symbol. The "twofold usage" of symbols, however, indeed, their intrinsic duality, is based on the chiasmus, the crisscrossing between representation (the symbol stands for a reality beyond itself) and being (the efficacious conferring of that reality by the symbol):

> Just as the sacrament not only symbolizes, in sensible species, an operation of Grace, but *is* also the real presence of God, which it causes to occupy a fragment of space and communicates to those who eat of the consecrated bread, provided that they are inwardly prepared, in the same way the sensible has not only a motor and vital significance, but is nothing other than a certain way of being in the world suggested to us from some point in space, and seized and acted upon by our body, provided that it is capable of doing so, so that sensation is literally a form of communion.[62]

Sensation is not *one* way of being in the world, as if it were one among many, but the *only* way of being: to be the communicant of the world is only another way of saying "to be" or "to exist." Merleau-Ponty makes that clear when he refuses to accept the idealist's position which would somehow require the sentient subject to cease from being in order to know. To know in this Eucharistic way, to follow Merleau-Ponty's "literal" metaphor, is to be. To be is nothing else than this continuous *pathos*: the wound of ek-sistence that realizes itself in co-existence:

> I am brought into relation with an external being, whether it be in order to open myself to it or to shut myself off from it. If the qualities radiate around them a certain mode of existence, if they have the power to cast a spell and what we called just now a sacramental value, this is because the sentient subject does not posit them as objects, but enters into a sym-

pathetic relation with them, makes them his own and finds in them his momentary law.[63]

Knowledge as this sympathetic relation ("sympathetic" here has the literal meaning of a reciprocal pathos, a suffering-together-with) is not the intellectualist knowledge afforded by an aloof distance between a distinct knower and the thing known. This knowledge is not comprehension, insofar as both ends are comprehended, the "subject" as well as the "object," so much so that one cannot distinguish any more between the two ("in this transaction between the subject of sensation and the sensible it cannot be held that one acts while the other suffers the action").[64] As Dionysius's narration of the Hierotheus episode has demonstrated, this knowledge is a μάθησις eventuated by πάθησις; knowledge as affection.

The double sense of *aesthesis* — the twofold paradox of perception occasioning affection but also of affection inaugurating perception — remains the implied mystery behind such oscular union between knowledge and being: on the one hand, being becomes again, as it was for the ancients, intelligible, that is, *sensible*[65] (but that does not mean that being stands now "explained" or even "explicable"); on the other hand, knowledge is not anymore mere understanding but relation and communion leading to the union of knower and known in *love*.[66] *There could be no light of knowledge without the burning fire of love.*

To our ears today such a statement sounds like an eccentricity, because for us love has lost its ontological dimension as that which drives us to be and enables us to know, degenerated as it has been into a feeling abandoned to the hands of psychologism. We have all become Lysiases in need of a Socratic palinode that would remind us that the union of knowledge and being is love. This is the only kiss philosophy has given us until today, although it has been neither always nor by everyone accepted. In the words of St. Bernard of Clairvaux:

> Two kinds of people therefore may not consider themselves to have been gifted with the kiss, those who know the truth without loving it, and those who love it without understanding it; from which we conclude that this kiss leaves room neither for ignorance nor for lukewarmness.[67]

Any hint of ignorance is to be properly expelled from the philosophical community — but what about lukewarmness? To understand the truth is a demand made to oneself by any self-respecting thinker — but to love it? How is one to love the truth in our age when truth is reduced to a set of facts or information that is said to correspond somehow to a dubious reality?

Even this very concept of reality (the totality of inert *res*) becomes extremely problematic in face of such truth that demands to be loved. A thing cannot be loved — as Augustine has shown us[68] — it can only be used. If truth is to be loved, and thus understood, then there can be neither truth nor understanding of the "real" world insofar as this world remains the "useful" world of things. If, despite its un-truthfulness, the world is nevertheless "loved," then the world *qua* world is only *mis*understood (as the person who, mistaken for a thing, is not "used" but misused and abused). If truth is the knowledge that loves as much as the love that understands, then only a person can be kissed with the kiss of truth, for Truth Himself has revealed Himself as a person (John 14:6).

eight
The Sabbath of Experience

you touched *me, and I am inflamed with love*

—Augustine, Confessions, X, 27

and while we spoke of the eternal Wisdom, longing for it and straining for it with all the strength of our hearts, for one fleeting instant we reached out and touched it.

—Augustine, Confessions, IX, 10

This brief passage from the ninth book of the *Confessions* marks the culmination of Augustine's beatific vision in the garden of Ostia — the third and last garden that would play an eminent role in the development of his narration. Augustine's story is structured as an ascent — from "the bodily pleasure" to "the whole compass of material things in their various degrees" and from there to "the heavens" and the planets until, moving ever higher, he passes from the meditation of "our own souls" to the contemplation of "that Wisdom by which all these things that we know are made, all things that ever have been and all that are yet to be."

This ecstatic *Himmelflug* is constructed in such a way as to stand as a close textual parallel of another, famous ascent of ancient literature. I refer, of course, to the ladder in Diotima's speech as it is recorded in Plato's *Symposium*. There, too, the philosopher is initiated into a gradual *anabasis* that mirrors that of Augustine: from the beauty of one body to that of many, then from physical beauty to that of theories, until one reaches the idea of the Beautiful itself. The parallelism between the two passages becomes all the more accentuated not on account of their many similarities (of structure and language)

143

but thanks to one difference: *attingimus eam*. Augustine, unlike Socrates, reaches out and touches what lies beyond creation, intangible. Augustine's "vision" ceases to be a mere apparition and becomes experience at that very moment when he can touch what the philosopher can only see:

> Especially significant here is the fact that as the spiritual senses are made (in Gregory of Nyssa, for example) to correspond to various degrees of a mystical nearness or ascent to God, there is an inversion in the traditional (Platonic) hierarchy of the senses which placed sight far above all. In the spiritual senses, sight and hearing are lowest (though not scorned), whereas smell and, even more, taste and touch are the most exalted. This was a development whose importance was to be second to none in the history of Western mysticism.[1]

How does this inversion that upsets the old hierarchy of the senses and their symbolism take place? How are we to explain that what Plato describes as "absolute, pure, unmixed, not polluted by human flesh or colors or any other rubbish of mortality" (*Symposium*, 211e) can now be touched? The answer lies hidden in a cave in the hills of Bethlehem.

It is indeed thanks to the singular event of the Incarnation, contrary to all reason and logic, that the Bishop of Hippo can succeed there where the Philosopher of Athens fails. For it is God who in His *kenosis* runs against the philosophical *anabasis* and, instead of moving away from the contingent human nature, as the philosopher would instruct us, comes and assumes the very "rubbish of mortality" from which reason has fled with contempt. God is no longer reserved and inaccessible, but He has come into contact with our nature on account of the human body that He assumed in the Incarnation.[2] His is a body available to our touch and willing to touch us. It is precisely at this point that Christianity parts ways with both classical antiquity and the other monotheistic religions. For both Judaism and Islam remain within the realm of religion which, following human reason, allows of no contact be-tween the human and the divine—as is put by Plato, "the god cannot be min-gled with the human" (θεὸς δὲ ἀνθρώπῳ οὐ μείγνυται; *Symposium* 203a)—a deep-seated position in Greek thinking, it seems, if we judge by its recurrence in ancient thought (most notably, Anaxagoras's maxim "other things have their portion in everything, but *nous* alone is infinite and self-powerful and mixed with nothing, but it exists alone itself by itself").[3] Contrary to all re-ligious thinking of pre- and post-Christian times, Christ is the God who, by deed and by speech, reaches out and touches us. Thus, at the end of the ser-mon on the mount, the evangelist adds a comment regarding the reception of Jesus' words: the crowds, Matthew says, are *struck* (ἐξεπλήσσοντο; 7:28) by His new message. Similarly, they are physically touched by Him in a series of encounters that follow between Jesus, on the one hand, and the sick, the disabled, and the possessed, on the other, who seek His help. The Gospel's emphasis on touch must have made a strong impression on the first followers of the new faith, for it is precisely in this way — that is, as a young healing god who reaches out and touches His people — that He was depicted on the walls of the Roman catacombs. To be sure, the ancient world had its own divine healers — with Asclepius being the most famous among them — but *nowhere* is Asclepius represented as touching his patients.[4] Unlike the apparitions of the Greek gods as well as the visitations of the Jewish prophets, Christ's revelation offers something radically new: it offers Himself in flesh. The divine Word is not anymore only to be heard but also to be touched. The prophets might have spoken His words and heard His voice, as St. Bernard observes; they, however, fall short in satisfying humanity's desire for infinitely more — for His very kiss — that is, for His touch.[5]

Among the many miracles related by the gospels, one episode in particular calls for a closer examination, as in it, the sense of touch is not only the medium through which the miracle is performed, but it also becomes the focal point of the narration. It is the healing of the woman with the flow of blood (Matt. 9:18–30; Mark 5:22–42; Luke 8:40–56). St. Mark's gospel offers us a more detailed version of the story:

> And, behold, there cometh one of the rulers of the synagogue, Jairus by name; and when he saw him, he fell at his feet,
>
> And besought him greatly, saying, My little daughter lieth at the point of death: I pray thee, come and lay thy hands on her, that she may be healed; and she shall live.
>
> And Jesus went with him; and much people followed him, and thronged him.
>
> And a certain woman, which had an issue of blood twelve years,
>
> And had suffered many things of many physicians, and had spent all that she had, and was nothing bettered, but rather grew worse,
>
> When she had heard of Jesus, came behind the multitude, and touched his garment.
>
> For she said, If I may touch but his clothes, I shall be whole.
>
> And straightway the fountain of her blood was dried up and she felt in her body that she was healed of that plague.
>
> And Jesus, immediately knowing in himself that power had gone out of him, turned him about in the multitude, and said, Who touched my clothes?
>
> And his disciples said unto him, Thou seest the multitude thronging thee, and sayest thou, Who touched me?
>
> And he looked round about to see her that had done this thing.
>
> But the woman fearing and trembling, knowing what was done in her, came and fell down before him, and told him all the truth.
>
> And he said unto her, Daughter, thy faith hath made thee whole; go in peace, and be whole of thy plague.
>
> While he yet spoke, there came from the ruler of the synagogue's house certain which said, Thy daughter is dead; why troublest the Master any further?

> As soon as Jesus heard the word that was spoken, he saith unto the ruler of the synagogue, Be not afraid, only believe.
>
> And he suffered no man to follow him, save Peter, and James, and John the brother of James.
>
> And he cometh to the house of the ruler of the synagogue, and seeth the tumult, and them that wept and wailed greatly.
>
> And when he came in, he saith unto them, Why make ye this ado, and weep? The damsel is not dead, but sleepeth.
>
> And they laughed him to scorn. But when he had put them all out, he taketh the father and the mother of the damsel, and them that were with him, and entereth in where the damsel was lying.
>
> And he took the damsel by the hand, and said unto her, *Talitha cumi,* which is interpreted, Damsel, I say unto thee, arise.
>
> And straightway the damsel arose, and walked; for she was of the age of twelve years. And they were astonished with a great astonishment.
>
> And he charged them straitly that no man should know it; and commanded that something should be given her to eat.

We notice that the passage (and the question of touch that it poses) is framed by two other stories: (a) the resurrection of the daughter of Jairus (which opens the narration but is interrupted by the episode with the bleeding woman) and, in Matthew's account, (b) the healing of the two blind men that concludes the narration. The common thread that binds these three episodes together is not so much their miraculous nature but rather the emphasis they place on the contact with Christ's body. The miraculous healings performed by Christ, however, do not always have to take place by means of His touch: indeed, there are a good number of instances when Christ heals by word alone;[6] in this case, however, it is touch itself (as physical contact, emotional reaction, sympathy, and knowledge) that becomes thematic.

It is the central story, that of the bleeding woman, that raises most emphatically the question of touch, as it distinguishes between two different "understandings" of touch. It is true that both the multitude and the bleeding woman "touch" Him; however, there is a qualitative difference in their touch. The difference is indicated by His question: "Who touched my clothes?" This question—given the circumstances of the moment (there was a crowd, after all, pressing him)—signals a paradox: "You see the people crowding you and yet you ask 'Who touched me?'"—or in Peter's words: "Master, the multitude throng thee and press thee and sayest thou, Who touched me?" (Luke 8:45). Why does Christ appear to be aware only of the *unapparent* touch of a woman who approached Him secretly, in other words, of what was supposed to remain unnoticed?

As there are those who do not see Him in seeing Him and those who have recognized Him without having ever seen Him (see John 9:39), similarly, there are those who touched Him without touching Him, without feeling what or whom they had touched. This is the "judgment" (κρίμα) for which

He has come into the World: *that they who do not see might see and those who see might be made blind* (John 9:39). One's failure to see Him as who He is has little to do with one's so-called spiritual senses. This doctrine, supported for the first time by Origen in his *De Principiis*,[7] introduced a distinction between the "common" senses and their "higher" counterparts. For example, in Book I of the *De Principiis* Origen writes:

> "You will find a divine sense." For he [Solomon] knew that there were in us two kinds of senses, the one being mortal, corruptible and human, and the other immortal and intellectual, which here he calls "divine." By this divine sense, therefore, not of the eyes but of a pure heart, that is, the mind, God can be seen by those who are worthy.[8]

It becomes immediately evident that what Origen calls a "divine sense" is not a sense at all, for it is the mind that "sees" God. There is nothing sensible or sensual, nothing physical or corporeal in such a "seeing." Insofar as it is not even the *heart* that sees God — for "blessed are the pure in heart for they will see God" (Matt. 5:8) — that is, insofar as this seeing is not the contemplation of God by a mystic, it only remains to be the conceptual understanding of God (by the *mind*, as Origen quite explicitly notes). Second, and running in parallel with this de-incarnational move of the senses, the "divine" or "spiritual" sense is reserved only for "those who are worthy." It is an elitist doctrine whose qualifications (only the pure, only the worthy) cancel out not only the corporeality but also the ecumenicity of the Revelation.

It is true, however, that the doctrine of the spiritual senses is developed later with such nuance and sophistication that would make it acceptable, granted that the Fathers who received it (St. Bernard of Clairvaux and Bonaventure — Gregory of Nyssa is still under too strong an influence from Origen) correct the Origenistic dualism for the sake of a spirituality grounded in the Incarnation. Bonaventure, most notably, devices a schema of stratification where the senses correspond to three major aspects of the Revelation: so, beginning from the lower and moving toward the apex of this spirituality of the senses, we find first seeing and hearing corresponding to *Verbum increatum*, smelling related to *Verbum inspiratum*, and finally, at the top of this configuration, tasting and touching are paired with *Verbum incarnatum*.[9] It is precisely this inversion of the old metaphysical schema that used to place sight at its top that accounts for what is particularly incarnational: in the Christian hierarchy of the senses touch cannot but occupy the highest and most exalted place.[10] "For Bonaventure," von Balthasar writes, "this is justified, because for him the earth is the most unpretentious, the humblest element and precisely for this reason was chosen to be the midpoint of the world and of the proofs of God's grace."[11]

For these reasons, this discussion has carefully avoided following Origen's doctrine of the spiritual senses — although it would have seemed very pertinent to the present work. Furthermore, it cannot be safely disengaged from his deficient Christology, and more important, from the tendency of Origenism toward spiritualizing the body on account of a (Gnostic and ultimately Platonistic) dualism. From a reading of part II, chapter VI of *De Principiis*, it becomes clear that Origen has difficulties admitting that the second Person of the Trinity "became flesh." For him, the Incarnation becomes a much more complex affair, involving the preexisting soul of the Son, which (having been assumed by Him eternally) assumes, in time, the human flesh: "This soul, then, acting as a medium between God and the flesh (*for it was not possible for the nature of God to mingle with a body apart from some medium*), there is born, as we said, the God-man."[12] Here we do not hear anymore a Father of the Church, or even a Christian speaking, but Plato himself (see *Symposium* 203a, quoted at the beginning of this chapter). Origen's comment on John 14:9 ("whoever sees me, sees the Father") is emblematic of this tendency:

> no one in his sense could say that, by saying this, Jesus refers to His body, sensible [αἰσθητόν] and visible [βλεπόμενον] as it is by humans . . . for if that were the case, then, even those who cried "Crucify Him, Crucify Him" or Pilate, having power over His person, would have seen God the Father, which is absurd. (*Contra Celsum*, VII, 43)

Indeed, it is absurd, but it is this very absurdity that strikes at the heart of the Incarnation. In another episode that becomes paradigmatic of such sensible spirituality, that of the Lord's transfiguration, the light of the glory of Christ — and, indeed, for the hesychasts and Palamites, the *uncreated* light! — is visible by these very physical eyes of the disciples. One cannot claim, at that moment at least, that the disciples were, as Origen would have it, spiritually perfect. Peter's betrayal is still to come, and so is the debate of "who, amongst them, is greater" (Luke 9:46) — and yet, in spite of such signs of miscomprehension, the grace is given to them to see a light that although it shines "like the sun" (Matt. 17:2) is not of this world. It is *through the body* of the apostles that the divine light of the transformed Lord is perceived and sensed, as it is *through the body* of Christ that the divine light shines. To refuse the former is to refuse the latter. Denying that their eyes did see the Invisible in Him and their hands did touch the Intangible in touching Him is to deny the Incarnation altogether. And that is precisely what Origen and his doctrine of the spiritual senses do. The sight that recognizes Him is not an altogether different or "higher" sight than the sight with which we perceive the material world around us. It has to be the same sight of our same eyes. For recognizing Him means also to recognize His physicality, His corporeality that is indispensable to Him. If we make Christ the object of a set of "purer," spiritual senses, it would mean that we separate and divide the inseparable and undividable union of natures in Him. It would mean that, not much unlike the Docetists, we have eyes only for a ghost. To see Him, to see a perfectly human and a perfectly divine being in Him, one needs a tactful touch: like the grasp which in front of the Other's otherness turns into a caress, so the hand that approaches

Him must be fortified with an absurd boldness, it must believe that it can do the impossible, that it can touch the intangible God in the contingent flesh of a Nazarene man. On the other hand, a touch that has not been informed with such an absurdity remains a mere "contact," no matter how spiritual or pure it might be. That is why, with regard to the "touch" of the multitude, the evangelists are using an altogether different terminology (συνθλίβοντα, ἀποθλίβουσι, συνέχουσι)—a vocabulary that is indicative of a touch without tact, equally blind as well as dumb.

To return to the miracle of the bleeding woman, we also need to question Christ's question: why does He ask? He knows that He has been touched ("for I became aware of the power [dynamis] coming out of me"; Luke 8:46). Is it possible that he does not know who has touched Him? Origen gives the following answer: it is not that Christ does not know who touched Him, but His question serves as the means through which the woman who touched Him is acknowledged and her faith made an example for posterity.[13] She had come almost in secret—behind Him—out of fear that the crowd or Christ's disciples or Christ Himself might forbid her to approach and touch Him—she was, after all, a woman and, even more, a woman bleeding, that is, an unclean woman according to the Law[14]—what chances did she have to touch the Master?

It is a question that a Pharisee might ask, as, indeed, it is asked by Simon the Pharisee in the episode that Luke narrates about the sinful woman who washed Jesus' feet.[15] Scandalized by Christ's tolerance in allowing a sinner to touch and kiss His feet, the Pharisee onlooker asks, "This man, if he were a prophet, would have known who and what kind of a woman is the one that touched him, for she is a sinner" (7:39). *That* He knew, for it was apparent to the eyes of everyone—but He also saw something that only one who is more than a prophet could know: he saw the genuine faith of these women, such that He could not find in the mind of a pious crowd or in the observances of a moralist Pharisee. In order, therefore, to show to the bleeding woman first and to the rest of the crowd as well that, although an "unclean" woman for the Law, nevertheless, she is a woman of a commendable faith, Christ looks around to see who was the one who touched Him. Her touching, although having cured her, had, however, remained unreciprocated—for now it is time for Him to "touch" her back. Thus, He turns (ἐπιστραφείς, στραφείς) toward her, in order to return to her her faith by acknowledging in public what she has done in secret. By doing so, He disqualifies her touch from being taken as idolatrous (and Himself from being regarded as a healing idol), for it was not the "magical" properties of the touch that have healed her, but her faith *in* the touch—her faith that she *can* touch Him, that *He* can be touched.

It is not of no importance that the bleeding woman touches the hem or the border (κράσπεδον) of His garment. There are two different metaphors at work in this phrase: (a) as "garment" is understood His flesh—there is a long exegetic tradition that understands the Incarnation of the Word as Its

149

clothing with human flesh and Its body as a garment fashioned (more precisely, "woven") by the Virgin Mary;[16] (b) the "edge" or the "border" of the garment is an allusion to a common metaphor among Classical authors that represents the human body in terms of a house.[17] In accordance with the latter metaphor, we are to understand the five senses (and in particular the "openings" of the sense organs) as the gates of the corporeal house. These gates are usually busy with the traffic of stimuli between the internal and the external world. The doors of the senses are thus functioning as a *liminem*, that is, as the threshold or the liminal space of the body. God stands by these gates ("Behold, I stand at the door and knock. If anyone hears my voice and opens the door, I will come in to him and dine with him, and he with me"; Rev. 3:20). In some cases, He is asked to come and enter "the house" of one's own body ("And behold, there came a man named Jairus . . . and he fell down at Jesus' feet, and he besought him that he would come into his house"; Luke 8:41); thus entering through our senses, He makes Himself manifest. In other cases, however, He "appears" bypassing the sensible, that is, once the doors of the senses are *shut* ("Then the same day at evening, being the first day of the week, when the doors were shut where the disciples were assembled for fear of the Jews, came Jesus and stood in the midst"; John 20:19). This sensory *huis clos*, evidenced time and again in mystical literature, comes as a result of the senses' exhaustion — exhaustion brought about by their ceaseless confrontation with the excess of the quotidian.

If one perceives a hesitancy to use at this point what the informed reader might have expected, that is, the terminology of the spiritual senses, it is only because the category of the "spiritual," as we have already seen, can all too easily collapse into an empty or "cheap" spiritualism. If called to give a name to the kind of sensible perception that would be more in line with the observations in this work, then, following Merleau-Ponty, one would rather speak of *sacramental* senses and *sacramental* perception. For we find in the sacraments and the rites of the Church this twofold character of the symbols spoken of in the previous chapter (that is, the unity or chiasmus of representation and being, form and content, the reference of the symbol to a reality beyond itself and, at the same time, the efficacious conferring of that reality by means of the symbol), a character that the present phenomenological inquiry has taken as its departing point. What the Church puts before us in the sacraments is nothing more than our own everyday actions, those same practices that constitute our everydayness: the breaking of the bread, the sharing of the cup, the washing of one's body, etc. The sacraments are not outwardly realities. They do not pretend to hide lofty but incomprehensible messages nor do they function as secret initiations to a sort of Eleusinian mysteries. What the Church reveals to us as mystery is the commonplace and the trivial: a meal, a bath, the loving bond between two people. In the repetition of their celebration (*kairos*), these acts of everydayness are now taken away from the corrupting succession of time (*chronos*), they are lifted up from the realm of necessity, that is, of nature, and instead, they become portals to another order, of an eschatology always to come and always already here. A glorious light is shed on the mundane, and as the corruptible becomes eternal, we come to realize that it is the ordinary and the familiar that instantiates the extraordinary and the mystical.

This simplicity could not have come to pass if it was not for the Incarnation; in fact, every sacrament and every rite hints back to the event of the Incarnation. The incense burnt in the church and the gold of the liturgical vessels and vestments are the incense and the gold brought by the Magi to the most powerless of humans (a baby) at the most humble of settings (a stable). Today, the sacraments repeat the very same act of bringing these gifts to the Bethlehem of our everyday. And as the Magi, with their journey and with their gifts, acknowledge much more than an infant lying in a manger, so, too, we acknowledge the extraordinary in the ordinary, we recognize the shadow, or rather the shine, that the eschaton casts upon the ephemeral:

> God, who had been only a circumference, was [now] seen as a center; and a center is infinitely small. It is true that the spiritual spiral henceforward works inwards instead of outwards, and in that sense is centripetal and not centrifugal. The faith becomes, in more ways than one, a religion of little things.[18]

* * *

The famous *noli me tangere*, uttered on the occasion of another encounter with a woman (John 20:17), far from being a taboo prohibition against touch in general, is only a warning against an unheeded touch that seeks to *grasp*: the folly that seeks to *hold* the resurrected body — without recognizing that it cannot be possessed.[19] Indeed, the explanation given by Christ comes as a surprise: "Touch me not, *for I am not yet ascended to my Father.*" If Christ's "touch me not" signified merely His aversion to Mary's touch, it would have made no sense to add, "for I am not yet ascended to my Father," as if it would become easier to touch Him *after* the ascension to the heavens. That difficulty, however, is removed once we read the passage in question not as a prohibition against touching, but as an admonition against a possessive holding,[20] in which case the phrase "for I am not yet ascended to my Father" is an etiological clause. Nevertheless, Christ's explanation sounds a bit curious if only because it rings with a promissory tone: "touch me not, for I am not yet ascended to my Father, however, as soon as I am with the Father, then it will be possible for you to touch me again." It is difficult to understand the meaning of such a statement, for one would have taken the exact opposite to be the case. We could touch Him only as long as He is here with us (and therefore not yet with the Father) — after the ascension no one could touch Him.

In chapter 6 of John's gospel, Christ speaks of His body as the bread of life given in the world to be eaten. It is a "harsh" saying, as the disciples acknowledge, that scandalizes a number of Christ's followers who would leave Him at this very moment for good (John 6:66). Of course, the passage in question has always been interpreted as a reference to the sacrament of the Eucharist: indeed, the expression "I am the living bread" (John 6:51) makes sense only once He pronounces over the bread "take, eat, this is my body" (Mark 14:22). But Christ goes on to add a different reference that might seem out of context:

> Many therefore of his disciples, when they heard this, said, This is a harsh saying, who can hear it? When Jesus knew in himself that his disciples murmured at it, he said unto them, Does this offend you? *What if ye shall see the Son of man ascend up where he was before?* (John 6:60–62)

This is a quite clear allusion to His Ascension, but how does it fit with the talk about His body? It would seem to us that the eucharistic distribution of His body, its "breaking up," is a result of His being "lifted up" in the Ascension. Indeed, the breaking of the host in liturgy evokes precisely the language and imagery of the Ascension. The specificity of Christ's body is being "sublated" in the body of Christ (the Church)—which is occasioned by the double movement of the ascent of Christ and the descent of the Spirit—and thus becomes appropriated by and common to all Christians.[21] The physical body of Christ, that is, His flesh, was always incubating His mystical body, that is, His Church, as much as the Church is today the singular vessel of His body and blood. Christ's flesh (its physicality and historicity) without the sacramental "sublation" of the Church is doomed to idolatry, as His kerygma (the ethical teaching of the Gospel), when it is not grounded on His eucharistic presence, is mere ideology.

* * *

It is time now to conclude this last chapter of our work on a note similar to the one that began it: the healing of blindness. John's narration of the healing of the man born blind might have served as the literary reference for Brueghel's painting by the same theme that occupies the central place of the *Allegory of Sight*. There are several curious details in the way that the story unfolds; as told by the fourth evangelist it reads as follows:

> And as Jesus passed by, he saw a man who was blind from his birth. And his disciples asked him, saying, Master, who did sin, this man, or his parents, that he was born blind? Jesus answered, Neither hath this man sinned, nor his parents: but that the works of God should be made manifest in him. I must work the works of the one who sent me, while it is day: the night cometh, when no one can work. As long as I am in the world, I am the light of the world. When he had thus spoken, he spat on the ground, and made clay of the spittle, and he anointed the eyes of the blind man with the clay, and said unto him, Go, wash in the pool of Siloam (which means, Sent). He went his way therefore, and washed, and came seeing. The neighbours

therefore, and they who before had seen him that he was blind, said, Is not
this he that sat and begged? (John 9:1–8)

The contrast between the light of Christ and the darkness of the world is
one of John's favorite and most often-used symbolisms. Less usual, however, is
the way that Christ heals the blindness (a form of darkness itself) of this man:
not by word but by "work" *(ergon)*. The kneading of clay mixed with spittle is
a reference to the creation of Man in Genesis (2:7); thus Christ shows that He
is the creator God who has the power to re-create what He has created (this
is, "the works of the one who sent me"). Ancient and modern exegetes note
how the name of the pool (Siloam, Shiloh in Hebrew) is a reference to Christ
Himself, as the One "sent" by the Father. The washing (and the healing that
comes as a result of it, the passing from the darkness of blindness to the light
of sight) in the pool of Siloam is taken as the *typos*, that is, the foreshadow-
ing, of baptism. The "rejection" of the Pharisees' spiritual blindness and the
confession that the blind man offers to Christ ("Do you believe on the Son
of Man? . . . Lord, I believe"; John 9:35–38) that functions as baptismal vow
strengthen that allegorical interpretation. Indeed, even before Tertullian's
and Augustine's readings of this passage as a baptismal prototype, the early
Christians depicted on the walls of the catacombs the healing of the blind
man as a symbol of baptism.[22] What remains curious, however, is the playful-
ness of Christ's gesture (as if in caressing): He who was sent sends him to the
one Sent (Siloam). Indeed, by sending him to Him (the Sent, Siloam), who
is no other than Himself, He sends him to Himself—for in washing in Him
(that is, in His name, Siloam, the one Sent), the blind man comes to see Him,
He who has sent him, as the one Sent by the Father.

Therefore, the healing of the blind man takes place thanks to two different "gestures": the first (the mixing of the clay and anointing of his eyes)
inscribes itself within the tradition of the Old Testament, as it refers back to
the creative work of God in Genesis; the second (the sending to the pool of
Siloam) anticipates the community of the New Testament and the sacraments
of the Church. The first (an *archaeological* or protological movement) obeys
the logic of "production"; the second (eschatologically oriented) unravels that
tradition. For, contrary to the account of Genesis, Christ's (re)creative work
takes place on the seventh day of the week, that is, on a Sabbath, and this
becomes the cause of the Pharisees' severe criticism, a criticism that takes the
form of a long interrogation (John 9:13–34). Christ's Sabbath is not the one
observed by the Pharisees, His Sabbath is the "night that comes when no one
can work," that is, the night when no longer He will be "in the world"—when
He will "rest" from all His work, after the work that is given to Him would be
proclaimed "accomplished," that is, the night of His death.

Homiletic evidence of the typological reading of Christ's death as the
Seventh Day of the new creation abounds. The present discussion will limit
itself to only two exemplary homilies by Gregory of Nyssa: *In Sanctum et Salu-*

tare Pascha and *De Tridui Spatio.*[23] In the opening of the former, Gregory immediately draws the connection between the Sabbath of the creation and the Holy Saturday of the Passion narrative: "The true repose [κατάπαυσις] of the Sabbath, the blessed one, on which the Lord rested [κατέπαυσεν] from his own works for the sake of the world's salvation by observing the Sabbath in the 'holiday' of death [τῇ ἀπραξίᾳ τοῦ θανάτου] has already come to an end." It is the latter homily, however, that establishes the typological parallel: "Here is the blessed Sabbath of the former cosmogony. By that Sabbath you may come to recognize *this* Sabbath, the day of the reposing [τῆς καταπαύσεως ἡμέραν], which God has blessed above all other days, for on this day the Only-begotten God truly rested [κατέπαυσεν] from all his work by the economy of death, observing the holiday of the Sabbath in his flesh."[24] The baptismal image of the blind man's washing in the pool of Siloam already foreshadows the Sabbath of His death—for as Paul writes, "as many of us as were baptized into Christ Jesus were baptized into His death . . . we were buried with Him through baptism into death" (Rom. 6:3–4).

Two different understandings of creation are combined in this passage, an understanding of creation as production and an understanding of creation as expression. The former can be identified with that particular function of touch described in the previous chapter as grasping, the latter with caressing. The conception of creation as production — ergonomic creation — obeys the logic of manu-facture *(ergon)*, that is, of a world that is molded by the divine hand as a potter gives shape to his clay. The concept of God as the cosmic architect is man's creation of God according to man's image and likeness. On the other hand, creation as expression — aorgic creation — renders the omnipresent reign of the *ergon* inoperative, by refusing to constitute products and things. It is a creation that does not take place as a process of forming matter (annihilating the nothing of creation's ex nihilo), but as the withdrawing of the Creator in order to let creation be[25] (by the Creator's "self-annihilation" in becoming that "*nihilum*" out of which the world is created).[26] There are further differences between these two distinct understandings of creation: the first presupposes a once-for-all creative act (and thus complicates things a bit, since it injects temporality at a moment where time is not supposed to have come to be and, therefore, creates the dilemma of a time "before" time),[27] while the second takes place in a continuous, perpetual movement where the world never ceases to be created (in each and every moment, a moment that is never momentary).

It would be safe to call that ergonomic understanding of creation *metaphysical,* insofar as it finds its philosophical legitimacy in Aristotle's *Physics* (as discussed in the previous chapter). The second understanding of creation, however, is equally part of the Western philosophical tradition, since, according to Jean-Luc Nancy, it "is followed through in Hegel and Schelling, among others, and, without doubt secretly in Heidegger, but was originally inscribed, as I have already suggested, within Kant's work."[28] Indeed, for Nancy, "the whole of the Kantian revolution turns around nothing else than the question of creation."[29] The nodal point of that question is none other than the possibility of experience as such: for Kant, the possibility of experience ultimately lies with the possibility of change, with change as a possibility for phenomena. Change, in turn, necessitates two principles, the "Principle of Permanence of Substance" (First Analogy) and the "Principle of Succession in Time, in accordance with the Law of Causality" (Second Analogy), what in the first edition of the *Critique* he, simply but tellingly, calls the "Principle of Production." Turning to these questions, we have not left the question of touch — and the touch of the intangible — behind us; we have only moved ahead in our inquiry. For substance and causality are inscribed within the provenance of *ergon* and thus the work of the hand.[30] In thinking such abstract principles, the philosopher has never ceased to contemplate the world in terms of the workshop: here lies the clay (the "substance" enduring through its numerous transformations of becoming), but here too we find the potter himself, the cause of such becomings.[31] From Aristotle's four causes to Kant's three analogies of experience, the world is given as product, and, therefore, whatever cannot be produced (or, in this case, re-produced), everything that does not conform with that ergonomy (the *nomos* of *ergon*), has to be excluded from experience — as an impossible experience or, what amounts to the same, an experience of the impossible. From the beginning of this work, however, we have been after such an impossible experience (seeing the invisible, touching the intangible), an experience that defies the principle of production and yet remains experience.[32]

Two different domains are associated with the language of production and causality, that of the courtroom and that of the marketplace. Aristotle's employment of a judicial language (the primary sense of αἰτία in Greek is legal, meaning guilt, blame, or imputation) reveals the world as an enormous crime scene. The philosopher, as the detective who arrives always too late, is called in order to seek out the ὑπ-αίτιον (the thing under accusation), and thus he summons the different αἰτίαι, as Kant would say, to the tribunal of reason. But what was the crime committed? Nothing else than that of existence. The philosopher's interrogation demands to know "why is there something rather than nothing?" Why and how did being come to be? And, indeed, such is one of the very first utterances of Greek philosophy, a pronouncement of guilt and penalty: διδόναι γὰρ αὐτὰ δίκην καὶ τίσιν ἀλλήλοις τῆς ἀδικίας κατὰ τὴν τοῦ χρόνου τάξιν (Anaximander, *Fragment 1*). The notion of existence as crime (and that of the guilt-ridden existent) is intrinsically linked with the notion of the creation as debt. Creation as production sustains an entire system of values, the value of work and, thus, that of the marketplace. For *ergon* is both the artifact as well as the labor directed toward the process of producing. The *ergon* assumes meaning only once it is placed within an economy, once it is inscribed in the logic of agora, of trade, commerce, and exchange. Nowhere is this more clearly evidenced than in a certain way of speaking ("theologically") about the Divine Economy in terms of the marketplace. According to such discourse, God's creation (His *ergon*) leaves us with an immense debt, a debt that no sacrifice, pain, or virtue could ever pay back. Humanity in its creation — *because* of its creation — is found under debt: it is nothing else but the price of our very own being that is negotiated here. Our Creator (as so aptly the Second Essay in Nietzsche's *Genealogy of Morals* has shown)[33] is also our Creditor that demands reimbursement. But who can repay such a high price? Only God, by becoming human, in order to pay God back on behalf of humanity. The image of Christ as the Redeemer has nothing to do with salvation strictly speaking ("*salvus*," i.e., "the healthy," operates within another metaphor, that of medicine). The discourse of redemption speaks of a ransom (Christ's life, or rather His death) offered to God as the payment that bought for us our freedom from the divine debt.

There are different ways, however, to think of the world, creation, and God, and along with them, a different thinking of the possibility of experience emergences, beyond causality and beyond production. We have already encountered it in the miracle of the blind man, but it is also to be found throughout the pages of the Gospel — indeed, the good news that the Gospel proclaims is nothing more but this: that the *ergon* has been brought to an end (the τετέλεσται announced from the cross), its completion is followed by a Sabbath, that is, the Seventh Day of the new creation — a creation that overcomes production. In the ἀργία of that Saturday, we have to imagine Christ, in the still silence of the tomb, "doing nothing" (τῇ ἀπραξία τοῦ θανάτου, as Gregory of Nyssa said). This is the suspension of ergonomy, the cessation of both *ergon* and *nomos* (κατάργησις). On the Eighth Day, the New Adam, the anarchic *arche* of the new creation (Rev. 3:15), is risen. That event cannot be mediated by any economical structure, ergonomical or otherwise, defiant as it is to all principles. The resurrected body of Christ gives birth to a new lineage, by being "the first to be born" (πρωτότοκος), born and not created, begotten and not made, without αἰτία and without ἀρχή. This is the anarchic event par excellence: "but Christ has indeed been raised from the dead, the first fruits [ἀπ-αρχή] of those who have fallen asleep" (1 Cor. 15:20); what kind of *arche* Christ has become is told by Paul in another of his *Letters*: "he is the beginning [ἀρχή], the firstborn [πρωτότοκος] from the dead, that in all things He may have the preeminence" (Colos. 1:18). This new beginning is effected through a series of καταργήσεις (the term in all probability is coined by Paul, as it does not occur in classical Greek literature). First, it is the realm of work and labor that is rendered inoperative, "and you, who once were alienated and enemies in your mind by toilsome works [ἔργοις τοῖς πονηροῖς], yet now He has reconciled you by Christ's physical body through death" (Colos. 1:21–22). Then, knowledge (or at least that kind of knowledge based on utility and function) follows: "whether there is knowledge, it will *vanish away* [καταργηθήσεται]" (1 Cor. 13:8), together with prophesy and everything that is partial, including beings themselves: "for God has chosen the base things of the world and the things which are despised, and the things which are not, *to bring to nothing* [καταργήσῃ] the things that are (1 Cor. 1:28). Finally, "comes the end, when He delivers the kingdom to God the Father, when He *puts an end* [καταργήσῃ] to all rule [ἀρχήν] and all authority [ἐξουσία] and power [δύναμις]" (1 Cor. 15:24).

This end, the end of the entire old order, of being and knowledge, of principles and reason, has been brought about in the sepulcher's stillness that followed the cry "It is finished." From His cross, God saw this world ending; from His tomb a new world has begun — "Behold, I make all things new" (Rev. 21:5).

NOTES

Introduction

1. The etymology that derives the beautiful *(to kalon)* from the call *(kaleo)* and thus understands beauty not in terms of symmetry, proportion, or harmony but in terms of an *attraction* was suggested by Plato, in his *Cratylus* (416c); Dionysius the Aeropagite inherits it from Plotinus (*Enneads*, I, 6) and adopts it in his *De Divinis Nominibus* (IV, 7, 701c).

2. "The doctrine of the beholding and perceiving *(Wahrnehmen)* of the beautiful ('aesthetics' in the sense of the *Critique of Pure Reason*) and the doctrine of the enrapturing power of the beautiful are complementarily structured, since no one can really behold who has not also already been enraptured, and no one can be enraptured who has not already perceived" (Hans Urs von Balthasar, *The Glory of the Lord: A Theological Aesthetics,* 7 vols., trans. Erasmo Leiva-Merikakis et al. (San Francisco: Ignatius Press, 1998), vol. I: *Seeing the Form,* 10; see also 125. (This work is divided into seven volumes.)

3. Heidegger, in *Holzwege,* trans. as *Off the Beaten Track* by Julian Young and Kenneth Haynes (Cambridge: Cambridge University Press, 2002), 50.

4. "In all these respects art, considered in its highest vocation, is and remains for us a thing of the past" (G. W. F. Hegel, *Aesthetics: Lectures on Fine Art,* 3 vols., trans. T. M. Knox [Oxford: Oxford University Press, 1975], vol. I, 10).

5. Martin Heidegger, *Nietzsche,* vol. 1, trans. David Farrell Krell (New York: Harper & Row, 1984), 194.

6. Ibid., 169.

7. See the work of Kevin Hart, especially the Introduction in *Counter-Experiences: Reading Jean-Luc Marion* (South Bend, Ind.: University of Notre Dame Press, in press).

8. I am aware of the irony of this statement, since for Nietzsche Christianity — or at least a certain Christianity — was synonymous with Platonism, the "Platonism of the masses," as he put it.

9. See Heidegger's *Nietzsche,* 200–210.

10. This relationship is the first thing that a phenomenology of the image should discover as, indeed, it does: "the original 'needs' the image in order to become manifest" (John Sallis, *Delimitations: Phenomenology and the End of Metaphysics* [Bloomington: Indiana University Press, 1986], 69).

11. Heidegger, "Introduction to 'What Is Metaphysics?'" in *Pathmarks,* ed. William McNeill (Cambridge: Cambridge University Press, 1998), 287–288.

12. Heidegger, "Letter on 'Humanism'" in *Pathmarks,* 269–270.

1. The Metaphysical Chiasm

1. Perhaps we should rethink the "idea of infinity," which for Descartes becomes sufficient evidence of the existence of God, as precisely that which comes from God — not "infinity" but the "idea" itself. Since any idea, insofar as it is given, is evidence of its giver, in this case (if not in every case), it is evidence of God. The etymology of the word seems to suggest as much: an ἰδέα (from ἰδεῖν, the aorist infinitive for the verb ὁράω, "to see") is an appearance — what appears is not autochthonous to the mind, but its origin is *elsewhere*, a point outside of and beyond us.

2. Jean-Luc Marion recently posed the very same question in a paper entitled "The Saturated Phenomenon," trans. Thomas A. Carlson, *Philosophy Today* 40 (spring 1996): 103–124; all subsequent page references are to this version of Marion's text. Reprinted in Janicaud et al., *Phenomenology and the "Theological Turn": The French Debate*, trans. Bernard G. Prusak, Thomas A. Carlson, and Jeffrey L. Kosky (New York: Fordham University Press, 2000), Part II: *Phenomenology and Theology*, 176–216. The theme of the saturated phenomenon was reworked by Marion and incorporated into sections 21 and 22 of his *Étant donné: Essai d'une phénoménologie de la donation* (Paris: Presses Universitaires de France, 1997); trans. Jeffrey L. Kosky as *Being Given* (Stanford, Calif.: Stanford University Press, 2002), 199–221. In the wake of Marion's publication a number of articles have appeared, all of them symptomatic of the perplexity that the thinking of the (im)possibility of the religious phenomenon was destined to cause. Some bore witness to the originality of Marion's thought even when he engages in a close reading of Husserl and Kant; others questioned the accuracy of this reading, which was not, for their taste, faithful enough. And yet others did not see it as a way of thinking at all, but rather as a transvestite theology which poses, or so they tell us, as phenomenology, a theology — with an agenda — that dares "not speak its name," that turns its readers into "catechumens." (I am echoing here, in disagreement, Dominique Janicaud's criticism as it is laid out in "The Theological Turn of French Philosophy" in *Phenomenology and the "Theological Turn"* [16–103, in particular 50–66]). For these critics Marion has to plead guilty for an abominable "reduction" that only *ravages* the reduction of phenomenology's founding father — "*reduces* religion to theology" — and which, as though this were not enough, "*particularizes* religion . . . as quite Christian — at best, monotheistic, and at worst, down right Catholic." Marion is therefore pronounced guilty of "theological colonialism" (see James K. A. Smith, "Liberating Religion from Theology: Marion and Heidegger on the Possibility of a Phenomenology of Religion," *International Journal for Philosophy of Religion* 46 [1999]: 17–33, at 23–24). From the time that phenomenology ceased to be a method of thinking and became the inherited property of a school with its by-laws and self-proclaimed police, we all have run the risk of being summoned in front of the tribunal of the judge, who would then read with a resonant voice the age-old accusation: "he introduces new gods to the city and he corrupts the youth" (*Apology*, 26c and 23d). For today's Anytoses and Meletoses, the fact that for Marion "God" is the "God of Abraham, Isaac, and Jacob," the God whom Jesus dared to call "Abba," that is to say, the God of the tradition within which Marion grew up, lives, and writes (as if it could have been otherwise), that fact amounts to a betrayal of rigorous science. For such thinkers, it seems, phenomenology ought to have been, to borrow Thomas Nagel's expression, *the view from nowhere*!

3. To safeguard mystical experience from both risks, that of impossibility and idolatry, and in order to maintain such experience as theologically tenable, the Eastern Church formulated a doctrine that distinguishes between the (impossible) experience of God in His essence and the actual experience of God in His workings or activities (energies). If the latter are still to occasion an experience *of* God, they need to be precisely that, that is, *of* God — uncreated and divine. Such a doctrine is first and seminally formulated by the Cappadocians, later by St. John Damascene, and finally received a full treatment in the polemical writings of St. Gregory Palamas. For further reading, see J. Meyendorff, *St. Gregory Palamas and Orthodox Spirituality* (New York: St. Vladimir's Seminary Press, 1974), and Duncan Reid, *Energies of the Spirit* (Atlanta, Ga.: American Academy of Religion, 1997).

4. Edmund Husserl, *Ideas Pertaining to a Pure Phenomenology and to Phenomenological Philosophy*, Book One (The Hague: Martinus Nijoff, 1983), §24, 44 (emphasis in the original).

5. Edmund Husserl, *Cartesian Meditations: An Introduction to Phenomenology*, trans. Dorion Cairns (The Hague: Martinus Nijhoff, 1970), §42, 89. All subsequent page references to Husserl's *Cartesian Meditations* are from this edition.

6. James K. A. Smith, "Respect and Donation: A Critique of Marion's Critique of Husserl," *American Catholic Philosophical Quarterly* 71, no. 4 (1988): 523–538, at 534.

7. Paul Ricœur, *Husserl: An Analysis of His Phenomenology*, trans. Eduard G. Bollard and Lester E. Embree (Evanston, Ill.: Northwestern University Press, 1967), 119.

8. The *Second Meditation* opens with the following remarks: "When we take into consideration that, for each kind of actual experience and for each of its universal variant modes (perception, retention, recollection, etc.), there is a corresponding pure phantasy, an 'as-if experience' [*Erfahrung als ob*] with parallel modes (as-if perception, as-if retention, as-if recollection, etc.), we surmise that there is also an *a priori* science, which confines itself to the realm of pure possibility (pure imaginableness) and, instead of judging about actualities of transcendental being, judges about [its] *a priori* possibilities" (§12, 27–28). In the *Third Meditation* the relationship between possibility and imagination becomes more explicit: "On this side a new universal concept of *possibility* arises, which, as mere 'imaginableness' (in a phantasying, *as if* something were), repeats in modified form all the modes of being, starting with the simple certainty of being . . . The *prefigurative intuition* of this verifying fulfillment furnishes actualizing evidence — not indeed of the being, but of the *possible being* [*Seinsmöglichkeit*] of the content in question" (§25, 59–59). In the *Fourth Meditation*, the development of the notion of the possible reaches its climax by a simple sentence that inverts a long philosophical tradition that goes as far back as Aristotle's primacy of actuality over possibility. Husserl writes: "In itself, then, the science of pure possibility precedes the science of actualities and alone makes it possible, as a science" (§34, 72). An echo of such an important conclusion is to be found in Heidegger's *Being and Time* where, a few words after a reference to Husserl, he writes: "Higher than actuality stands possibility. We understand phenomenology solely by seizing upon it as a possibility" (Martin Heidegger, *Being and Time*, trans. Joan Stambaugh [New York: State University of New York Press, 1996], §7, 34).

9. For a discussion of the shortcomings that this reasoning by analogy entails for

intersubjectivity in general, see Jean-Luc Marion, *Prolegomena to Charity*, trans. Stephen Lewis (New York: Fordham University Press, 2002), 160–163.

10. Already the problem of a phenomenological experience of God is posed against the background of incarnation (and the Incarnation). If someone were to say here that Christ does have a body and therefore things are made easier because I could "physically" perceive Him, that would have been a faulty step — once again, what our senses perceive in Christ is only His flesh, but the flesh hides as much as it reveals the Logos.

11. The reverse is also the case: an excessive intuition that remains blind (and blinding) insofar as it lacks the corresponding concepts. One finds an example of such a case in Luke's narration of the post-Paschal apparition of Christ to two disciples on their way to Emmaus (Luke 24:13–25). For a phenomenological reading of that passage see Jean-Luc Marion, "They Recognized Him; and He Became Invisible to Them," *Modern Theology* 18, no. 2 (April 2002), 145–152.

12. And so the entire patristic tradition in both East and West is in agreement in taking the Old Testament theophanies as a series of "incarnations" of the Logos prior to His proper Incarnation. Augustine is the only exception in this hermeneutical consensus (see *De Trinitate*, books II–IV). For a survey of the pre-Augustinian fathers and for a discussion on Augustine's shift of exegesis, see Kari Kloos, "Seeing the Invisible God: Augustine's Reconfiguration of Theophany Narrative Exegesis," *Augustinian Studies* 36, no. 2 (2005): 397–420.

13. Gregory of Nyssa, *Ad Theophilum*, GNO, III, I, 123.

14. The key term in Dionysius's vocabulary that expresses the proportional manifestation of God in each and every being is ἀναλογία. The divine things are revealed "in proportion to the capacity" of each intellect (κατὰ τὴν ἀναλογίαν ἑκάστου τῶν νοῶν; *DN*, I, 1, 588A); the illuminations that proceed from the Good are "analogous to each of the beings" (ταῖς ἑκάστου τῶν ὄντων ἀναλόγοις ἐλλάμψεσιν; *DN*, I, 2, 588D); the participation to the hyperessential Union is "analogous to those who partake" (κατὰ μέθεξιν ἀνάλογον τοῖς μετέχουσι; *DN*, II, 5, 641D); as is their participation to the Good beyond goodness (ἐν μετουσίᾳ γίνεσθαι κατὰ τὴν σφῶν ἀναλογίαν; *DN*, IV, 2, 696C). How much different is Dionysius's *analogia* from Husserl's analogical presentation of the Other! Whereas for Husserl the Other's body is presented as analogous to my flesh, for Dionysius the Other is presented in giving Himself analogously to me. The movement of inverse intentionality is already outlined here.

15. Gregory of Nyssa, *Ad Theophilum*, GNO, III, I, 124.

16. For Sartre the Other as he or she appears to me through the look that looks-at-me is the best resistance against the solipsistic argument: "This resistance indeed is based on the fact that the Other is given to me as a concrete evident presence which I can in no way derive from myself and which can in no way be placed in doubt nor made the object of a phenomenological reduction or of any other ἐποχή" (J.-P. Sartre, *Being and Nothingness*, trans. Hazel E. Barnes [New York: Washington Square Press, 1956], 362–363)

17. The possibility of "being-seen-by-the-Other" is already implicit in the *Fifth Cartesian Meditation*. As Husserl moves from the single monad to the intersubjective communion of monads he notices that it is the Other as well that perceives me as I perceive him, *as Other*: "If, with my understanding of someone else, I penetrate more deeply into him, into his horizon of ownness, I shall soon run into the fact that, just as his animate bodily organism lies in my field of perception, so my animate organism

lies in his field of perception and that, in general, he experiences me forthwith as an Other for him, just as I experience him as *my* Other" (§56, 129–130; emphasis in the original). Note that the development of all culture and society is based on this simple reciprocity of looks and experiences between an I and an Other alone.

18. Sartre, *Being and Nothingness*, 349; emphasis in the original.

19. The structure of the inverse intentionality that is being described here is, at least as structure, implied already in Levinas's analysis of manifestation: *"Revelation* constitutes a veritable inversion *objectifying cognition"* (*Totality and Infinity: An Essay on Exteriority*, trans. Alphonso Lingis [Pittsburgh, Penn.: Duquesne University Press, 1969], 67; emphasis in the original).

20. See, for example, Descartes's argument about the piece of wax *(cera)* (in *Meditationes de Prima Philosophia* §§29–31), which concludes as follows: *Fieri enim potest ut hoc quod video non vere fit cera; fieri potest ut ne quidem oculos habeam, quibus quidquam videatur; sed fieri plane non potest, cum videam, sive (quod jam non distinguo) cum cogitem me videre, ut ego ipse cogitans non aliquid sim. Simili ratione, si judico ceram esse, ex eo quod hanc tangam, idem rursus efficietur, videlicet me esse* (*Ouvres de Descartes* VII [Paris: Librairie Philosophique Vrin, 1957], 33.9–33.16).

21. The expression belongs to Hans Urs von Balthasar from his analysis of St. John of the Cross's mystical visions (see *The Glory of the Lord: A Theological Aesthetics*, Vol. III: *Studies in Theological Style: Lay Style* [San Francisco: Ignatius Press, 1983], 126). A similar expression is to be found in a classical example of theophany, that of Dionysius in Euripides' *Bacchae*, where the god appears as ὁρῶν ὁρῶντα (470).

22. Jean-Luc Marion, *In Excess: Studies of Saturated Phenomena*, trans. Robyn Horner and Vincent Berraud (New York: Fordham University Press, 2002), 77.

23. Ibid., 78.

24. Ibid., 79.

25. Ibid., 112.

26. Ibid., 113; emphasis added.

27. The term was coined by the Russian theologian and philosopher Pavel Florensky (see "Against Linear Perspective," in *Utopias: Russian Modernist Texts 1905–1940*, ed. Catriona Kelly [London and New York: Penguin Books, 2002], 70–75). I am here greatly indebted to Prof. Nicholas Constas, who introduced me to the thought of Florensky and generously shared with me his thoughts on the impact that Florensky's work could have on current philosophical thinking. For an excellent description of this unique technique as well as its historical and theoretical genealogy, see Nicholas Constas, "Icons and the Imagination," *Logos* 1 (1997): 114–127, and Gary M. Gurtler, S.J., "Plotinus and Byzantine Aesthetics," *Modern Schoolman* 66 (1989): 275–284. To cite only an example from Gurtler's analysis: "Classical perspective achieves its affect by foreshortening, making some lines of a scene shorter than they really are to produce the illusion of three dimensions on a flat surface. The result is significant, freezing the world at one point of space and time. One becomes, as it were, fixated in only one of the infinitely numerous possible points of view." The inverse perspective "by abstracting from the specificity of time and space . . . presents a timeless quality that takes the viewer out of the isolation of his particular moment and into the presence of the eternal. Instead of one point of view, the whole of reality is included" (275).

28. Jean-Luc Marion, *God without Being*, trans. Thomas A. Carlson (Chicago: University of Chicago Press, 1991). Hereafter cited parenthetically as *GWB*, followed by the page number. For a comprehensive treatment of Marion's philosophy and its

theological implications, see Robyn Horner's *Jean-Luc Marion: A Theo-Logical Introduction* (London: Ashgate, 2005) as well as the earlier *Rethinking God as Gift: Marion, Derrida and the Limits of Phenomenology* (New York: Fordham University Press, 2001).

29. See also Marion's comments regarding the "crossing out" of God's name; "We cross out the name of God only in order to show ourselves that his unthinkableness *saturates* our thought — right from the beginning, and forever" (GWB, 46; my emphasis).

30. See also Marie-José Baudinet's remarkable article "The Face of Christ: The Form of the Church" in *Fragments for a History of the Human Body*, Part One, ed. Michael Feher, Ramona Naddaff, and Nadia Tazi (New York: Zone Books, 1989), 149–155, and, more recently, Marie-José Mondzain's *Image, Icon, Economy*, trans. Rico Franses (Stanford, Calif.: Stanford University Press, 2005). One could argue that Mondzain's efforts of setting the iconoclastic controversy against the background of the theological (and political) polysemy of the term "economy" are better captured by the palaiologism "iconomy," that is, the economy of the image (for the pun of "iconomy," see Baudinet's essay, 149).

31. A claim that Levinas would never accept: "The Other is not the incarnation of God" (*Totality and Infinity*, 79) since "[f]or a Jew, incarnation is neither possible nor necessary" (*Difficult Freedom: Essays in Judaism*, trans. S. Hand [Baltimore: Johns Hopkins University Press, 1990], 15).

32. Ricœur, *Husserl*, 138; my emphasis.

33. Richard Kearney, *The God Who May Be: A New Hermeneutics of Religion* (Bloomington: Indiana University Press, 2001), 19. It is telling, I believe, that in Sartre's own version of Hades (*No Exit*), it is precisely this face-to-face relationship with the Other that makes the Other to be hell. Sartre reverses the entire model down to the slightest detail; where for the Greeks the underworld is defined as the absence of seeing (Hades), the Sartrean hell is the place of constant and compulsory vision (the lights never turn off, one cannot sleep, one has no eyelids, etc.).

34. S. Kierkegaard, *The Concept of Anxiety*, Kierkegaard's Writings 8, trans. Reidar Thomte (Princeton, N.J.: Princeton University Press, 1980), 123 and 124.

35. Not to be confused with the *exaiphnes* (also translated as the "sudden"). See chapter 3 of the present work.

36. Ibid., 128–129.

37. Of course, the ecclesial understanding of the Eucharist plays with both meanings of communion. The Eucharist is the actual communion one receives, but also the means of communion, first, among the participants themselves and, through this relationship, with the one participated (Christ). There are other far-reaching and essential considerations about the Eucharist that need to be taken into account; first of all, its eschatological character is of paramount importance. As an event that unfolds in a time beyond time (in the temporality of *kairos* and not of *chronos*), in the Christic chiasmus of the horizontal axis of history with the vertical, in the consecrating descent of the Holy Spirit, the Eucharist bridges the divisions and cancels out the fragmentations effected by the categories of space and time. Theologically understood, the catholicity of the Eucharist (and therefore, of the Church) means that every time the broken bread and the common cup are shared by the faithful, the event of the Church, in her geographical and historical entirety, is occasioned. Simply put, around the eucharistic table are present all of those who believed, believe, and will believe in Christ's death

and resurrection, from the time of His Incarnation to the time of His second coming, regardless of their physical (race, gender, age) or social (class, educational, moral) differences. These differences are not simply obliterated for the sake of a homogeneous uniformity; they are rather "lifted up" in the "negation" (κατάργησις, *Aufhebung*) effected by the assumption of the fullness of human nature in the "collective person" (κοινόν πρόσωπον) of Christ (as Cyril of Alexandria notes, see *PG*, 73, 161c). They were introduced by the fall of the old man, Adam, and they were overcome by the resurrection of the new man, the second Adam, "so that God may be all in all" (1 Cor. 15:28). Last, one should also pay attention to the praying practice of the Church: all the prayers are phrased and expressed from a communal "we" (e.g., "*Our* Father . . ."). How little sense would it make for one in the Church to say "*my* Father . . ."!

38. One problem, however, remains unresolved: what happens (to me) if, or when, the Other refuses, or simply is unable, to see in me his or her Other? What happens when for the Other I am not another Other, but only a third? What happens when the reciprocity of the prosopic relationship is never returned? Isn't it, then, the case that my rejection by the Other breaks down the symmetry of love? Doesn't the Other's unavailability turn my chance to live Paradise into the experience of everyday hell? How, then, do we account for the fact that the very same "structure" of being a *prosopon* can either be my salvation or my condemnation depending on such fragile and arbitrary factors as chance, infatuation, preference, etc.?

39. In the translation of H. Lawrence Bond, in *Nicholas of Cusa, Selected Spiritual Writings* (New York: Paulist Press, 1997), 241.

40. Hans Urs von Balthasar, *The Glory of the Lord: A Theological Aesthetics, vol. I: Seeing the Form*, trans. Erasmo Leiva-Merikakis (San Francisco: Ignatius Press, 1998, 301–302).

41. It is none else than Christ Himself who employs the literal meaning of this understanding "Saul, Saul, why are you persecuting *me?*" (Acts 9:4). He didn't say *them* (the followers of the new faith that Paul did persecute) but *me*, making Paul's mistreatment of others a personal matter that not only concerned Him but also was directed against Him: "I am Jesus, whom you are persecuting" (Acts 9:5). Paul's mistake in this instance is his failure to recognize *Him* in *them*, or better yet, Christ's "consubstantiality" *(homoousia)* with each and every human.

42. Translated by H. Lawrence Bond, in *Nicholas of Cusa*, 243.

43. Jorge Luis Borges, *Selected Poems* (bilingual edition), ed. A. Coleman (New York: Viking, 1999), 81 (translation has been slightly modified).

44. For a theological and historical treatment of the iconoclastic controversy, see Bishop Ambrosios Giakalis's *Images of the Divine: The Theology of Icons at the Seventh Ecumenical Council* (Leiden: Brill, 2005); for a recent assessment of the philosophical implications of iconoclasm see Kevin Hart's essay "The Profound Reserve," in *After Blanchot: Literature, Criticism, Philosophy*, ed. Leslie Hill and Dimitris Vardoulakis (Dover: University of Delaware Press, 2006), 35–57.

45. Aristotle, *Categories*, VII (6a 37). Nicephorus's text reads as follows: "Οὐκ ἄκαιρον δὲ οἶμαι ἐν τῷ παρόντι, καὶ τοῦτο προθεῖναι τῷ λόγῳ, ὅτι ἡ εἰκών σχέσιν ἔχειν πρός τό ἀρχέτυπον, καί αἰτίου ἐστίν αἰτιατόν· ἀνάγκη οὖν διά τοῦτο καί τῶν πρός τι εἶναί τε ταύτην καί λέγεσθαι. Τά δέ πρός τι, αὐτά ἅπερ ἐστὶν, ἑτέρων εἶναι λέγεται, καί ἀντιστρέφει τῇ σχέσει πρός ἄλληλα· ὥσπερ ὁ πατήρ υἱοῦ πατήρ, καί ἔμπαλιν ὁ υἱός πατρός λέγεται υἱός, ὡσαύτως καί φίλος φίλου . . . Οὕτως οὖν καί ἀρχέτυπον, εἰκόνος ἀρχέτυπον· καί εἰκών, ἀρχετύπου εἰκών· καί οὐκ ἄν τις ἄσχετον εἰκόνα τοῦ τινος εἰκόνα

φαίη. Ἅμα γάρ συνεισάγεται καί συνεπιθεωρεῖται θατέρῳ τὸ ἕτερον" (And I think it is not inappropriate to add this as well to the argument: that the icon expresses a relationship with the original and is the effect of a cause. For this reason it is necessary that the icon belongs and is classified among those things that express relation. The things that express relation are called what they are on the grounds of their relationship to something different [than themselves] and their reciprocal relationship with each other, for example, a "father" is the father of a son and a "son" is called so insofar as he is the son of a father, in a similar way a "friend" is someone's friend. In the same way too, an original always implies its icon and an icon is that of its original. One could not say that something is an icon without the relationship with this someone [whom the icon represents]. What is different is introduced and regarded together with the other.) From *Antirrheticus I, PG,* 100 (277 D).

46. Let me note here that the key term *perichoresis* is first used in this context (by Gregory of Nyssa in his *Epistle 101, PG,* 37, 181C) and only later applied (by Pseudo-Cyril, in his *De Trinitate, PG,* 77, 1144B) on the relationship of the Persons in the Trinity.

47. In Maximus's *Epistula XV* ("On the Common and the Particular, i.e., on the Essence and the Hypostasis"), *PG,* 91 (556 AC).

48. Kalistos Timothy Ware, "The Transfiguration of the Body," in *Sacrament and Image,* ed. A. M. Allchin (London: Fellowship of S. Alban and S. Sergius, 1967), 30.

49. For further criticism on the artistic misuse of the icons, see Philip Sherrard, "The Art of the Icon," in *Sacrament and Image.*

50. Yannis Ziogas, *The Byzantine Malevitch* (Athens: Stachy Publications, 2004).

51. John Scotus Eriugena, *Periphyseon* III, 678CD.

52. Alain Besançon, *The Forbidden Image,* trans. Jane Marie Todd (Chicago: University of Chicago Press, 2000), 372.

53. Ziogas, *The Byzantine Malevitch,* 81.

2. The Existential Chiasm

1. Sophocles, *Antigone,* 909–912, trans. F. Storr (Cambridge: Loeb Classical Library, 1981).

2. Shakespeare, *Hamlet,* act 5, scene 1, 126–134.

3. See, among others, *Being as Communion* (New York: St. Vladimir's Seminar Press, 1985); "Communion and Otherness," *St. Vladimir's Theological Quarterly* 38, no. 4 (1994): 347–361; "Human Capacity and Human Incapacity," *Scottish Journal of Theology* 28 (1975): 401–448; "On Being a Person: Towards an Ontology of Personhood," in *Persons, Divine and Human* (Edinburgh: T&T Clark, 1991).

4. Miroslav Volf, *After Our Likeness: The Church as the Image of the Trinity* (Grand Rapids, Mich.: Wlliam B. Eerdmans, 1998); see, in particular, 87, 115, and 181–185

5. Ibid., 181–182.

6. Thus, the paradox that the individual is higher than the universal "cannot be mediated, for all mediation [and thus thought and language] takes place only by virtue of the universal; it is and remains for all eternity a paradox, impervious to thought." S. Kierkegaard, *Fear and Trembling,* 56.

7. W. D. Ross, *Aristotle's Metaphysics,* vol. II (Oxford: Oxford University Press, 1924), cxv.

8. See among others, Gregory Vlastos's "The Individual as Object of Love in

Plato," in *Platonic Studies* (Princeton, N.J.: Princeton University Press, 1981); John Crosby's *Personalist Papers* (Washington: Catholic University Press, 2004); Zizioulas's *Being as Communion*, esp. ch. 1; and Linda Zagzebski, "The Uniqueness of Persons," *Journal of Religious Ethics* 29 (2001): 401–423.

9. That was the infamous chasm by Mt. Taegetus called "Apothetai"; see Plutarch, *Lykurgus* 16.1–16.2.

10. "ἡ μὲν γὰρ ποίησις μᾶλλον τὰ καθόλου, ἡ δὲ ἱστορία τὰ καθ' ἕκαστον λέγει" (*De Arts Poetica*, 1451b 5–7).

11. For more on this discussion, see chapter 8 of the present work.

12. See, for example, *Fear and Trembling*, 55: "the single individual is higher than the universal." And again, "the single individual as the single individual is higher than the universal."

13. Hegel, *Aesthetics: Lectures on Fine Art*, vol. II, 803; emphasis added.

14. See John Sallis, *Shades: Of Painting at the Limit* (Bloomington: Indiana University Press, 1998).

15. "As transcendental I, the 'I think' accomplishes *no individuation*. Because it exerts a pure abstract function, 'the representation "I" does not contain in itself the least manifoldness and it is absolute (although merely logical) unity.' It unifies the manifold precisely because it remains an empty unity, orphan of all particularity." Jean-Luc Marion, *Being Given*, 252 (emphasis in the original).

16. "For in receiving what gives itself (the phenomenon), the receiver receives its effects, therefore receives itself from it—it is individualized by facticity . . . and receiving itself as a being given, frees itself from the subsistence of a substratum, in short, from the subjectivity of the 'subject.'" Ibid., 261.

17. More specifically, 256–258 for Husserl and 259–262 for Heidegger.

18. What Husserl's phenomenology lacks (and which Heidegger's corrective accords) is in Marion's words "unsubstitutable individuation, irremissible ipseity" (258). But Heidegger fails to liberate Dasein from the old remnant of subjectivism insofar as he grounds selfhood on self-constancy (*Ständigkeit des Selbst*). The questions that Marion raises against such a move are all concerned with individuation. "As a result," he asks, "wouldn't individuation itself also become problematic?" And a few lines later he asks again: "Can we ever base an individuation on it [i.e., the collectivity of Dasein]?" (261).

19. Ibid., 257.

20. Ibid., 268.

21. Ibid.

22. Jean-Luc Marion, *Prolegomena to Charity* (New York: Fordham University Press, 2002), 98.

23. *Being Given*, 265.

24. Ibid.

25. Ibid., 268.

26. Ibid., 271.

27. For more on the medical as well as the ethical implications of chimerism, see N. Yu, M. S. Kruskall, J. J. Yunis, et al., "Disputed Maternity Leading to Identification of Tetragametic Chimerism," *New England Journal of Medicine* 346 (May 16, 2002): 1545–1552.

28. "Toward A Fourth Reduction?" in *After God: Richard Kearney and the Religious Turn in Continental Philosophy*, ed. John Panteleimon Manoussakis (New York:

Fordham University Press, 2006). The idea of a fourth reduction was conceived in common by Richard Kearney and myself as a supplement to Marion's third reduction. In what ways our reduction may supplement Marion's should become clear from the remainder of this chapter. Originally, Richard Kearney and I had thought of publishing our thoughts in a single text under a double signature. Later, however, differences in emphasis and interpretation emerged, and so we decided to publish our texts separately but next to each other in the opening section of *After God*.

29. The number 3 is a simplification for the sake of our argument (although Dominique Janicaud in "The Theological Turn of French Phenomenology" counts the same three reductions, namely, the transcendental [Husserl], the existential [Heidegger], and the one suggested by Marion that is left unnamed [in *Phenomenology and the "Theological Turn*," 31 and 56–62]). A more in-depth inquiry would have identified more kinds of phenomenological reductions — indeed, in Husserl alone one could count at least three different ways: the Cartesian, the psychological, and the ontological. See Dan Zahavi, *Husserl's Phenomenology* (Stanford, Calif.: Stanford University Press, 2003), 47.

30. I use the term "paradox" as Marion has defined it in *Being Given*, §23, and in *In Excess*, chapter 5.

31. "La Banalité de la saturation," in *Le Visible et le révélé* (Paris: Cerf, 2005), 143–182.

32. For more on this, consult Richard Kearney's "Epiphanies of the Everyday" in *After God*.

33. These expressions occur throughout the *Works of Love*; for their specific meaning see *Works of Love*, trans. H. V. Hong and E. H. Hong (Princeton, N.J.: Princeton University Press, 1995), 72 ff.

34. Sartre's phenomenological analysis of my relation with others is a good example of such functionalism: "others are those forms which pass by in the street, those magic objects which are capable of acting at a distance and upon which I can act by means of determined conduct. I scarcely notice them; I act as if I were alone in the world. I brush against 'people' as I brush against a wall; I avoid them as I avoid obstacles . . . Those 'people' are functions: the ticket-collector is only the function of collecting tickets; the café waiter is nothing but the function of serving the patrons. In this capacity they will be most useful if I know their *keys* and those 'master-words' which can release their mechanisms" (*Being and Nothingness*, 495). This is what Marion playfully calls "inter-objectivity" (*Prolegomena to Charity*, 162). As we have seen in the previous chapter, for Sartre it is the look of the Other that is alone capable of resisting the organization of my relation with others into this mechanics.

35. Metropolitan of Pergamon John (Zizioulas), "Communion and Otherness," 354. At this point Zizioulas is coming very close to Duns Scotus's *haecceitas* — a point to which we will return later in this chapter.

36. Kierkegaard, *Works of Love*, 87.

37. Ibid., 88. The full passage runs as follows: "In other words, when the dissimilarity hangs loosely in this way, then in each individual there continually glimmers that essential other, which is common to all, the eternal resemblance, the likeness."

38. "On Personality, Grace and Free Will," in *The Sermons and Devotional Writings of Gerard Manley Hopkins*, ed. Christopher Devlin, S.J. (London: Oxford University Press, 1959), 146–159.

39. Ibid., 147.

40. This was the conclusion of a paper on Marion that Prof. Westphal read at The Breakthrough of Phenomenology and Theology Conference organized by Boston University's Philosophy Department on April 27, 2001. Forthcoming in the *International Journal for Philosophy of Religion*.

41. "The crucial point in this discussion is that we ought to deal with the other, not as he appeared yesterday or as he is today, but as who he will be in the future and at the eschaton, namely, as a fellow and as a neighbor in the Kingdom. For it is the future — that is, their place in the Kingdom — that gives to each being its true character." Metropolitan of Pergamon John (Zizioulas), "Eucharist and the Kingdom of God," *Synaxis* (in Greek), 52 (1994): 81–97, at 92. Zizioulas's commitment to eschatology forces him to distinguish between two ontologies, the *protological* ontology that is nothing else but the "worldly" attitude, and the *eschatological* ontology. According to the first, whatever has happened cannot be eradicated or erased; our acts and decisions form our facticity, which is, in this case, tantamount to our being. Thus even God is constrained by our past. On the other hand, for eschatological ontology (which for Zizioulas is reflected in the Eucharist) it is not the past but the future, unseen, unknown, and surprising, as it might be, that determines our being and our existence: "the sinner is not ontologically determined by who he *was* [i.e., a sinner], but by who he *will be* [i.e., a saint]." See "Church and the Eschaton" (in Greek) in *Church and Eschatology*, ed. Pantelis Kalaitzidis (Athens: Kastaniotis, 2001), 43.

42. Kierkegaard, *Works of Love*, 89.

43. Thus each person *in its relational character* as *prosopon* (and not *in se* as in Augustine's *De Trinitatis*) could be understood as a *vestigium Christi* and, by extension, a *vestigium trinitatis*. Here and throughout our analysis of personhood's relatedness we take the Trinity as our archetypal paradigm, of which personal relation, I suggest, is a trace. However, certain precautions need to be taken: the notion of a trace, as it has been used by Levinas and Derrida, carries the connotation of an absent signified of which the trace is only a signifier (trace as lack). I, on the other hand, favor an understanding of the trace as efficacious sign rather than empty signifier, as mark rather than lack. (For the problematic of the trace, see Emmanuel Levinas, "*La Trace de l'Autre*," in *Tijdschrift voor Filosofie* 3 (1963), 605–623; Jeffrey Bloechl, *The Face of the Other and the Trace of God* (New York: Fordham University Press, 2000); Michael J. MacDonald, "Jewgreek and Greekjew: The Concept of Trace in Derrida and Levinas," *Philosophy Today* (1991): 215–227; and Kevin Hart, *The Trespass of the Sign: Deconstruction, Theology and Philosophy* (New York: Fordham University Press, 2000). One final caveat is offered by Kevin Hart who, in a more recent essay, writes: "[w]e can never aspire to the divine perichoresis, and to do so would be to slight the excellence we enjoy as creature of flesh and blood" ("The Kingdom and the Trinity," in *Religious Experience and the End of Metaphysics*, ed. Jeffrey Bloechl [Bloomington: Indiana University Press, 2003], 165). *Pace* Hart, we would like to argue that we *should* aspire to imitate the divine perichoresis, as far as it is humanly possible and not only in spite of our "flesh and blood" (as in the doctrine of the *theosis*) but especially *because of* them (see also note 3 above). In accordance with Hart's discussion of the relation between the Kingdom and the Trinity, I believe that the *communio personarum* cannot, in turn, succeed in becoming a trace of the Trinity unless it exemplifies first the "structure" of the kingdom (and hence our insistence on the eschatological character of the person).

44. This term is borrowed from Alfred North Whitehead's *Process and Reality*

(1960); I wish to acknowledge, at the same time, the original work advanced by the studies of Harold H. Oliver, such as *A Relational Metaphysic* (The Hague: Martinus Nijhoff, 1981) and *Relatedness: Essays in Metaphysics and Theology* (Macon, Ga.: Mercer University Press, 1984).

45. This, of course, creates the puzzle that asks how can an experiencing be prior to the person who experiences and to what is experienced? Isn't experience always experience of someone and of something? Translated into the language of personhood: what comes first, the person qua *prosopon*, or the relation that establishes him or her as person? This question might look rather trivial in itself (indeed, like the chicken-and-the-egg puzzle); it assumes, however, quite important dimensions once transferred to the theological discourse: what or who constitutes the Trinity, the (person of the) Father who begets the Son and proceeds the Spirit, or something common and anterior to all of the three Persons, namely, their relationship? To decide this problem is to decide where to assign priority: to the hypostasis of the persons (as is usually done in the East, e.g., the Cappadocians) or to the essence of the Godhead (as is usually done in the West, e.g., Augustine). In other words, is God first a Trinity and then a Unity or first One and then distinguished into the three Persons? Neither position is without its problems. Our dyadic understanding of *prosopon* as *topos* (i.e., personal substance) and *tropos* (i.e., personal relation) — and thus *at once* topical and tropical — cuts through this dilemma.

46. We find glimpses of this insight in a number of phenomenological analyses, to quote only two eloquent instances here: "Man and the world are relative beings, and the principle of their being *is* the relation" (Jean-Paul Sartre, *Being and Nothingness*, 407). And again: "There is vision, touch, when a certain visible, a certain tangible, turns back upon the whole of the visible, the whole of the tangible, of which it is part, or when suddenly it finds itself *surrounded* by them, or when between it and them, and through their commerce, is formed a Visibility, a Tangible in itself, which belongs properly neither to the body qua fact nor to the world qua fact — as upon two mirrors facing one another where two indefinite series of images set in one another arise which belong really to neither of the two surfaces, since each is only the rejoinder of the other, and which therefore form a couple, a couple more real than either of them" (Merleau-Ponty, *The Visible and the Invisible*, trans. Alphonso Lingis (Evanston, Ill.: Northwestern University Press, 1968), 139.

47. David Bohm, *Quantum Theory* (London: Constable, 1954), 161; my emphasis. For a philosophical appropriation of quantum theory, see Oliver, *A Relational Metaphysic*. I am greatly indebted to Prof. Oliver's analysis.

48. Pavel Florensky, *The Pillar and Ground of the Truth*, trans. Boris Jakim (Princeton, N.J.: Princeton University Press, 1997), 35. One can provide further evidence for the centrality of relation, for instance, Dionysius the Aeropagite's captivating remark that ἡ δὲ σχέσις σώζει καὶ εἶναι ποιεῖ ("it is relation that saves and creates Being"; *DN*, IV, 23:21).

49. W. Norris Clarke, S.J., *Explorations in Metaphysics: Being, God, Person*, (South Bend, Ind.: University of Notre Dame Press, 1994), 216.

50. On the paradoxes of sensation, see Maurice Merleau-Ponty, "Eye and Mind," in *The Primacy of Perception*, trans. Carleton Dallery, ed. James M. Edie (Evanston, Ill.: Northwestern University Press, 1964), and Michel Henry's two seminal books, *L'essence de la manifestation* (Paris: Presses Universitaires de France, 1963) and *Phénoménologie matérielle* (Paris: Presses Universitaires de France, 1990). For a more

in-depth discussion of this topic in relation to Merleau-Ponty and Michel Henry, see chapter 7 of the present work.

51. See Marion, *Prolegomena to Charity*, especially chapters 4 and 7; and more recently, *Le Phénomène érotique* (Paris: Grasset, 2003). Brian Gregor's analysis of the erotic in his "Eros That Never Arrives" (*Symposium* 9, no. 1 [2005]: 67–88) is most pertinent to this discussion. See, for example, Gregor's conclusion: "Love moves beyond essence, beyond quiddity, but not beyond personality" (82).

52. E. H. Gombrich, *Shadows: The Depiction of Cast Shadows in Western Art* (London: National Gallery Publications, 1995); see in particular 17–26. For the analysis on shadows I am indebted to Ilias Papagiannopoulos's *Beyond Absence: Essay on the Human Person on the Traces of Sophocles's Oedipus Rex* (Athens: Indiktos, 2005), 101–106 (in Greek).

53. "First Principle and Foundation," in *The Sermons and Devotional Writings of Gerard Manley Hopkins*, 123.

54. *Haecceitas* is not a term that occurs frequently in the writings of Duns Scotus — in fact it seems that Scotus uses this neologism for the first (and only?) time in the *Reportatio Parisiensis*, II, xii, 5.

55. "Ultima realitas entis," in *Ordinatio*, n. 188.

56. At least once, Hopkins himself makes the allusion to Scotus: "Is not this pitch or whatever we call it then the same as Scotus's [ha]*ecceitas*?" in *The Sermons and Devotional Writings of Gerard Manley Hopkins*, 151.

57. Jean-Paul Sartre, *Being and Nothingness*, 451; emphasis in the original.

58. *Ordinatio*, n. 186.

59. "Non est igitur 'ista entitas' materia vel forma vel compositum, in quantum quodlibet istorum est 'natura'" (*Ordinatio*, n. 188); and "illa entitas quam addit singulare super speciem, non est entitas quiditativa" (*Ordinatio*, n. 197).

60. "singulare autem non habet definitionem propriam, sed tantum definitionem speciei, et ita non est de ipso demonstrario propria, sed tantum demonstration quae est de specie (non enim habet passionem propriam, sed tantum passionem speciei)" (*Ordinatio*, II, n. 193).

61. *The Sermons and Devotional Writings of Gerard Manley Hopkins*, 146; my emphasis.

62. Ibid.

63. See the editor's commentary (Appendix II) in *The Sermons and Devotional Writings of Gerard Manley Hopkins*. Fr. Devlin presents Hopkins's argument from the essay in discussion here ("On Personality . . .") in the following points: "a) . . . Personality is prior to existence. b) A man's personality is also distinct from his human nature. Two different persons can have exactly the same nature . . . c) Personality is the same as freedom" (338).

64. For Marion's comments on Scotus, see Jean-Luc Marion, "Une Époque de la métaphysique," in *Jean Duns Scot ou la revolution subtile*, ed. Christine Goémé (Paris: FAC, 1982), 87–95. Marion uses Scotus's *haecceitas* at some length in his *Prolegomena to Charity* (95–98). For Marion it is love that discloses the "unsubstitutable particularity" (as he translates the *haecceitas*) of the other, beyond essence and beyond "beingness" (95). In Marion's account, the *haecceitas* has also the power to surpass my consciousness's intentionality by inverting it: "*haecceitas* does not reproduce, as a symmetrical reply, the egoity of an I; it reverses it" (98). Inverse intentionality is thus made the effect of the Other's *haecceitas* on me. It is interesting, then, to imagine what

would be the effect of God's "haecceitas" on my consciousness — what else than the bestowing of particularity, that is, the constitution of *haecceitas* itself?

65. I have followed a similar argument with regard to God's existence in my "From Exodus to Eschaton," *Modern Theology* 18, no. 1 (2002): 95–107.

66. From a theological perspective, Miroslav Volf writes: "this means that each human being *is constituted into a person by what in each case is a different relation of God to that human being.* A human being becomes a person and enters thus into existence as human being because he 'is addressed by God equiprimally with regard to both God and to himself and is called to communion with God.' On the one hand, God's call is general and is the same for everyone. This grounds common humanity and the equal dignity of every human being. At the same time, however, that call must be specific to each individual; otherwise, abstract personhood, or universal human nature, would be created through the call, but not each particular person distinct from all others, that is, the concrete human being. Unless God's relation to every person is specific in every case, and unless God calls every human being by name (see Gen. 3:9), no human being can declare, 'I believe that God created *me.*'" *After Our Likeness*, 182; emphasis in the original.

67. As well as a "micro-eschatology" as Richard Kearney calls it in his "Epiphanies of the Everyday" (in *After God*).

68. Ibid.

69. "The best formulation of the reduction is probably that given by Eugene Fink, Husserl's assistant, when he spoke of 'wonder' in the face of the world" (Merleau-Ponty, *Phenomenology of Perception* [London: Routledge, 2002], xv).

70. For the event of the Incarnation from a phenomenological perspective, see Michel Henry, *Incarnation: Une philosophie de la chair* (Paris: Seuil, 2000).

71. "car l'idée de la révélation chrétien est qu'au bout du compte *rien n'est révélé,* rien sinon la fin de la révélation elle-même, sinon cesi que la révélation veut dire que le sens se dévoile purement comme sens, en personne, mais en une personne telle que tout le sens de cette personne consiste à se révéler . . . ce qui est révélé est le révélable." Jean-Luc Nancy, "La Déconstruction du Christianisme," *Les Études Philosophiques* 4 (1998), 511 (emphasis in the original).

72. A case in point here could be the Greek as well as the Eastern attitudes of personhood. Because Plato and Buddha (to mention two names representative of two different systems of thought) lack the solid ground for an incarnational understanding of the human person, they are forced to come up with its substitute: an endless series of reincarnations. What is lost, however, in the process of reincarnation is the specificity of the person, who by being many is really none. Reincarnation, in fact, is really a process of *de-fleshment.* No wonder, then, that for both systems flesh is a prison, the worthless shell of the soul, from which one has to flee, toward a faceless and depersonalized Nothing. Slavoj Žižek does not hesitate to see an ideological affinity between the *Bhagavad-Gita* and the Nazi ideology that led to the Holocaust: "if external reality is ultimately just an ephemeral appearance, then even the most horrifying crimes eventually *do not matter* . . . Here it is difficult to resist the temptation to paraphrase this passage [from the *Bhagavad-Gita's* account of the meeting of Krishna with Arjuna, 44–45 in W. Johnson's translation] as the justification for the burning of Jews in the gas chambers to their executioner, caught in a moment of doubt: since 'he who thinks it to be the killer and he who thinks it to be killed, both know nothing,' since 'the self kills not, and the self is not killed,' therefore 'you ought not to grieve for any' burned

Jew, but 'looking alike on pleasure and pain, on gain and loss, on victory and defeat,' do what you were ordered to do." Žižek concludes, "no wonder the *Bhagavad-Gita* was Heinrich Himmler's favorite book: it is reported that he always carried a copy in his uniform pocket" (*The Puppet and the Dwarf: The Perverse Core of Christianity* [Cambridge, Mass.: MIT Press, 2003], 32).

73. And the community that the *prosopon* creates, i.e., the ecclesial event (not to be confused with the merely ecclesiastical).

74. An interesting observation about the character of the early Church is the Christian community's choice of (a) a name for themselves and (b) the architectural style according to which they built their meeting places (i.e., their churches). The name "ecclesia" predates Christianity. It was used by the ancient Greek polis for the assembly of its citizens (*ekklesia* means to "call together"), a body with a purely civic function. The architectonic rhythm that the first Christians chose to build their churches after was neither, as one might expect, the style of the *Naos*, the Greco-Roman religious center, nor that of the Judaic Temple, but something altogether different. The early Christian community made a conscious choice for the *basilica*, that is, a civic forum with no religious connotations whatsoever. It is interesting to note here that the Greco-Roman temple housed only the cultic statue of the god or goddess, whereas the worshiping people were required to stay outside of the temple. The Christian church inverted this model: the church is built to house the "assembly of the faithful," the *ecclesia*, who, gathered in His name, *is* the manifestation of God. See Fred S. Kleiner and Christian J. Mamiya, *Gardner's Art through the Ages*, vol. I (Boston: Wadsworth, 2005), 310. It is perhaps in light of such evidence that political theorists, such as Marcel Gauchet, speak of Christianity as "a religion for departing from religion" or the "religious" after religion (see M. Gauchet, *The Disenchantment of the World: A Political History of Religion* [Princeton, N.J.: Princeton University Press, 1997]).

75. In one of his earlier phenomenological studies, *Existence and Existents*, Levinas does not hesitate to go as far as to identify the sacred with the nocturnal *il y a*: "The impersonality of the sacred in primitive religions, which for Durkheim is the 'still' impersonal God from which will issue one day the God of advanced religions, on the contrary describes a world where nothing prepares for the apparition of a God. Rather than to a God, the notion of the *there is* leads us to the absence of God, the absence of any being" (trans. Alphonso Lingis [The Hague, Martinus Niijhoff, 1978], 61). What allows the identification of the *il y a* with the religious category of the sacred is their common denial of the face of the Other (note how Levinas speaks of the "*impersonality* of the sacred"). To fully understand what is at stake here, one needs to be aware of the linguistic as well as semantic nuances behind the distinction of the "sacred" and the "saintly" (cf. E. Benveniste's *Le Vocabulaire des institutions indoeuropéennes* [Paris 1969], vol. II, 180), two terms that are unfortunately used interchangeably, although they name two diametrically different worldviews. Freud utilized this distinction in his study of Judaism, *Moses and Monotheism*, and Levinas has dedicated an entire volume to the subject (*Du sacré au saint* [Paris: Éditions Minuit, 1977]). I wish to acknowledge Prof. Thanos Lipowatz, whose erudition on this matter helped me understand better the conceptual difference between these two terms.

3. The Aesthetical Chiasm

1. Kierkegaard, *Either/Or*, trans. Howard V. Hong and Edna H. Hong (Princeton, N.J.: Princeton University Press, 1987), 68.

2. Heidegger, *Being and Time*, 391/427.

3. Ibid., 311/338.

4. See Sartre's remark: "ce qui sépare l'antérieur du postérieur c'est précisément *rien*" (*L'Être et le néant: Essai d'ontologie phénoménologique* [Paris: Gallimard, 1977], 64). Before Sartre, Augustine had said, "But the two times, past and future, how can they *be*, since the past is no more and the future is not yet? On the other hand, if the present were always present and never flowed away into the past, it would not be time at all, but eternity. But if the present is only time, because it flows away into the past, how can we say that it *is*? For it is, only because it will cease to be. Thus we can affirm that time is only in that it tends toward not-being (*Confessions*, XI, xiv, 219). See also *Being and Time*, 391/427.

5. That could be named as the Greek view—but already Plato sets forth what would become the proper Christian view of Time, i.e., that Time is *created*. Time is created not only in the same way that the Cosmos is created but together with it (see Augustine). As a creature, Time shares with Cosmos its "cosmetic" element, that is, its beautiful arrangement. Therefore, if there is an aesthetics of the cosmos (of the creation), it ought to be an aesthetics of the Chronos as well.

6. Heidegger, *Being and Time*: "The Moment brings existence to the situation and discloses the authentic 'There'" (319/348). "The present, as the Moment, discloses the today authentically" (362/397), "the Moment that lies in resoluteness" (353/387).

7. Kierkegaard, *The Concept of Anxiety*, 90.

8. Metropolitan of Pergamon John D. Zizioulas, "Towards an Eschatological Ontology," unpublished paper delivered at King's College in 1999 (7 in the ms.).

9. Jean-Yves Lacoste, *Experience and the Absolute: Disputed Questions on the Humanity of Man*, trans. Mark Raftery-Skehan (New York: Fordham University Press, 2004), 138.

10. Ibid., 137.

11. "Der Anfang bleibt als Ankunft," in Martin Heidegger, *Elucidations of Hölderlin's Poetry*, trans. Keith Hoeller (New York: Humanity Books, 2000), 195.

12. Lacoste, *Experience and the Absolute*, 137.

13. "Towards an Eschatological Ontology."

14. Dietrich Bonhoeffer, *Works, Vol. 6: Ethics*, trans. Reinhard Krauss, Charles C. West, and Douglas W. Stott (Minneapolis: Fortress Press, 2005), 160.

15. Ibid., 169.

16. Ibid., 158.

17. Ibid.

18. Lacoste, *Experience and the Absolute*, 89.

19. See Raymond E. Brown, *The Gospel of John and Epistles of John: A Concise Commentary* (Collegeville, Minn.: Liturgical Press, 1988), 19.

20. See Georges Florovsky, *Bible, Church, Tradition: An Eastern Orthodox View, Collected Works*, vol. I (Vaduz: Belmont, 1987), 35–36.

21. Lacoste, *Experience and the Absolute*, 138. "Reconciled existence," Lacoste writes on the next page, "takes place therefore in an *interim between the eschatological blessings already granted and the eschatological blessings that still remain within an economy of promise*" (emphasis in the original).

22. See Richard Kearney, "Epiphanies of the Everyday: Toward a Micro-Eschatology," in *After God*, ed. John Panteleimon Manoussakis (New York: Fordham University Press, 2006), 3–20.

23. Kierkegaard, *Either/Or*, 57.

24. Jean-Paul Sartre, *The Psychology of Imagination* (Secaucus: Citadel Press, 1972), 280; my emphasis.

25. "it must be that queer thing; The instant . . . this queer thing, the instant, is situated between the motion and the rest; it occupies no time at all, and the transition of the moving thing to the state of rest, or of the stationary thing to being in motion, takes place to and from the instant . . . it occupies no time in making it and at that moment it cannot be either in motion or at rest. The same holds good of its other transitions. When it passes from being in existence to ceasing to exist or from being nonexistent to coming into existence, it is then between certain motions and states; it is then neither existent nor nonexistent, and it is neither coming into existence nor ceasing to exist" (translation by F. M. Cornford). Another translation reads as follows: "this strange thing in which it is at the time of changing really exist?—What thing? The moment . . . there is this curious nature which we call the moment lying between rest and motion, not being in any time; and into this and out of this what is in motion changes to rest, and what is at rest to motion . . . And it will be in the same case in relation to the other changes, when it passes from being into cessation of being, or from not-being into becoming—then it passes between certain states of motion and rest, and neither is nor is not, nor becomes nor is destroyed" (translation by B. Jowett).

26. "οὔτε ἄχρονον πάντῃ, οὔτε ἔγχρονον, ἀλλ᾽ ὁμοῦ καὶ τὸ ἄχρονον ἔγχρονον, καὶ τὸ ἔγχρονον ἄχρονον . . . τό τε ἔγχρονον αἰωνίζεταὶ πως καὶ οὐσίωται τὸ γενητόν, καὶ αὖ τὸ αἰώνιον χρονίζεται, καὶ τὸ ὂν τῇ γενέσει συμπλέκεται, καὶ ἔστι μὲν ἡ ψυχή τὸ συναμφότερον" (*Dubitationes et Solutiones De Primis Principiis, In Platonis Parmenidem*, ed. Car. Aem. Ruelle [Brussels, 1964], reprint of the 1899 edition, 263).

27. At this point we should address the bias that characterizes some contemporary discussions of the *kairos*. For example, Agamben's analysis of temporality in the history of philosophy distinguishes two schemata, both equally paradigmatic of the failures of the West—the cyclical movement of Greek time and the linear movement of Christianity. His preference lies with neither of these, but with the *kairos* that he attempts to present as the exclusive characteristic of Gnosis. He then goes on to say: "The elements for a different concept of time lie scattered among the folds and shadows of the Western cultural tradition. We need only to elucidate these, so that they may emerge as the bearers of a message which is meant for us and which it is our task to verify. It is in Gnosticism, that failed religion of the West, that there appears an experience of time in radical opposition to both the Greek and the Christian versions. In opposition to the Greek circle of experience and the straight line of Christianity, it posits a concept whose spatial model can be represented by a broken line. In this way it strikes directly at what remains unaltered in classical Antiquity and Christianity alike: duration, precise and continuous time. The cosmic time of Greek experience is denied by Gnosticism in the name of the world's absolute estrangement from God (God is the *allotrios*, the supreme other), whose providential work cannot be a matter of preserving cosmic laws, but of breaking them. The impetus toward redemption of Christian linear time is negated because, for the Gnostic, the Resurrection is not something to be awaited in time, to occur in some more or less remote future; it has already taken place" (Giorgio Agamben, "Time and History: Critique of the Instant and the Continuum," in *Infancy and History: The Destruction of Experience*, trans. Liz Heron [London: Verso, 1993], 100–101). Such understanding of Christian eschatology is rather superficial, for eschatology, as we have seen, is in its essence

non-messianic, since the Messiah has already come. It was He, in any case, who eloquently expressed the mystery of the *kairos* when He said, ἔρχεται ὥρα καὶ νῦν ἐστιν, that is, "the hour is coming and *now* is" (John 4:23, 5:25: "Most assuredly, I say to you, the hour is coming, and now is, when the dead will hear the voice of the Son of God; and those who hear will live"). The Christian experience of time is to be sought nowhere else but in the event that constitutes the Christian community, that is, in the Eucharist. There, at the moment of the consecration, the celebrant says, "remembering Your passion on the Cross, Your entombment, Your resurrection and Your glorious and Second coming." Not only the Resurrection, Christ's and ours, but even that very Second Coming, has already taken place from the Eucharist's point of view. That explains how the Christian community can recall it in memory: as an event already realized. Strangely, it is Agamben himself who in his commentary on the epistle to the Romans (*Le Temps qui reste: un commentaire de l'Épître aux Romains* [Paris: Bibliothèque Rivages, 2000]) offers a much different, and evidently more sophisticated, reading of kairological time in Paul. See also "The Time That Is Left," *Epoché* 7, no. 1 (2002): 1–14.

28. *Gesamtausgabe*, 60, 102.

29. *The Concept of Anxiety*, 87–88.

30. *Gesamtausgabe*, 60: Über Zeit und Augenblick (biblischer Sprachgebrauch nicht zufällig; die ausdrückliche Charakterisierung des Wann, kein objectiv gleichgültiges Wann; καιρός entscheidend). Und wie bestimmt er dieses Wann? Nicht durch objektive Zeitangabe, sonder durch das *Wie*, und zwar *Wie* als bezogen gleich auf den Bezug zu dem *Wie*, denn der Bezug bzw. Vollzug ist das Entscheidende des Wann! (150).

31. And thus we part ways with the solely existential understanding of Bultmann's kairological eschatology. See Rudolf Bultmann, *History and Eschatology* (Edinburgh: T&T Clark, 1957).

32. See Alexander Golitzin, "'Suddenly, Christ': The Place of Negative Theology in the Mystagogy of Dionysius Aeropagites," in *Mystics: Presence and Aporia,* ed. Michael Kessler and Christian Sheppard (Chicago: University of Chicago Press, 2003). Golitzin mentions — besides Dionysius — the *Acts of Judas Thomas*, Athanasius's *Life of Anthony*, and Ephrem the Syrus's *Hymns on Nature* and *Hymns on Paradise*. An examination of these texts allows Golitzin to conclude with the following words: "thus, again, we find the term linked with the mystical vision, Christ, light, and the liturgies of both heaven and earth" (24). Beyond the milieu of early Christian literature, one finds frequent references to *exaiphnes* as indicating divine manifestation in the work of Philo of Alexandria (cf. *De Somnis, Quod Deus sit immutabilis, De sacrificiis Abeli et Caini, De mutatione nominum*). For a recent treatment of the *exaiphnes* in Philo, see Jean-Louis Chrétien, *The Unforgettable and the Unhoped For*, trans. Jeffrey Bloechl (New York: Fordham University Press, 2002), 99–118.

33. The entire *Third Letter* of Dionysius the Aeropagite attests to the relation of the exaiphnes with the Incarnation. Here is Dionysius's *Third Letter* in its entirety: "'Suddenly' *[exaiphnes]* means that which has come forth unexpectedly and from the hitherto invisible into manifestation. And I think that here theology is suggesting the philanthropy [i.e., the Divine Economy] of Christ. The superessential has proceeded out of hiddenness to become manifest to us by becoming a human being. Yet He is also hidden, both after the manifestation, and, to speak more divinely, even within it. For this is the hidden of Jesus, and neither by rational discourse, nor by intuition can

His mystery be explained. But instead even when spoken, it remains ineffable, and when conceived, unknowable."

34. For an analysis of the *exaiphnes* in these texts, see Golitzin, "'Suddenly, Christ.'"

35. "Ἐξαίφνης ἐστι τὸ παρ' ἐλπίδα, καὶ ἐκ τοῦ τέως ἀφανοῦς εἰς τὸ ἐμφανές ἐξαγόμενον" (*PG*, 3, 1069 B).

36. "Εἰσεῖδεν ἐξαίφνης οὐκ ἰδών ὅπως, ἀλλ' ἡ θέα πλήσασα φωτός τὰ ὄμματα οὐ δι' αὐτοῦ πεποίηκεν ἄλλο ὁρᾶν, ἀλλ' αὐτὸ τὸ φῶς τὸ ὅραμα ἦν" (*Enneads*, VI, 7, 36:19–20).

37. "δι' οὐ γὰρ ἐφωτίσθη, τοῦτό ἐστιν, ὅ δεῖ θεάσασθαι" (*Enneads*, V, 3, 17:36).

38. "ἐν δὲ τῷ πορεύεσθαι ἐγεντο αὐτὸν ἐγγίζει τῇ Δαμασκῷ, ἐξαίφνης τε αὐτόν περιήστρεψε φῶς ἐκ τοῦ οὐρανοῦ . . . ἠγέρθη δὲ Σαῦλος ἀπὸ τῆς γῆς, ἀνεῳγμένον δε τῶν ὀφθαλμῶν αὐτοῦ *οὐδέν* ἔβλεπεν" (Acts 9:3, 8).

39. The phenomenology of the *inapparent* begins with Husserl's categorial intuition (from the *Logical Investigations*) and culminates in Heidegger's last seminars (especially the Seminar in Zähringen in 1973). See M. Heidegger, *Four Seminars*, trans. A. Mitchell and F. Raffoul (Bloomington: Indiana University Press, 2003), 64–81 and 89.

40. Karsten Harries, *Infinity and Perspective* (Cambridge, Mass.: MIT Press, 2001).

41. This is the groundbreaking insight in the eschatology of the Metropolitan of Pergamon John Zizioulas; see "Towards an Eschatological Ontology" and "Church and the Eschaton."

42. As we already have seen, Jean-Luc Nancy writes that "car l'idée de la révélation chrétien est qu'au bout du compte *rien n'est révélé*, rien sinon la fin de la révélation elle-même, sinon cesi que la révélation veut dire que le sens se dévoile purement comme sens, en personne, mais en une personne telle que tout le sens de cette personne consiste à se révéler . . . ce qui est révélé est le révélable" (Jean-Luc Nancy, "La Déconstruction du Christianisme, *Études Philosophiques* 4 [1998], 511, emphasis in the original).

43. Edmund Husserl, *Logische Untersuchungen*, vol. 2, part 1, section 2 (Tübingen: Max Niemeyer Verlag, 1968), 25. "In these we discover as a common circumstance the fact that certain objects or states of affairs of whose reality someone has actual knowledge indicate to him the reality of certain other objects or states of affairs, in the sense that his belief in the being of the one is experienced (though not at all evidently) as motivating a belief or surmise in the being of the other" (*Logical Investigations*, trans. J. N. Findlay [modified] [New York: Humanities Press, 1970], 270).

44. See Jacques Derrida, *Speech and Phenomena and Other Essays on Husserl's Theory of Signs*, trans. David B. Allison (Evanston, Ill.: Northwestern University Press, 1973), especially 27–31.

4. Prelude

1. For a good overview of the history of ontology's and epistemology's (and even theology's) reduction to language see Haralambos Ventis's *The Reductive Veil: Post-Kantian Non-representationalism versus Apophatic Realism* (Katerini: Epektasis Publications, 2005).

2. I cite here three aphorisms indicative of this position: "language is at once the house of being and the home of human essence" (Martin Heidegger, "Letter on

'Humanism,'" in *Pathmarks*, 274); "The limits of my language mean the limits of my world" (Ludwig Wittgenstein, *Tractatus logico-philosophicus*, *Werkausgabe* I [Frankfurt: Suhrkamp, 1989], 5.6); "there is nothing outside of the text" (Jacques Derrida, *Of Grammatology*, 158, and *Limited Inc.*, 136).

3. Referring to Wittgenstein's work I use the following abbreviations: *PI* for *Philosophical Investigations* (trans. G. E. M. Anscombe [Oxford: Blackwell, 1997]); *Tractatus* for *Tractatus logico-philosophicus* (trans. D. F. Pears and B. F. McGuinness [London: Routledge, 1961]); and *Zettel* for *Zettel* (trans. G. E. M. Anscombe and G. H. von Wright [Oxford: Blackwell, 1967]).

4. Augustine, *Confessions*, Book I, viii, trans. F. J. Sheed (Indianapolis: Hackett, 1993), 9. The translation has been slightly modified. Wittgenstein's quotation is shorter. It should be noted that scholars of St. Augustine have criticized Wittgenstein for focusing exclusively on this autobiographical paragraph from the *Confessions* and thus failing to take into account Augustine's treatment of language in his earlier dialogue *De Magistro*. For more on the subject, see M. F. Burnyeat, "Wittgenstein and Augustin 'De Magistro'," *Proceedings of the Aristotelian Society* 61 (1987): 1–24; P. Bearsley, "Augustin and Wittgenstein on Language," *Philosophy* 58 (1983): 229–236.

5. See, among others, Sidney Cavell, *Philosophical Passages: Wittgenstein, Emerson, Austin, Derrida* (Oxford: Blackwell, 1995), 125–186; S. Mulhall, *Inheritance and Originality* (Oxford: Clarendon Press, 2001), 29–43; and F. Kerr, *Theology after Wittgenstein* (Oxford: Blackwell, 1986), 38–42.

6. One should recall at this point that the first part of the Saussurean *General Linguistics* opens with a similar gesture: Saussure begins by challenging the general assumption that holds language "as a naming process only — a list of words, each corresponding to the thing that it names" (*Course in General Linguistics*, trans. Wade Baskin [New York: McGraw-Hill, 1959], 65, hereafter abbreviated as *CGL*).

7. That Wittgenstein's early view of language shows some kind of affinity with that of Augustine is noted by Mulhall: "It should, however, be equally clear that Wittgenstein takes Augustine's picture of language and the Tractarian idea of language to be linked; the extremity of the Tractarian idea would, after all, only look tenable if its author's starting point is something like the Augustinian picture" (37).

8. At a later point in the analysis, Wittgenstein brings back this thesis in order to rebut it further. He writes: "Let us first discuss *this* point of the argument: that a word has no meaning if nothing corresponds to it. — It is important to note that the word 'meaning' is being used illicitly if it is used to signify the thing that 'corresponds' to the word. That is to confound the meaning of a name with the bearer of the name. When Mr. N. N. dies one says that the bearer of the name dies, not that the meaning dies. And it would be nonsensical to say that, for if the name ceased to have meaning it would make no sense to say 'Mr. N. N. is dead'" (*PI*, 40). For example, when an atheist uses the word "God," his or her statements are still meaningful regardless whether the bearer of the word denies the reality of the bearer of the name. We can still speak of "God" in a meaningful way without being, immediately, concerned with (proving or not) His existence.

9. "But what is language? It is not to be confused with human speech" (*CGL*, 9).

10. See *CGL*, 22–23, 88–89, and 110.

11. "For we can avoid ineptness or emptiness in our assertions only by presenting the model [the language-game] as what it is, an object of comparison — as, so to

speak, a measuring rod; not as a preconceived idea to which reality *must* correspond" (*PI*, 131).

12. On the arbitrariness of the sign in Saussure, see *CGL*, 67 ("The bond between the signifier and the signified is arbitrary . . . I can simply say: *the linguistic sign is arbitrary*"). In Wittgenstein, see *PI*, 497 ("The rules of grammar may be called 'arbitrary'") and 520; *Zettel*, 331 ("the rules of grammar are arbitrary"); and Garth Hallett, *A Companion to Wittgenstein's Philosophical Investigations* (Ithaca, N.Y.: Cornell University Press, 1977), 69 ("In this sense they [the rules of language] are arbitrary, like the rules of a game").

13. "He felt that he would not get far with Hegel because he seemed 'to be always wanting to say that things which look different are really the same'. . . he placed himself at the opposite pole: 'my interest is in showing that things which look the same are really different.' He was thinking, as a motto for his book [the *Philosophical Investigations*], of the phrase 'I'll teach you differences'" (Kerr, *Theology after Wittgenstein*, 36).

14. See, for instance, the comment that Wittgenstein makes: "The word 'God' is amongst the earliest learnt — pictures and catechisms, etc. But not with the same consequences as with *pictures* of aunts. I wasn't shown that which the picture pictured" (*Lectures and Conversations on Aesthetics, Psychology, and Religious Belief*, ed. Cyril Barrett [Berkeley: University of California Press, 1966], 59).

15. *Wittgenstein's Lectures in Cambridge 1932–1935*, ed. Alice Ambrose (Oxford: Blackwell, 1979), 32.

16. F. Kerr, *Theology after Wittgenstein*, 147.

17. L. Wittgenstein, *Lectures and Conversations*, 59.

18. P. Ricœur, *The Conflict of Interpretations*, ed. Don Ihde (Evanston, Ill.: Northwestern University Press, 1974), 69.

19. "Semiology and Medicine," in *The Semiotic Challenge*, trans. Richard Howard (New York: Hill and Wang, 1988), 210.

20. As D. Z. Phillips aptly points out: "We cannot separate concepts from practice, from what we do, because it is only *in practice*, in what we do, that concepts have their life and meaning" (*Wittgenstein and Religion* [London: St. Martin's Press, 1993], xiii).

21. "The masses have no voice in the matter, and the signifier chosen by language could be replaced by no other . . . No individual, even if he willed it, could modify in any way at all the choice that has been made . . . it is bound to the existing language" (*CGL*, 71; see also 10).

22. *Thought and Knowledge* (Ithaca, N.Y.: Cornell University Press, 1977), 212. D. Z. Phillips rejects the validity of such term, which he calls "an aberration" and assures us that "Wittgenstein did not hold this view, and neither is it held by those influenced by him in the philosophy of religion" (*Wittgenstein and Religion*, 30). Certain comments, however, made by an illustrious member of the Vienna Circle, Rudolph Carnap, seem to lead us to a different conclusion: "those nonrational areas, on the one hand," writes Carnap of poetry, love, and religion, "and science, on the other hand, can neither confirm nor disprove one another" (*The Logical Structure of the World*, trans. Rolf A. George [Berkeley: University of California Press, 1967], 293). And he continues: "what about 'nonrational knowledge,' for example, the content of a mystical, ineffable view of God? It does not come into a relation with any knowledge within

the limits that we have so far staked out; it can neither be confirmed nor disconfirmed by any of it; there is no road from the continent of rational knowledge to the island of intuition"; he advises us, at the end, to keep "the heterogeneity" between reason and faith "clearly seen and emphasized" (294–295).

23. This is, of course, an old problem. It goes as far back as the Eunomian controversy in the fourth century A.D. Eunomius held that the *name* of God could give us access to His *essence* "with which it exactly corresponds" (see L. R. Wickham, "*Syntagmation* of Aetius the Anomean," *Journal of Theological Studies* 19 [1968], 537). Such an opinion was harshly castigated by the Cappadocian Fathers and in particularly Gregory of Nyssa, who in a series of treatises (*Contra Eunomium*) showed that names do not and cannot indicate the essence of God (they cannot tell us *what* God is), but they are "signifiers" that can show us *who* and *how* He is (i.e., as Father, Son, etc.) (see Gregory of Nyssa, *Contra Eunomium* in *Gregorii Nysseni Opera*, vol. 2, ed. Werner Jaeger [Leiden: E. J. Brill, 1960]). We will return at greater length to this controversy in the next chapter.

24. See Wittgenstein's comments on the phrase "Jesus is the Lord" in *Culture and Value*, trans. Peter Winch (Chicago: University of Chicago Press, 1980), 33.

25. There are two texts in which the image of *khora* appears: "Khora" (1993), an essay published in the volume *On the Name* (Stanford, Calif.: Stanford University Press, 1995) and originally written for a volume in honor of Jean-Pierre Vernant (*Poikilia: Études offertes à Jean-Pierre Vernant*, 1987), and *Comment ne pas parler: Dénégations* (1987) later translated in English ("How to Avoid Speaking: Denials") and published in the volume *Derrida and Negative Theology*, ed. Harold Coward and Toby Forshay (New York: State University of New York Press, 1992).

26. For a reading equally attentive to Plato and Derrida, see John Sallis, *Chorology: On Beginning in Plato's Timaeus* (Bloomington: Indiana University Press, 1999).

27. "How to Avoid Speaking," 100.

28. Ibid., 104.

29. Ibid., 77. Derrida misreads the theoretical background of Dionysius's theology, which, albeit Christianized, remains Neoplatonic. His misreading then consists in failing to understand what Reiner Schürmann aptly observes, namely, that "upholding the incognizability [i.e., the apophaticism] and the non-being of the one, henology turns Plato against himself" (*Broken Hegemonies*, trans. Reginald Lilly [Bloomington: Indiana University Press, 2003], 143). As Schürmann continues: "[a]greeing with Plato, Plotinus holds that to be is to be intelligible. But contrary to Plato, he discovers that when we speak of intelligible things we always speak of multiple things, be it only of the duality of knowing and known. Now, nothing which implies otherness — or even more so, multiplicity — can be first. Intelligence and being will be derivative because they are intrinsically multiple. This is why, in the Plotinian universe, no being can claim supreme standing. Thus, if it is 'due to the one' that all beings are beings, the one is not itself to be found among them . . . The expression 'supreme Being' thus amounts to nonsense" (ibid.). For the same argument from a scholar of Dionysius see Eric Perl's remarks cited in subsequent notes.

30. Jacques Derrida, *Margins of Philosophy*, trans. Alan Bass (Chicago: University of Chicago Press, 1982), 6 (emphasis in the original). Derrida himself refers to this passage and the ensuing debate with Jean-Luc Marion in "How to Avoid Speaking: Denials," n. 2, 131.

31. Most notably in John D. Caputo's work *The Prayers and Tears of Jacques Der-*

rida (Bloomington: Indiana University Press, 1997). Caputo's analysis can be simplified in the following three steps: (a) *différance* is not God; (b) *différance* is "emblematized by . . . *khora*" (*Prayers and Tears,* 2) and therefore, (c) God is not *khora*. Richard Kearney has convincingly described the dangers to be avoided, as a result of this polarization between God and *khora*, in the chapter "God or *Khora*" from his *Strangers, Gods and Monsters* (London: Routledge, 2003).

32. Jacques Derrida, "How to Avoid Speaking," 108.

33. "Khora," 89.

34. "How to Avoid Speaking," 108.

35. Nowhere is God's lack of otherness more beautifully expressed than in Nicholas of Cusa's dialogue *De Li non Aliud.* Nicholas mentions his influences in the very beginning of his work (the Abbot has been reading Plato's *Parmenides* and Proclus's commentary of the same dialogue, Peter is reading and translating Proclus's *Theology of Plato,* Ferdinand has been reading Aristotle, and Nicholas himself has been studying the works of Dionysius). I will cite a passage of the dialogue and let the reader judge for oneself whether this confirms Derrida's argument of hyperessentiality:

"Ferdinand: Do you wish to say that Not-other is an affirmation or a negation or some such kind of thing?

Nicholas: Not at all. Rather, before all such things . . .

Ferdinand: Does Not-other posit something, or does it remove something?

Nicholas: It is seen prior to all positing and removing.

Ferdinand: Therefore, it is not a substance or a being or one or any other thing whatsoever.

Nicholas: This is my view.

Ferdinand: By the same token, it is neither not-being nor nothing.

Nicholas: This too I regard as surely the case.

Ferdinand: I am following you, Father, as best I can. And it seems to me most certain that Not-other is not comprehended either by way of affirmation or by way of negation or in any other way . . .

Nicholas: . . . Not-other cannot receive otherness or change" (IV, 12, trans. Jasper Hopkins [Minneapolis: Arthur J. Banning, 1987], 1113–1114). It is worth noticing, however, that after Nicholas has reached the most rigorous negation, denying any name and attribute to God, including those of Being, Truth, Goodness, and the One, he supplements the radical transcendence of the Not-other with an equally radical immanence:

"Ferdinand: If I understand you rightly, Not-other is seen before all things in such way that it cannot be absent from any of the things which are seen after it, even if these things are contradictories.

Nicholas: Indeed, this is my view about the truth of the matter" (IV, 14, 1115).

Let us not assume that Nicholas, attempting to negate otherness as a predicate for God, affirms sameness. God as the Not-other stands beyond our conceptual dyads:

"Nicholas: Not-other is not other; nor is it *other* than other [i.e., same]; nor is it other in an other" (VI, 20, 1118).

36. See Eric Perl's masterful exposition of the similarities but also the differences between Neoplatonism and deconstruction in "Signifying Nothing: Being as Sign in Neoplatonism and Derrida," in *Neoplatonism and Contemporary Thought,* vol. 2, ed. Harris R. Baine (Albany: State University of New York, 2002). Perl explains: "no *being* can be the first principle, for to be a being, i.e., to be, is to be derivative" (133). The

One's transcendence of being is, then, logically complemented by its omnipresence in being: "precisely in order to be not somewhere, not any thing, and so not derivative, [the One] must be everywhere, all things" (136).

37. Plotinus, *Enneads*, VI, 9, 8:29–35.

38. "Signifying Nothing," 136.

39. Indeed, *Transcendence and Self-transcendence* is the title of Westphal's book (Bloomington: Indiana University Press, 2004).

40. For instance, see 96, 98, 117, and 137–138.

41. For Kant as a successor of negative theology's legacy, see Hans Urs von Balthasar, *The Glory of the Lord*, vol. V, *The Realm of Metaphysics* (1991), 489–496.

42. Jacques Derrida, "Above All, No Journalists!" in *Religion and Media*, ed. Hent de Vries and Samuel Weber (Stanford, Calif.: Stanford University Press, 2001).

43. As was recently argued by Giorgio Agamben, *Potentialities: Collected Essays in Philosophy*, trans. Daniel Heller-Roazen (Stanford, Calif.: Stanford University Press, 1999), 220–239. For my response to Derrida's arguments, see "The Revelation According to Jacques Derrida," in *Other Testaments: Derrida and Religion*, ed. Kevin Hart and Yvonne Sherwood (London: Routledge, 2005).

44. In his polemical text "On a Hyphen" and the ensuing discussion with Eberhard Gruber, Jean-François Lyotard claims, with a dose of sarcasm, that the hyphen which unities (and separates) Jew and Christian in the expression "Judeo-Christian" "is the highest thought of which Europe has been capable" (*The Hyphen: Between Judaism and Christianity*, trans. Pascale-Anne Brault and Michael Naas [New York: Humanity Books, 1999], 57). Historically, Lyotard argues, the Judeo-Christian hyphen came to be embodied in the flesh, so to speak, of a man that shared both identities: "Shaoul and Paulus" (15). That is why Lyotard's meditations on the hyphen are soon turned into a reading of Paul's letters. The image, however, that assumes a predominant role throughout Lyotard's text is that of the "Voice" (always with a capital "V"). This Voice, of course, is none other than the voice that proclaims "Hear, O Israel . . ." "Adam's desire to speak the language of the Voice," Lyotard informs us, led to his expulsion from Paradise (14). For the Voice is never to be given voice, that is, *flesh* — if Paul breaks with the letter of the Law, it is always, according to Lyotard, because he "acts the perpetually desired Voice instead of acting its letter" (22). In the new era, marked by the advent of Christianity, "the Voice is vocalized, because it offers itself up to be partitioned out, far from paradise, in the abjection of suffering, abandonment, and death. So that reading is in vain. For presence is real, in the Host" (23). That constitutes a major offence as it violates "the interdiction against figuration, which is an interdiction against incarnation, against the temptation to make the Voice itself speak, to make it speak directly and visibly" (24). Lyotard explains: "The Hebraic law forbidding images is not some artistic or ritualistic idiosyncrasy, but a declaration of suspicion concerning the 'visible.' 'Visible' must be understood in the extended sense that Augustine gives it in the *Confessions* as any figure that presents itself as sensible, including the audible. No images mean no transfer onto the imaginary of presence" (59–60). Such statements only confirm our suspicion that iconoclastic convictions mask anti-Incarnational ideologies.

45. For some time a mosque, Kariye Camii or Kariye Djami is used today as a museum. For a detailed analysis and further information on the monastery, its history, and its iconography see A. Underwood, *The Kariye Djami*, 3 vols. (New York: Bollingen Foundation, 1966).

5. Interlude

1. Cant. 3:1–4, in the version of the Septuagint.

2. Οἱ ζητοῦντες τόν Κύριον οὐκ ἐλατωθήσονται παντός ἀγαθοῦ, as a verse of the matins goes — "those who seek God shall not be deprived of any good." What this verse says is that those who are seeking (the God, the source of all good) and who therefore have *not* what they are seeking (for otherwise they would not seek it in the first place) "shall not be deprived" of what they seek — *as if*, and indeed this *is* the case, as if they always had it. The difference between "having" and "not having" collapses. For Florensky, who meditates on this very verse, "it turns out that those who have not are identical to those who have" (*The Pillar and Ground of the Truth*, 32).

3. The biblical passage of Adam's name-giving *(onomatothesia)* to creation must have had a certain bearing in the mind of the Christian bishop and exegete (Gen. 2:19: "And out of the ground the Lord God formed every beast of the field, and every fowl of the air; and brought them unto Adam to see what he would call them: and whatsoever Adam called every living creature, that was the name thereof"). Radical conventionalism could not have been a choice for Gregory. On the other hand, the dangers of linguistic naturalism (à la Eunomius) were imminent and had to be refuted. The hermeneutical thesis was a rather elegant solution.

4. On the one hand, there is the often-attested axiom on the impossibility of such vision: "no one can ever see God" (Ex. 33:20, John 1:18, 1 Tim. 6:14); the passage in question, however (Matt. 5:8), says, "Blessed are the pure in heart for they shall see God."

5. *De Beatitudinibus*, PG (Migne), vol. 44, 1268.

6. Ibid. Dionysius, in the *Divine Names* (a treatise that by its very subject matter had to face this problem), makes use of the same distinction. For "effects," however, Dionysius is using δυνάμεις instead of ἐνέργειαι: "For what is divine and everything which is manifested to us are known by their participations alone. But these — whatever they are in their proper source and foundation — are beyond intellect and beyond all being and knowledge. Thus, if we would name the hiddenness beyond being either 'God,' or 'being,' or 'life,' or 'light,' or 'logos,' we would understand nothing other than the powers [δυνάμεις] which are brought forward out of it into us" (*DN*, II 645A), trans. John D. Jones (Milwaukee: Marquette University Press, 1980), 123.

7. For an evaluation of Gregory's philosophy of language in the light of modern linguistics and post-modern theories, see Alden A. Mosshammer, "Disclosing but Not Disclosed: Gregory of Nyssa as Deconstructionist," in *Studien zu Gregor von Nyssa und der Christlichen Spätantike*, ed. Hubertus R. Drobner and Christoph Klock (Leiden: Brill, 1990), 99–123. Mosshammer "translates" Gregory's position of the ineffable and unknowable nature of God as "a signified without a signifier" (103).

8. However, the differences between Plotinus's usage of *diastema* and Gregory's might not be as stark as T. Paul Verghese seems to suggest ("Διάστημα and διάστασις," in *Gregor von Nyssa und die Philosophie*, ed. Heinrich Dörrie et al. [Leiden: Brill, 1976], 243–260). In both Plotinus and Nyssa *diastema* belongs to the created world, and it is conceived in juxtaposition to eternity (αἰών) that pertains only to God. Verghese's reading of the Soul as ἀδιάστατον (246), a thesis that Gregory could not accept and therefore the point where the two thinkers part ways, is not clearly supported by the text (*Ennead*, III, 7, 13, 63), as it heavily depends on how one understands the preceding clause: "εἰς ὅ γάρ ἐθελήσει." Does the ἀδιάστατον modify this ὅ? Even if we

take ἀδιάστατον to mean the soul, it is far from evident that this is the created (human) soul. Plotinus probably has in mind the eternal (and thus without *diastema*) ψυχήν τοῦ παντός, the Hypostasis Soul, cited a few lines below. I thank Gary Gurtler, S.J., for bringing this point to my attention.

9. In Plotinus, *Ennead* I, 5, 7, 24; in Gregory of Nyssa, *CE* II, 226.

10. *Diastema* is often grouped by Gregory together with color, shape, volume, and other similar attributes of bodies (see *Hex.*, 14; *De Anima*, 124); they all belong to a class of names he calls "circumscribed" (ὀνόματα περιγραπτικά; *Cant.* 157), that is, names of things that occupy space. In *CE*. I, 246, he explicitly links the κτιστὴν οὐσίαν with the "*diastemic* extension" of time and space (διαστηματικῇ τινι παρατάσει . . . χρόνῳ καὶ τόπῳ περιειργομένη).

11. As translated by David L. Balas (slightly modified) in his "Eternity and Time in Gregory of Nyssa's *Contra Eunomium*" in *Gregory von Nyssa und die Philosophie* (cited above), 139. The original text reads as follows: Πολύ γὰρ τὸ μέσον καὶ ἀδιεξίτητον, ᾧ πρὸς τὴν κτιστὴν οὐσίαν ἡ ἄκτιστος φύσις διατετείχισται. Αὕτη πεπεράτωται, ἐκείνη πέρας οὐκ ἔχει· αὕτη τοῖς ἰδίοις μέτροις κατὰ τὸ ἀρέσαν τῇ σοφίᾳ τοῦ πεποιηκότος ἐμπεριείληπται, τῆς δὲ μέτρον ἡ ἀπειρία ἐστίν· αὕτη διαστηματικῇ τινι παρατάσει συμπαρεκτείνεται, καὶ χρόνῳ καὶ τόπῳ περιειργομένη, ἐκείνη ὑπερεκπίπτει πᾶσαν διαστήματος ἔννοιαν . . . ἐν ταύτῃ τῇ ζωῇ καὶ ἀρχὴν τοῖς οὖσι καὶ τέλος ἔστιν ἐπινοῆσαι, ἡ δὲ ὑπέρ τὴν κτίσιν μακαριότης οὔτε ἀρχὴν οὔτε τέλος προσίεται, ἀλλ' ὑπέρ τὸ ἐν ἑκατέρῳ σημαινόμενον πέφυκεν ἀεὶ ὡσαύτως ἔχουσα καὶ ἐφ' ἑαυτῆς βεβηκυῖα, οὐ διαστηματικῶς ἔκ τινος εἴς τι τῇ ζωῇ διοδεύουσα.

12. John Milton, *Paradise Lost*, book 4.

13. L. Wittgenstein, *Tractatus*, 5.6.

14. *In Ecclesiasten Homiliae*, GNO V, 412.

15. In Scot Douglass's translation in "A Critical Analysis of Gregory's Philosophy of Language: The Linguistic Reconstitution of Metadiastemic Intrusions," in *Gregory of Nyssa, Homilies on the Beatitudes*, Proceedings of the Eighth International Colloquium on Gregory of Nyssa, Paderborn, September 14–18, 1998, ed. Hubertus R. Drobner and Albert Viciano (Leiden: Brill, 2000), 455. The passage in Greek reads as follows: Ὡς γὰρ οὐ κρατεῖται πνεῦμα ἐν ὕδατι, ὅταν τινὶ τῶν βαρυτέρων συγκατασπασθὲν ἐναποληφθῇ τῷ βάθει τοῦ ὕδατος, ἀλλ' ἐπὶ τὸ συγγενὲς ἀνατρέχει, τὸ δὲ ὕδωρ πολλάκις τῇ ἀναδρομῇ τοῦ πνεύματος συνεπαίρεται, ἐν λεπτῇ τινι καὶ ὑμενώδει τῇ ἐπιφανείᾳ τῷ ἀερῶδει κύκλῳ περικυρτούμενον, οὕτω καὶ τῆς ἀληθινῆς ζωῆς τῆς ἐγκειμένης τῇ σαρκὶ πρὸς ἑαυτὴν μετὰ τὸ πάθος ἀναδραμούσης καὶ ἡ περὶ αὐτὴν σὰρξ συνεπήρθη, ὑπὸ τῆς θεϊκῆς ἀθανασίας ἀπὸ τῆς φθορᾶς συνανωσθεῖσα ἐπὶ τὸ ἄφθαρτον.

16. "Jesus answered and said unto him, Verily, verily, I say unto thee, Except a man be born from above, he cannot see the kingdom of God. Nicodemus said unto him, How can a man be born when he is old? Can he enter the second time into his mother's womb, and be born? Jesus answered, Verily, verily, I say unto thee, Except a man be born of water and of the Spirit [ἐξ ὕδατος καὶ πνεύματος], he cannot enter into the kingdom of God" (John 3:3–5).

17. "Know ye not, that those baptized into Jesus Christ were baptized into his death? Therefore we are buried with him by baptism into death: that like as Christ was raised up from the dead by the glory of the Father, even so we also should walk in newness of life" (Rom. 6:3–4).

18. "Both λεπτός and ὑμήν have sexual connotations in respect to virginity. The 'circle of air' is impenetrable. If the water pierces the membrane, the ὑμήν, and enters

the space, the bubble ceases to exist. One of Gregory's main critiques of Eunomius is his audacity in entering, penetrating, this space" (Scot Douglass, "A Critical Analysis of Gregory's Philosophy of Language," 456). Here the violence of speech is comparable to that of "rape." The image of virginal hymen, especially in the context of Christ's birth, is a clear allusion to the importance of the Virgin Mary as the sacred *khora* that contains the uncontainable (see the hermeneutics of hyphenation in chapter 5). As Douglass points out: "Because of this function, the space of the Virgin's womb is both finite and infinite, that is, localized yet 'broader than the heavens.' Her womb contains the incontainable, and therefore, is literally κεχαριτωμένη. Like other *metadiastemic intrusions*, it is an impenetrable space. To penetrate the womb, to break the ὑμήν, is to destroy one of the metaphorical poles used to construct this space, Mary's virginity" (460). As the 3rd Ecumenical Council (Ephesus, 431) reminds us, any attack on the status of Mary is an attack on the status of Christ and vice versa.

19. Etymologically, the two words, *hymn* and *hymen*, are related; they derive from the Sanskrit term *syūman* (for "band"). See Edward Ross Wharton, *Etymological Lexicon of Classical Greek* (Chicago: Ares Publishers, 1974), 127. *Hymen* is also the nuptial hymn (the mythological context provided by the legend that wants Hymenaios, son of Aphrodite, to have died on the first night of his wedding). Hjalmar Frisk remarks on the relation of the terms ὑμήν and ὕμνος: "Formal am nächster liegt umzweifelhaft Auschluß an ὑμήν (wie λιμήν: λίμνη, ποιμήν: ποίμνη, u.a.), u.zw. im ursprünglichen Sinn von 'Band, Naht'. . . Die Erklärung kann sich auf eine antike Auffassung stützen (z.b. ὑφάνας ὕμνον), dieser Auffassung sich unmittelbar ergebende Anknüpfung an ὑφὴ, ὑφαίνω" (*Griechisches Etymologisches Wörtbuch*, vol. II [Heidelberg: Carl Winter, 1970], 965). The hypothesis that the common metaphor behind both terms is that of weaving (the hymeneal membrane and the hymnal composition are each similarly "woven" into one "fabric") could provide further evidence for a Marian imagery of weaving (Mary's womb as the loom workshop where Christ's body was woven). For the latter, see Nicholas Constas, "Weaving the Body of God: Proclus of Constantinople, the Theotokos and the Loom of the Flesh," *Journal of Early Christian Studies* 3, no. 2 (1995): 169–194, and more recently, *Proclus of Constantinople and the Cult of the Virgin in Late Antiquity, Homilies 1–5, texts and translations* (Leiden: Brill, 2003).

20. The parallelism between iconic seeing and hymnological hearing has already been noted by Jean-Luc Marion's treatment of Dionysius (*The Idol and Distance*, trans. Thomas A. Carlson [New York: Fordham University Press, 2001]). Marion characterizes the inclusion of "the practice of language within the hierarchical play of distance" as "amount[ing] to treating [language] as an *icon*" (183); God's anonymity "introduces the play of the *icon*" (185); later Marion speaks of "[t]he *iconic* depth of language" (186), which is reflected in praise, for "[p]raise plays the role of a language appropriate to the distance that *iconically* comprehends language itself" (187). The emphasis has been added.

21. *De Visione Dei*, 37. English translation by H. Lawrence Bond (in *Nicholas of Cusa, Selected Spiritual Writings* [New York: Paulist Press, 1997]). Latin edition by Adelaida Dorothea Riemann (in *Opera Omnia*, vol. VI [Hamburg: Felix Meiner, 2000]).

22. Ibid.

23. Ibid., 40.

24. Ibid.

25. From the *Cherubic Wanderer*, quoted by Martin Heidegger, *The Principle of Reason*, trans. Reginald Lilly (Bloomington: Indiana University Press, 1991), 35–40.

26. Milan Kundera, *The Unbearable Lightness of Being*, trans. Michael Henry Heim (New York: Harper & Row, 1984), 94.

27. No thinker has written more eloquently on this subject and with a greater passion than Arthur Schopenhauer (*The World as Will and Representation* [New York: Dover Publications, 1966], vol. I, §52). Schopenhauer begins his discussion of music with a confession of weakness — this is not the shortcoming of the thinker in articulating properly his subject, but rather the failure of thinking itself in grasping what lies beyond it: "I recognize, that it is essentially impossible to demonstrate this explanation, for it assumes and establishes a relation of music as *a representation to that which of its essence can never be representation*, and claims to regard music as *the copy of an original that can itself never be directly represented*" (257; my emphasis). In the heart of this paradox we find again the strange logic that governs the *icon*. As the icon visualizes the Invisible, so music too lends sensibility and form to that which exceeds the senses or the ideas. The iconic character of music (and the hymn in particular) will be underscored later in this chapter. "[M]usic, since it passes over the Ideas, is also quite independent of the phenomenal world, positively ignores it, and, to a certain extent, could still exist even if there were no world at all, which cannot be said of the other arts" (ibid.). Music is, then, placed at the threshold of *diastemic* distinction. What Schopenhauer seems to be saying is that music is "*in* this world but not *of* this world"; or as he puts it, music "expresses the metaphysical to everything physical in the world, the thing-in-itself to every phenomenon" (262). That is why "the composer reveals the innermost nature of the world, and expresses the profoundest wisdom, in a language that his reasoning faculty does not understand, just as a magnetic somnambulist gives information about things of which she has no conception when she is awake" (260). In Bryan Magee's words: "The great composers are the great metaphysicians, penetrating to the centre of things and giving expression to truths about existence in a language that our intellects are unable even to comprehend, let alone translate into concepts or words" (*The Tristan Chord: Wagner and Philosophy* [New York: Metropolitan Books, 2001], 171).

28. "Music always expresses the immediate in its immediacy . . . the immediate is the indeterminate" (Kierkegaard, *Either/Or*, 70). "Reflection is implicit in language, and therefore language cannot express the immediate. Reflection is fatal to the immediate, and therefore it is impossible for language to express the musical" (71).

29. Theodor W. Adorno, *Quasi una Fantasia: Essays on Modern Music*, trans. Rodney Livingstone (London: Verso, 1992), 2.

30. Denys Turner, "Faith, Reason and the Eucharist: Music as a Model for Their Harmony" (unpublished paper delivered at the Boston College Bradley Medieval Lecture Series, November 18, 2005).

31. Ibid.

32. According to Schopenhauer it is a mere coincidence that the same medium is used for both activities: "even the *vox humana* is for it originally and essentially nothing but a modified tone, just like that of an instrument . . . Now in this case it is an accidental circumstance that this very instrument serves in a different way as the organ of speech for the communication of concepts" (*The World as Will and Representation*, vol. II, 448).

33. That words have only a secondary function in song and hymn is evident from

a number of observations: (a) that language in songs does not have to, and often does not, obey the rules of language; (b) that we do not have to know or to understand the language of a song in order to enjoy it (this is the case of opera, where often the text can be, from the listener's experience, irrelevant to the music itself); (c) while in language the simultaneous talk of two or more persons becomes immediately incomprehensible and the result is an experience of meaningless noise, in music polyphonic singing is perceived in quite contrary terms, namely, as harmonious. This is because in the case of language words play the important role; when I am listening to someone talking, I do not pay attention to the sounds his or her vocal apparatus makes but rather to the words he utters. However, both (the "sounds" and the "words") are physically the same — it is my attitude that changes. When, on the other hand, I am listening to a song, the words themselves fade into the background of my attention, and are only perceived as the "vehicle" of music, as sounds. A paradigmatic case of this disparity between music and language is the one described by Slavoj Žižek (*The Fragile Absolute — or, Why Is the Christian Legacy Worth Fighting For?* [London: Verso, 2000]): "The duet from *The Marriage of Figaro* in *The Shawshank Redemption* (the cinema version of King's story) is an exemplary case of the effect of the sublime which relies on the contrast between the poverty and horror of real life and the sudden intrusion of this Other Space. The black convict (Morgan Freeman), whose commentary we hear, claims that he doesn't know what the two ladies are singing about, and it is perhaps better that he doesn't know, but all the men listening to them were, for a brief moment, free . . . What we have here is the effect of the sublime at its purest: the momentary suspension of meaning which elevates the subject into another dimension in which the prison terror has no hold over him. It is deeply significant that the duet is from Mozart (and incidentally, a rather trifling one: the duet from Act III in which the Countess dictates to Susanna the letter destined to trap her unfaithful husband) — can one imagine a more startling contrast than the one between mid-twentieth-century American prison life and the universe of late-eighteenth-century aristocratic love intrigue? *So the true contrast is not simply between the prison horror and the 'divine' Mozart's music but, within music itself, between the sublime dimension of music and the trifling character of its content.* More precisely, what makes the scene sublime is that the poor prisoners, unaware of this trifling content, directly perceive the sublime beauty of the music" (158–159, my emphasis).

34. Ἡδὲ τοῦ παντὸς διακόσμησις ἁρμονία τὶς ἐστι μουσικὴ πολυειδῶς καὶ ποικίλως κατά τινα τάξιν καὶ ῥυθμόν πρὸς ἑαυτὴν ἡρμοσμένη καὶ ἑαυτῇ συνᾴδουσα καὶ μηδέποτα τῆς συμφωνίας ταύτης διασπωμένη, εἰ καὶ πολλὴ τις ἐν τοῖς καθ᾽ ἕκαστον ἡ τῶν ὄντων διαφορὰ θεωρεῖται (*In Inscriptions Psalmorum*, GNO V, 30–31). This is a fascinating locus classicus in the history of ideas: it dates back to the Pythagorean "music of the spheres," and finds its way into Kepler's third law of planetary motion and Schopenhauer's cosmic tonalities, up to string theory of modern physics (see Schopenhauer, *The World as Will and Representation*, vol. I, 258–259; Brian Greene, *The Elegant Universe* [New York: Vintage Books, 1999], 135 ff.).

35. Such a cosmic hymnody is described by Psalm 148:1–13: "Praise ye the Lord. Praise ye the Lord from the heavens: praise him in the heights. / Praise ye him, all his angels: praise ye him, all his hosts. / Praise ye him, sun and moon: praise him, all ye stars of light. / Praise him, ye heavens of heavens, and ye waters that be above the heavens. / Let them praise the name of the Lord: for he commanded, and they were created. / He hath also established them for ever and ever: he hath made a decree

which shall not pass. / Praise the Lord from the earth, ye dragons, and all deeps / Fire, and hail; snow, and vapours; stormy wind fulfilling his word / Mountains, and all hills; fruitful trees, and all cedars / Beasts, and all cattle; creeping things, and flying fowl / Kings of the earth, and all people; princes, and all judges of the earth / Both young men, and maidens; old men, and children / Let them praise the name of the Lord: for his name alone is excellent; his glory is above the earth and heaven."

36. Δείκνυσι δὲ τοῦτο καὶ ἡ ὀργανικὴ τοῦ σώματος ἡμῶν διασκευὴ πρὸς ἐργασίαν μουσικῆς φιλοτεχνηθεῖσα παρὰ τῆς φύσεως. Ὁρᾷς τὸν τῆς ἀρτηρίας αὐλόν, τὴν τῆς ὑπερῴας μαγάδα, τὴν διὰ γλώττης καὶ παρειῶν καὶ στόματος, ὡς διὰ χορδῶν καὶ πλήκτρου, κιθαρῳδίαν (*In Inscriptions Psalmorum*, GNO V, 33).

37. After the title of Angelus Silesius's fragment 366 ("A heart that is calm in its ground, God-still, as he will, / Would gladly be touched by him: it is his lute-play"). See Heidegger, *The Principle of Reason*, 68.

38. Kierkegaard, *Fear and Trembling*, 35.

39. See, for example, chapter 3 of the present work, where I asserted that "in the mystical language of Christian Neoplatonism, the *exaiphnes* becomes emblematic of the sacred time of divine presence, in its tripartite manifestation: historically (in the Incarnation), personally (in visions and apparitions), and eschatologically (in the sacraments of the Church)."

40. "The Indescribable is here accomplished" (*Faust* II, Act V, 12108–12109).

41. Ἀπαγγελῶ τὸ ὄνομά σου τοῖς ἀδελφοῖς μου, ἐν μέσῳ ἐκκλησίας ὑμνήσω σε.

42. "But where it is a matter of God and the divine, the word *hymnein* almost replaces the word 'to say'"; Hans Urs von Balthasar, *The Glory of the Lord*, vol. II: *Studies in Theological Styles: Clerical Styles*, trans. Andrew Louth et al. (San Francisco: Ignatius Press, 1984), 173. For Balthasar this is far from being accidental: "the 'hymnic' is therefore for Denys a methodology of theological thinking and speaking" (160). Von Balthasar counts 108 times of such a replacement in the *Divine Names* (173, n. 81). Marion follows suit: "Denys tends to substitute for the *to say* of predicative language another verb, ὑμνεῖν, to praise" (*ID*, 184 and n. 68, where Marion provides a sampling of textual evidence).

43. Dionysius raises this question himself in *DN*, I 593B: "And if [the superessential ray] is above language and knowledge and any kind of intellection and essence . . . and there is neither sensation nor imagination, neither opinion nor name, neither language nor contact or science of it, how is then our *On the Divine Names* treatise supposed to examine the superessential divinity, since it has been shown to be unnameable and ineffable?"

44. The variations of this theme are countless; here are some instances: God is beyond παντός λόγου καὶ πάσης γνώσεως καὶ ὑπὲρ νοῦν (I 593B); παντὸς λόγου καὶ νοῦ καὶ σοφίας (VII 865D); νοῦ παντός καὶ λόγου (VII 868D); πάντα λόγον καί νοῦν ὑπεραῖρον (VII 869D); οὔτε νοεῖται οὔτε λέγεται οὔτε ὀνομάζεται (VII 872A); ὑπὲρ πάντα καὶ ὅρον καὶ λόγον (IX 913C); ὑπὲρ πάντα καὶ λόγον καὶ νοῦν (XIII 981A); τὸ ὑπὲρ πᾶν ὄνομα καὶ πάντα λόγον καὶ γνῶσιν (XIII 981B).

45. John D. Jones's translation, 110, modified. Jones is right, in this context as elsewhere, to break into verse.

46. Contrary to what Derrida claims in his "How to Avoid Speaking": "how can one deny that the encomium qualifies God and *determines* prayer, *determines* the other, Him to whom it addresses itself, refers, invoking Him even as the source of prayer? How can one deny that, in this movement of determination (which is no lon-

ger the pure address of the prayer to the other), the appointment of the *trinitary* and hyperessential God distinguishes Dionysius's *Christian* prayer from all other prayer?" (111, emphasis in the original).

47. Rainer Maria Rilke, *The Book of Hours: Prayers to a Lowly God*, bilingual edition, trans. Annemarie S. Kidder [Evanston, Ill.: Northwestern University Press, 2001], 7–9.

6. Postlude

1. After John D. Jones's translation, 131, largely modified for accuracy; emphasis added.

2. That makes it immediately a controversial locus in the debate regarding the authenticity and authorship of the Dionysian corpus — a debate that, for our purposes, is irrelevant.

3. See, for example, Hans Urs von Balthasar's comments on the subject: "The whole theology of the Areopagite is for him a single, sacred *liturgical* act" (*The Glory of the Lord*, vol. 2, 153) and "because all theology is for him a glorious *celebration* of the divine mysteries and therefore has its archetype and pattern in the *liturgical* songs of heavens" (160), and finally "theology is exhausted in the act of wondering *adoration* before the unsearchable beauty in every manifestation" (170; my emphasis). See also Alexander Golitzin, "'Suddenly Christ': The Place of Negative Theology in the Mystagogy of Dionysius Areopagites," in *Mystics: Presence and Aporia*, ed. Michael Kessler and Christian Sheppard (Chicago: University of Chicago Press, 2003).

4. Thus, confirming Marion's much-debated statement, only the celebrant (as hymnologist) is the true theologian (see Marion, *God without Being*, 153).

5. *DN*, VII, 1, 868A.

6. See Zizioulas (Metropolitan of Pergamos), *Being as Communion*: "By developing the 'liturgy of the word' as an integral part of the eucharistic liturgy, the Church did nothing but eschatologize the historical, i.e., make the apostolic kerygma come to the Church not simply from the side of the past but simultaneously from the side of the future" (191). A note on the same page explains how the eschatological character of the readings is indicated: "this is why the reading is traditionally *sung* and not just read didactically" (emphasis in the original). It is rather unfortunate that the liturgical practice in most churches today has effaced the eschatological/doxological intonation of the readings by substituting it with a prosaic, didactic reading that reflects a rather secular understanding of the function of the Scripture in liturgy.

7. "Διώκω δε εἰ καὶ καταλάβω, ἐφ᾽ ᾧ καὶ κατελήμφθην ὑπὸ Χριστοῦ Ἰησοῦ."

8. For a fuller treatment of this oblivion, see K. Rahner, *Hearers of the Word*, trans. M. Richards (New York: Herder and Herder, 1969). I thank Gary Gurtler, S.J., for bringing this work to my attention.

9. Hans Urs von Balthasar, *Explorations in Theology*, vol. II: *Spouse of the Word* (San Francisco: Ignatius Press, 1991), 475.

10. The only systematic attempt to such a phenomenology that I am aware of is the work of Don Ihde (see *Listening and Voice: A Phenomenology of Sound* [Athens: Ohio University Press, 1976]; "Studies in the Phenomenology of Sound," *International Philosophical Quarterly* [1940], 232–251; and "Some Auditory Phenomena," *Philosophy Today* 10, no. 4 [1966], 227–235). The reference to *akoumena* is taken from F. Joseph Smith's study "Heidegger and Insights Leading to a Phenomenology of Sound," quoted by Ihde in *Philosophy Today*.

11. Von Balthasar, *Spouse of the Word*, 476.

12. "Studies in the Phenomenology of Sound," 238.

13. Ibid., 249.

14. What is described here would correspond to Marion's second mode of manifestation (surprise) of the givenness of *l'adonné*. Marion writes: "the interloqué, resulting from a summons, is taken and overwhelmed (taken over or surprised) by a seizure. But this seizure determines him all the more radically as it remains (or can remain) of indeterminate origin. The call surprises by seizing the gifted without always teaching him what it might be. It reduces him to merely watching for, freezes him in place, puts him in immobile availability for what might not finally come or indeed ever begin. The gifted gives all his attention to an essentially lacking object; he is open to an empty gap. Such a gap, imposed on the *self/me* without giving him knowledge of it, therefore contradicts all ecstasy of knowledge, by which the transcendental I constituted, in front of itself and in an on principle transparent evidence, the object. Surprise, this obscure and suffered seizure, contradicts intentionality, this known and knowing ecstasy deployed by the I at its own initiative" (*Being Given*, 268–269).

15. Von Balthasar, *Spouse of the Word*, 475–476, my emphasis.

16. In particular chapter 5 ("The Ear of the Virginal Body": The Poetics of Sound in the School of Proclus) in *Proclus of Constantinople and the Cult of the Virgin in Late Antiquity.*

17. Theodotus of Ancyra (hom. 4), as quoted by Constas, ibid., 279.

18. Proclus (hom. 36), as quoted by Constas, ibid., 280.

19. As quoted by Constas, ibid., 281.

20. See ibid., 306.

21. Ibid., 312.

7. Touch Me, Touch Me Not

1. Elias Canetti, *Crowds and Power*, trans. Carol Stewart (New York: Farrar, Straus and Giroux, 1962), 15.

2. Ibid., 207.

3. Ibid., 15; emphasis added.

4. According to Sartre's analysis, first I learned to use my body as an instrument and then to recognize it as my body: "The child has known for a long time how to grasp, to draw toward himself, to push away, and to hold on to something before he first learns to pick up his hand and to look at it. Frequent observation has shown that the child of two months does not see his hand as *his* hand. He looks at it, and if it is outside his visual field, he turns his head and seeks his hand with his eyes as if it did not depend on him to bring the hand back within his sight" (*Being and Nothingness*, 469).

5. "Far from the body being first *for us* and revealing things to us, it is the instrumental-things which in their original appearance indicate our body to us. The body is not a screen between things and ourselves; it manifests only the individuality and the contingency of our original relation to instrumental-things" (ibid., 428).

6. Ibid., 217.

7. Martin Heidegger, *Parmenides*, trans. André Schuwer and Richard Rojcewicz (Bloomington: Indiana University Press, 1992), 80.

8. Heidegger, *What Is Called Thinking?* 16.

9. See, for example, David M. Levin, ed., *Modernity and the Hegemony of Vision* (Berkeley: University of California Press, 1993), and Jay Martin, *Downcast Eyes:*

The Denigration of Vision in Twentieth-Century Thought (Berkeley: University of California Press, 1993).

10. S. H. Rosen, "Thought and Touch: A Note on Aristotle's *De Anima*," *Phronesis* (1961), 132.

11. According to W. D. Ross's commentary, the metaphor of touch in this context implies "(1) the absence of any possibility of error . . . (2) the apparent absence of a medium in the case of touch. τό θιγεῖν means an apprehension which is infallible and direct." *Metaphysics*, vol. II (Oxford: Oxford University Press, 1924), 277.

12. Heidegger, *The Principle of Reason*, 48.

13. Heidegger, "On the Essence and Concept of Φύσις in Aristotle's *Physics* B1," in *Pathmarks*, 185.

14. We should note here that the description of the body's subjectivity (the For-itself) in Sartre's *Being and Nothingness* (404–445) bears the telling subtitle "facticity"—the subject-body is already from the beginning posited as the product of a "facere."

15. "From the beginning of Aristotle's thematic observations in the *Physics*, the kind of being called φύσει ὄντα is contrasted with that of τέχνη ὄντα. The former is that which brings itself forth by arising out of itself, the latter is that which is brought forth through human planning and production." Heidegger, "Anaximander's Saying," in *Off the Beaten Track*, 244.

16. "How does the causal theory of nature arise? Could natural causality impose itself on the mind because before all else man experiences *himself* as a cause? He fabricates works. Beside these, he observes things that grow and that he does not fabricate. Nature is a *cause, too*. Could his causal conception of nature then arise out of his experience of human fabrication, as a transposition of it? For Heidegger, only because there is a cause of artefacts—namely, man—has '*phusis* been taken from the outset as "cause,"' as the *other cause*." R. Schürmann, *Heidegger On Being and Acting: From Principles to Anarchy*, trans. Christine-Marie Gros (Bloomington: Indiana University Press, 1987), 86.

17. For the origin of the term *energeia* out of craftsmanship and tool-making as well as for its role in Aristotle's thought, see Stephen Menn, "The Origins of Aristotle's Concept of Ἐνέργεια: Ἐνέργεια and Δύναμις," in *Ancient Philosophy* 14 (1994), 73–114.

18. See Richard Sorabji, "Body and Soul in Aristotle," in *Articles on Aristotle*, vol. 4: *Psychology and Aesthetics*, ed. J. Barnes, M. Schofield, and R. Sorabji (London: Duckworth, 1979), 47. The same can be said about the consciousness phenomenologically defined: "consciousness is aware of itself *in so far as it is consciousness of a transcendent object*" (Jean-Paul Sartre's *The Transcendence of the Ego*, trans. Forrest Williams and Robert Kirkpatrick [New York: Hill and Wang, 1960], 40; Sartre's emphasis). On the basis of this principle, Sartre judges the transcendental Ego a superfluous and rather harmful addition to any phenomenology: "When I run after a streetcar, when I look at the time, when I am absorbed in contemplating a portrait, there is no *I*. There is consciousness *of the streetcar-having-to-be-overtaken*, etc., and non-positional consciousness of consciousness. In fact, I am then plunged into the world of objects; it is they which constitute the unity of my consciousness; it is they which present themselves with values, with attractive and repellent qualities—but *me*, I have disappeared; I have annihilated myself" (48–49).

19. Jean-Louis Chrétien, *The Call and the Response*, trans. Anne A. Davenport (New York: Fordham University Press, 2004), 84; my emphasis.

20. Ibid., 120.

21. Sartre, *Being and Nothingness*, 417.

22. Ibid.

23. Ibid., 419.

24. "Thus the perception of my body is placed chronologically *after* the perception of the body of the Other." Ibid., 469–470; my emphasis.

25. Ibid., 447; my emphasis.

26. As Aristotle noted earlier regarding the *nous*: παρεμφαινόμενον γὰρ κωλύει τὸ ἀλλότριον καὶ ἀντιφράττει· ὥστε μηδ' αὐτοῦ εἶναι φύσιν μηδεμίαν ἀλλ' ἢ ταύτην, ὅτι δυνατός, that is, "the intrusion of any other characteristic would be obstructive [of its knowing the things], therefore it must have no characteristic, absolutely none but this: the capacity [to be everything else]" (429a 20–22).

27. This is a posthumous note made by Freud — Derrida plays with the ambiguity of the phrase "the soul is extended (or distended), she knows (or I know) nothing about it"; Jacques Derrida, *Le Toucher: Jean-Luc Nancy* (Paris: Éditions Galilée, 2000), 21 ff.

28. Rosen, "Thought and Touch," 136.

29. See Conrad Phillip Kottak, *Anthropology* (New York: McGraw-Hill, 2004), 109–113.

30. S. Zuckerman, *The Social Life of Monkeys and Apes* (London, 1932) as quoted by Canetti, *Crowds and Power*, 214.

31. Ibid., 214.

32. Ibid., 216.

33. Chrétien, *The Call and the Response*, 89–90.

34. Sartre, *Being and Nothingness*, 511.

35. Ibid., 511–512.

36. Levinas, *Totality and Infinity*, 259.

37. "It is not an intentionality of disclosure but of search: a movement unto the invisible" (ibid., 258).

38. Ibid., 258; emphasis added.

39. "Alongside of the night as anonymous rustling of the *there is* extends the night of the erotic, behind the night of insomnia the night of the hidden, the clandestine, the mysterious, land of the virgin . . . immersed in the false security of the elemental" (ibid., 258–259). Jacques Derrida has dedicated a chapter of his *Le Toucher: Jean-Luc Nancy* to Levinas's phenomenology of the caress (chapter IV, "L'intouchable ou le vœu d'abstinence"), where he does not fail to note that the Levinasian caress *inverts* the structure of the ethical (see, in particular, 107). See also Ellen T. Armour's comment: "Levinas's description of the caress amounts to an inversion (or even perversion) of the ethical" ("Touching Transcendence," in *Derrida and Religion*, ed. Kevin Hart and Yvonne Sherwood [London: Routledge, 2005], 355).

40. Sartre, *Being and Nothingness*, 507.

41. Ibid., 506–507.

42. Ibid., 508.

43. "The subjectivity of sensibility, taken as incarnation, is an abandon without return, maternity, a body suffering for another, the body as passivity and renouncement, a pure undergoing." Emmanuel Levinas, *Otherwise than Being, or Beyond Essence*, trans. Alphonso Lingis (Pittsburgh, Penn.: Duquesne University Press, 1981), 79.

44. Sartre, *Being and Nothingness*, 508.

45. Ibid., 460.

46. Ibid., 461.

47. Ibid., 463.

48. Levinas, *Otherwise than Being,* 76–77.

49. Proclus, *Elements of Theology,* Part III, preposition xv, "Πᾶν τὸ πρὸς ἑαυτὸ ἐπιστρεπτικὸν ἀσώματόν ἐστιν" (ed. E. R. Dodds [Oxford: Clarendon Press, 1963]). The body cannot convert or return to itself, therefore it is the only corporeality.

50. See Sorabji, "Aristotle on Demarcating the Five Senses," in *Articles on Aristotle,* vol. 4, 88.

51. Meister Eckhart, *Sermon 48* (in the Classics of Western Spirituality), trans. Edmund Colledge, O.S.A., and Bernard McGinn (Paulist Press, 1981), 197; emphasis added.

52. The problematic of this paragraph would remind a reader of Kant with certain passages (if only in reverse) from the *Critique of Pure Reason.* Indeed, Aristotle's description of the mechanism of perception seems to suggest that a priori judgments (the soul's immediate knowledge of the forms) cannot, in fact, be anything else but synthetic (as given by experience).

53. This is indeed the sole principle on which von Balthasar's theological aesthetics is built. He describes it in the opening pages of the first volume of his *Herrlichkeit* as follows: "The doctrine of the beholding and perceiving *(Wahrnehmen)* of the beautiful ('aesthetics' in the sense of the *Critique of Pure Reason*) and the doctrine of the enrapturing power of the beautiful are complementarily structured, since no one can really behold who has not also already been enraptured, and no one can be enraptured who has not already perceived" (10; for concrete application of this double structure throughout Balthasar's work see *The Glory of the Lord,* vol. I, 119, 125, 135, 151, and 182).

54. "Each one of us is a fragment of a man" (ἕκαστος οὖν ἡμῶν ἐστιν ἀνθρώπου ξύμβολον; *Symposium* 191d).

55. See, for instance, Merleau-Ponty's remark: "If one wants metaphors, it would be better to say that the body sensed and the body sentient are as the obverse and the reverse, or again, as two segments of one sole circular course which goes above from left to right and below from right to left, but which is but one sole movement in its two phases" *(The Visible and the Invisible,* 138).

56. Michel Henry, *Philosophy and Phenomenology of the Body,* trans. Girard Etzkorn (The Hague: Martinus Nijhoff, 1975), 119.

57. These are the questions raised by Henry in that chapter entitled "The Twofold Usage of Signs" (ibid.). I disagree, however, with the solution suggested by Henry: the unity of the two phenomena is neither to be grounded on the effortlessness of motion (122), nor on the abstraction of an "organic" body that synthesizes the two phenomena on the basis of their being "equally at our disposal" (123). For Henry, the ultimate concept on which he traces his reading of Maine de Biran is movement in its most vulgar sense, that of locomotion: "Therefore, it is movement which maintains the being of the organic body at the same time as it confers upon it its unity and its belonging to the ego" (126). For Henry, "*I* move, therefore *I* am." The problem with such a thesis is that it has not advanced a single step since Aristotle's *Physics* and the casting of being in terms of *kinesis* (see my comments on the ergological difference above).

58. Ibid., 115–116.

59. "What we intend to signify when we speak of ontological dualism is merely

the necessity of the existence of this sphere of absolute subjectivity without which our experience of the world would not be possible" (ibid., 117).

60. Modern philosophy, on the other hand, has consistently thought of man as a thing: it is not an accident that for both Descartes and Spinoza man is defined as *res cogitans* ("Sed quid igitur sum? Res cogitans"; *Meditations*, II; see also *Ethics*, II).

61. Cf. Pavel Florensky's similar observation: "strictly speaking, only a person is known and only by a person" (*The Pillar and Ground of Truth*, 56).

62. Maurice Merleau-Ponty, *Phenomenology of Perception*, trans. Colin Smith (London: Routledge, 2002), 246.

63. Ibid., 248.

64. Ibid.

65. *Sensible* is used here in both senses of the word, as sensory and as making sense *(sinnvoll)*.

66. ἡ δὲ γνῶσις ἀγάπη γίνεται ("for knowledge becomes love," Gregory of Nyssa, *An et res.*, *PG*, 46, 96). See also "What Love Knows," in Marion's *Prolegomena to Charity*, 153–169.

67. *On the Song of Songs*, 8: 6 (vol. I, trans. Kilian Walsh, OCSO [Kalamazoo, Mich.: Cistercian Publications, 1971], 49).

68. Augustine, *De Doctrina Christiana*, I, 3 ff.

8. The Sabbath of Experience

1. Nicholas James Perella, *The Kiss Sacred and Profane* (Berkeley: University of California Press, 1969), 39.

2. Touch and contact, if not the prevailing paradigms, are certainly very important metaphors, employed often by the Fathers, most notably the Cappadocians, as almost "technical" terms to describe the event of the Incarnation. See, for example, Gregory of Nyssa's *Catechetical Oration* (PG, 45, 49A: τί ἐπαισχύνονται τῇ ὁμολογίᾳ τοῦ Θεόν ἀνθρωπίνης ἅψασθαι φύσεως;) and Basil the Great's *Letter 262* (PG, 32, 973C: ἔπειτα, πῶς εἰς ἡμᾶς διέβη ἡ τῆς ἐνανθρωπήσεως ὠφέλεια, εἰ μὴ τό ἡμέτερον σῶμα, τῇ θεότητι *συναφθέν*, κρεῖττον ἐγένετο τῆς τοῦ θανάτου ἐπικρατείας;). The terminology of "contact" (σύναψις) is preferred over the language of "change" (τροπή or μεταβολή) with regard to the Incarnation, for in contact both natures — the divine and the human — are united without confusion or change, that is, in accordance with the Christological dogma as it would come to be famously defined later in Chalcedon.

3. Ἡμὲν ἄλλα παντὸς μοῖραν μετέχει, νοῦς δὲ ἐστιν ἄπειρον καὶ αὐτοκρατές καὶ μέμεικται οὐδενί χρήματι, ἀλλὰ μόνος αὐτὸς ἐπ᾽ ἑωυτοῦ ἐστιν. (Fragment 12, in Diels-Kranz, *Die Fragmente der Vorsokratiker*, vol. II, Berlin, 1935).

4. See, for example, the exhaustive collection of Asclepius's representations in the *Lexicon Iconographicum Mythologiae Classicae* (Zurich: Artemis Verlag, 1984).

5. Bernard of Clairvaux, *On the Song of Songs*, 2:5 (vol. I, 11).

6. See, for example, the episode with the centurion, narrated by Matthew earlier (Matt. 8:5–13). The centurion, very much alike Jairus, asks Christ to heal his servant. But contrary to Jairus, when Christ agrees to visit his house in order to heal his servant, the centurion deems himself unworthy of such a visit: "Lord, I am not worthy that thou should come under my roof: but speak the word only, and my servant shall be healed" (8:8).

7. Origen based this idea on a textual variation of Prov. II, 5, that is not found

in the critical text of the LXX. The doctrine of the spiritual senses influenced greatly not only Origen's own exegetical work but also the subsequent tradition (see, e.g., Gregory of Nyssa's hermeneutical principle as it is applied throughout the *Commentary on the Song of Songs* and defined in the following words: "we learn *in passim* something more, another doctrine of this book's philosophy, namely that our sense [αἴσθησις] is somehow dual, a carnal one [σωματική] and one divine, as the Proverbs mention somewhere that 'you will find a divine sense'; the soul's effects [τοῖς ψυχικοῖς ἐνεργήμασι] stand in analogy with the senses of the body"; *GNO*, VI, 34). For a more detailed exposition of Origen's doctrine of the spiritual senses see K. Rahner, "Le Debut d'une doctrine des cinq sens spirituels chez Origène," *Revue d'Ascétisme et de Mysticisme* 13 (1932): 113–145.

    8. *On First Principles*, I:9, trans. G. W. Butterworth (Gloucester: Peter Smith, 1973), 14.

    9. Von Balthasar, *The Glory of the Lord*, vol. 2, 321–333.

    10. "So in the presence of God, the worldly tree of the senses seems to be inverted, and the lowest sense [i.e., touch] becomes the highest" (ibid., 324, n. 311).

    11. Ibid.

    12. Origen, *On First Principles*, 110; emphasis added.

    13. *Die griechischen christlichen Schriftsteller der ersten drei Jahrhunderte: Origenes Werke*, ed. E. Klostermann, vol. XII, Fragment 182 (Leipzig, 1941).

    14. As John Chrysostom points out (in *In Matthaeum*, XXXI, PG 57, 371).

    15. "And one of the Pharisees desired him that he would eat with him. And he went into the Pharisee's house, and sat down to dine. And, behold, a woman in the city, which was a sinner, when she knew that Jesus sat to dine in the Pharisee's house, brought an alabaster box of ointment, and stood at his feet behind him weeping, and began to wash his feet with tears, and did wipe them with the hairs of her head, and kissed his feet and anointed them with the ointment" (Luke 7:36–38).

    16. See chapter 5, n. 19.

    17. See Christopher M. McDonough's study on a passage from Ovid's *Fasti*, "Carna, Proca and the *Strix* on the Kalends of June," *Transactions of the American Philological Association* 127 (1997), 315–344, especially 331.

    18. G. K. Chesterton, *The Everlasting Man* (San Francisco: Ignatius Press, 1993), 172.

    19. Indeed, on several other occasions, the resurrected Christ not only does not prohibit the touch of the disciples but urges it. The exhortation to doubting Thomas— "put your finger here and see my hands and reach out your hand and put it into my side" (John 20:27)—is famous. Luke's gospel records a more telling episode: to the disciples fearing that they see a ghost, Christ says, "touch me and see; a ghost does not have flesh and bones, as you see me have" (24:39), and to further prove His corporeality He asks to be given some food to eat.

    20. "Do not hold on to me" is the translation that the New International Version gives; "stop holding on to me" is how the New American Bible translates the passage in question. Other translations that follow a similar interpretive line are "do not hold me" (Worldwide English) and "stop clinging to Me" (New American Standard Bible).

    21. A masterful theological exposition of the connection between the doctrine of Ascension and the Eucharist (as well as the Eucharistic Ecclesiology) is to be found in Douglas Farrow's *Ascension and Ecclesia: On the Significance of the Doctrine of the*

Ascension for Ecclesiology and Christian Cosmology (Grand Rapids, Mich.: Eerdmans, 1999). I regret that Farrow's beautiful treatment of the Ascension came to my attention once this work was completed and thus too late to be taken into full account.

22. See Brown, *The Gospel of John and Epistles of John,* 56.

23. Werner Jaeger (ed.), *Gregorii Nysseni Opera,* vol. IX (Leiden: Brill, 1940–).

24. Quotations taken from 309 and 274, respectively. The last passage has properly become part of the Eastern Church's office for the matins of Holy Saturday. I would like to thank Nicholas Constas for bringing these texts to my attention.

25. It is God's withdrawal that occasions God's giving (in this case, His creating), as Marion has demonstrated in the five studies that are included in his *The Idol and Distance.* Only such withdrawal can qualify the distance (another key term in Marion's work) of God's transcendence. It is not accidental that we speak here of *distance* and not of *difference* (see chapters 4 and 5 of the present work).

26. What Jean-Luc Nancy calls the *"extranéation* of the self" in "Dies Illa: (From One End to the Infinite, Or of Creation)," *Journal of the British Society for Phenomenology* 32 (2001), 275, n. 18. By "the Creator's self-annihilation," I understand both the self-contraction of God (the *tsim-tsoum* of the Kabala) and Christ's double "self-contraction," who, as Paul writes, "being in very nature God, did not consider equality with God something to be grasped, *but made himself nothing,* taking the very nature of a servant, being made in human likeness. And being found in appearance as a man, he humbled himself and became obedient to death — even death on a cross!" (Phil. 2:6–8).

27. All of these are, of course, old questions addressed by Origen (see, e.g., Tzamalikos's *The Concept of Time in Origen* [Bern: Peter Lang, 1991]) and Augustine (see, in particular, book XI of the *Confessions*).

28. Nancy, "Dies Illa," 267.

29. Ibid., 275, n. 19.

30. "Elle [l'idée platonicienne] s'est formée en partie parce que l' homme s'est générale intéressé à ses modes de production, à ce qu'il peut produire lui-même, et pour chercher l'*ousia,* l'essence, la substance, il a cherché de quelle façon il construisait des objets, il fabriquait des objets. Ainsi, au lieu de l'idée de présence génerale, nous avons comme point de départ l'idée d'une fabrication d'objets ou d'ouvres d'art qui peuvent être très belles mais *ergon*" (Jean Wahl, *Sur l'interprétation de l'histoire de la métaphysique d'après Heidegger* [Paris: Centre de Documentation Universitaire, 1951], 30).

31. "what strikes the mind in the Greek classical age is that there is becoming, and first of all a becoming of which man is the author and master. Both metaphysics and logic derive from the astonishment before what *our hands can make* out of some material" (Schürmann, *From Principles to Anarchy,* 99; emphasis added).

32. An alternative to the experience founded upon the concept of production and work is offered by "the experience of the Absolute" as exemplified in liturgy. A short passage from Lacoste's *Experience and the Absolute* should suffice in showing the direction that our thought should follow: "the liturgical experience eludes the network of *bonum utilis* by virtue of its essence, and . . . we would not do justice to liturgy were we to fail to understand its uselessness . . . [Liturgy] produces nothing that could possibly be handled, admired, sold, or given. It is utterly foreign to the logic of *action:* it does not set itself up so as to furnish a solution to the problems of the polis, even though it resolves, in a symbolic manner which demands that the limits of the symbol be surpassed, the contradictions of political and social experience. This requires, then,

that we specify by what logic liturgy can resist modernity's equation of Being and doing in order to appear as the rather remarkable figure we will call 'inoperativity,' the refusal to enter into any logic of production in the name of a logic bound up with more urgent stakes" (77–78).

33. "God himself sacrifices himself for the guilt of mankind, God himself makes payment to himself, God as the only being who can redeem man from what has become unredeemable for man himself—the creditor sacrifices himself for his debtor, out of love (can one credit that?), out of love for his debtor!" (F. Nietzsche, *The Genealogy of Morals*, trans. Walter Kaufmann and R. J. Hollingdale [New York: Vintage Books, 1989], 90).

BIBLIOGRAPHY

Adorno, Theodor W. *Quasi una Fantasia: Essays on Modern Music.* Translated by Rodney Livingstone. London: Verso, 1992.

Agamben, Giorgio. *Potentialities: Collected Essays in Philosophy.* Translated by Daniel Heller-Roazen. Stanford, Calif.: Stanford University Press, 1999.

———. *Le Temps qui reste: un commentaire de l'Épître aux Romains.* Paris: Bibliothèque Rivages, 2000. Translated by Patricia Dailey as *The Time That Remains.* Stanford, Calif.: Stanford University Press, 2005.

———. "Time and History: Critique of the Instant and the Continuum." In *Infancy and History: The Destruction of Experience,* trans. Liz Heron, 95–107. London: Verso, 1993.

———. "The Time That Is Left." *Epoché* 7, no. 1 (2002): 1–14.

Aristotle. *Μετά τά Φυσικά. Scriptorum Classicorum Bibliotheca Oxoniensis.* Edited by W. Jaeger. Oxford: Oxford University Press, 1957.

———. *Περί Ψυχῆς. Scriptorum Classicorum Bibliotheca Oxoniensis.* Edited by W. Jaeger. Oxford: Oxford University Press, 1961.

———. *Τά Φυσικά. Scriptorum Classicorum Bibliotheca Oxoniensis.* Edited by W. Jaeger. Oxford: Oxford University Press, 1936.

Armour, Ellen T. "Touching Transcendence." In *Derrida and Religion,* ed. Kevin Hart and Yvonne Sherwood. London: Routledge, 2005.

Augustine. *Confessions.* Translated by F. J. Sheed. Indianapolis: Hackett, 1942.

Austin, J. L. *How to Do Things with Words.* 1962. Cambridge, Mass.: Harvard University Press, 1975.

Bailly, Christoph. *Adieu: essai sur la mort des dieux.* La Tour d'Aigues: Éditions de l'Aube, 1989.

Balas, David, L. "Eternity and Time in Gregory of Nyssa's *Contra Eunomium.*" In *Gregory von Nyssa und die Philosophie,* ed. Heinrich Dörrie, Margarete Altenburger, and Uta Schramm. Leiden: Brill, 1976.

Balthasar, Hans Urs von. *Explorations in Theology. Vol. II: Spouse of the Word.* San Francisco: Ignatius Press, 1991.

———. *The Glory of the Lord: A Theological Aesthetics.* 7 vols. Translated by Erasmo Leiva-Merikakis et al. San Francisco: Ignatius Press, 1982–1991.

Barthes, Roland. "Semiology and Medicine." In *The Semiotic Challenge,* trans. Richard Howard, 202–213. New York: Hill and Wang, 1988.

Bataille, Georges. *L'Expérience intérieure.* Vol. I of *Somme athéologique.* Paris, 1945.

———. *Histoire de l'œil.* Paris: Pauvert, 1967.

———. *Somme athéologique.* 3 vols. Paris: Gallimard, 1945–1954.

Baudinet, Marie-José. "The Face of Christ: The Form of the Church." In *Fragments for a History of the Human Body,* part 1, ed. Michael Feher, Ramona Naddaff, and Nadia Tazi, 149–155. New York: Zone Books, 1989.

Bearsley, P. "Augustin and Wittgenstein on Language." *Philosophy* 58 (1983): 229–236.

Benjamin, Walter. *Gesammelte Schriften.* Edited by Rolf Tiedemann and Hermann Schweppenhäuser with the assistance of Theodor W. Adorno and Gershom Scholem. Frankfurt: Suhrkamp, 1972–1989.

Bibliography

Bergson, Henri. *Les deux sources de la morale et la religion*. Paris: Presses Universitaires de France, 1932, 1951.

Bernard of Clairvaux. *On the Song of Songs*. 4 vols. Translated by Kilian Walsh, OCSO. Kalamazoo, Mich.: Cistercian Publications, 1971.

Besançon, Alain. *The Forbidden Image*. Translated by Jane Marie Todd. Chicago: University of Chicago Press, 2000.

Birault, Henri. "Philosophie et théologie: Heidegger et Pascal." In *Heidegger*, ed. Michel Haar, 514–541. *Cahier de l'Herne*. Paris: Éditions de l'Herne, 1983.

Birus, Hendrik. "'Ich bin, der ich bin': über die Echo eines Namens." In *Juden in der deutschen Literatur: ein deutsch-israelisches Symposium*, ed. Stéphane Moses and Albrecht Schöne, 25–53. Frankfurt: Suhrkamp, 1986.

Bloechl, Jeffrey. *The Face of the Other and the Trace of God*. New York: Fordham University Press, 2000.

———, ed. *Religious Experience and the End of Metaphysics*. Bloomington: Indiana University Press, 2003.

Bohm, David. *Quantum Theory*. London: Constable, 1954.

Bonhoeffer, Dietrich. *Works, Vol. 6: Ethics*. Translated by Reinhard Krauss, Charles C. West, and Douglas W. Stott. Minneapolis: Fortress Press, 2005.

Borges, Jorge Luis. *Selected Poems* (bilingual edition). Edited by A. Coleman. New York: Viking, 1999.

Boyarin, Daniel. *A Radical Jew: Paul and the Politics of Identity*. Berkeley: University of California Press, 1994.

Brkic, Pero. *Martin Heidegger und die Theologie: ein Thema in dreifacher Fragestellung*. Mainz: Matthias Grünewald, 1994.

Brown, Raymond E. *The Gospel of John and Epistles of John: A Concise Commentary*. Collegeville, Minn.: Liturgical Press, 1988.

Bultmann, Rudolf. *History and Eschatology*. Edinburgh: T&T Clark, 1957.

Burnyeat, M. F. "Wittgenstein and Augustin 'De Magistro.'" *Proceedings of the Aristotelian Society* 61 (1987): 1–24.

Capelle, Philippe. *Philosophie et théologie dans la pensée de Martin Heidegger*. Paris: Éditions du Cerf, 1998.

Caputo, John D. *Heidegger and Aquinas: An Essay on Overcoming Metaphysics*. New York: Fordham University Press, 1982.

———. *The Mystical Element in Heidegger's Thought*. New York: Fordham University Press, 1986.

———. *The Prayers and Tears of Jacques Derrida: Religion without Religion*. Bloomington: Indiana University Press, 1997.

———. *Radical Hermeneutics: Repetition, Deconstruction, and the Hermeneutic Project*. Bloomington: Indiana University Press, 1987.

Carabine, Deirdre. *The Unknown God: Negative Theology in the Platonic Tradition, Plato to Eriugena*. Louvain: Peeters Press, W. B. Eerdemans, 1995.

Carnap, Rudolph. *The Logical Structure of the World*. Translated by Rolf A. George. Berkeley: University of California Press, 1967.

Cavell, Stanley. *Philosophical Passages: Wittgenstein, Emerson, Austin, Derrida*. Oxford: Blackwell, 1995.

Certeau, Michel de. *La Fable mystique: XVI'–XVII' siècle*. Paris: Gallimard, 1982.

———. "La Fiction de l'histoire: l'écriture de Moise et le monothéisme." In *L'Écriture de l'histoire*. Paris: Éditions du Seuil, 1975.

Chrétien, Jean-Louis. *L'Appel et la réponse*. Paris: Éditions de Minuit, 1992. Translated by Anne A. Davenport as *The Call and the Response*. New York: Fordham University Press, 2004.

———. *L'Arche de la parole*. Paris: Presses Universitaires de France, 1999.

———. "La Réserve de l'être." In *Martin Heidegger*, ed. Michel Haar, 233–260. *Cahier de l'Herne*. Paris: Éditions de l'Herne, 1983.

———. *The Unforgettable and the Unhoped For*. Translated by Jeffrey Bloechl. New York: Fordham University Press, 2002.

Clarke, W. Norris, S.J. *Explorations in Metaphysics: Being, God, Person*. South Bend, Ind.: University of Notre Dame Press, 1994.

Coakley, Sarah A. *Powers and Submissions: Spirituality, Philosophy and Gender*. Oxford: Blackwell, 2002.

———. *Religion and the Body*. New York: Cambridge University Press, 1997.

———. *Re-thinking Gregory of Nyssa*. Oxford: Blackwell, 2003.

Constas, Nicholas. "Icons and the Imagination." *Logos* 1 (1997): 114–127.

———. *Proclus of Constantinople and the Cult of the Virgin in Late Antiquity, Homilies 1–5, Texts and Translations*. Leiden: Brill, 2003.

———. "Weaving the Body of God: Proclus of Constantinople, the Theotokos and the Loom of the Flesh." *Journal of Early Christian Studies* 3, no. 2 (1995): 169–194.

Courtine, Jean-François. *Heidegger et la phénoménologie*. Paris: Vrin, 1990.

———. "Les Traces et le passage du Dieu dans les *Beiträge zur Philosophie* de Martin Heidegger." *Archivio di Filosofia* 1, no. 3 (1994): 519–538.

Coward, Harold, and Toby Foshay, eds. *Derrida and Negative Theology*. Albany: State University of New York Press, 1992.

Critchley, Simon. *The Ethics of Deconstruction: Levinas and Derrida*. Oxford: Blackwell, 1992.

———. *Ethics-Politics-Subjectivity: Essays on Derrida, Levinas and Contemporary French Thought*. London: Verso, 1999.

Crosby, John. *Personalist Papers*. Washington: Catholic University Press, 2004.

Dahlstrom, Daniel. "Heidegger's Religious Turn: From Christianity and Metaphysics to God." Unpublished paper presented at the XXXIV Heidegger Conference, Marshall University, Huntington, W.V., May 20, 2000.

Damascius Diadochos. *Dubitationes et solutiones de primis principiis, in Platonis Parmenidem*. Edited by Car. Aem. Ruelle. Brussels, 1964; reprint of 1899 ed.

Dastur, Françoise. "Le 'Dieu extrême' de la phénoménologie. Husserl et Heidegger." *Archives de Philosophie* 63 (2000): 195–204.

———. "Heidegger et la théologie." *Revue philosophique de Louvain* 2, no. 3 (1994): 226–245.

Derrida, Jacques. "Above All, No Journalists!" In *Religion and Media*, ed. Hent de Vries and Samuel Weber, 56–93. Stanford, Calif.: Stanford University Press, 2001.

———. *Adieu à Emmanuel Levinas*. Paris: Galilée, 1997.

———. "Comment ne pas parler: dénégations." In *Psyché: inventions de l'autre*, 535–595. Paris: Galilée 1987. Translated by Ken Frieden as "How to Avoid Speaking: Denials," in *Derrida and Negative Theology*, ed. Harold Coward and Toby Foshay, 73–142. Albany: State University of New York Press, 1992.

———. *De l'esprit: Heidegger et la question*. Paris: Galilée, 1987.

———. "Donner la mort." In *L'Éthique du don: Jacques Derrida et la pensée du don*, ed. Jean-Michel Rabaté and Michael Wetzel, 11–108. Paris: Métailié-Transition, 1992.

———. *Donner le temps: la fausse monnaie*. Paris: Galilée, 1991.

———. *D'un ton apocalyptique adopté naguère en philosophie*. Paris: Galilée, 1983.

———. *L'Écriture et la différence*. Paris: Éditions du Seuil, 1967.

———. *Éperons: les styles de Nietzsche*. Paris: Flammarion, 1976.

———. "Foi et savoir: les deux sources de la 'religion' aux limites de la simple raison." In *La Religion*, ed. Jacques Derrida and Gianni Vattimo, 9–86. Paris: Éditions du Seuil, 1996. Translated by Samuel Weber as "Faith and Knowledge: The Two Sources of 'Religion' at the Limits of Reason Alone," in *Religion*, ed. Jacques Derrida and Gianni Vattimo, 1–78. Stanford, Calif.: Stanford University Press, 1998.

————. "How to Avoid Speaking: Denials." In *Derrida and Negative Theology*, ed. Harold Coward and Toby Forshay, 73–142. New York: State University of New York Press, 1992.

————. "La Main de Heidegger (*Geschlecht II*)." In *Psyché: inventions de l'autre*, 415–451. Paris: Galilée, 1987.

————. *Le Toucher: Jean-Luc Nancy*. Paris: Éditions Galilée, 2000.

————. "L'Oreille de Heidegger." In *Politiques de l'amitié*. Paris: Galilée, 1994.

————. *L'Oreille de l'autre: otobiographies, transferts, traductions. Textes et débats avec Jacques Derrida, sous la direction de Claude Lévesque et Christie V McDonald*. Montreal: VLB, 1982.

————. *Limited Inc.* Evanston, Ill.: Northwestern University Press, 1977.

————. *Marges de la philosophie*. Paris: Éditions de Minuit, 1972. Translated by Alan Bass as *Margins of Philosophy*. Chicago: University of Chicago Press, 1982.

————. *Mémoires d'aveugle: l'auto-portrait et autres ruines*. Paris: Éditions de la réunion des musées nationaux, 1990.

————. "Mochlos: Or, The Conflict of the Faculties." In *Logomachia*, ed. R. Rand, 1–34. Lincoln: University of Nebraska Press, 1992.

————. *Of Grammatology*. Baltimore: Johns Hopkins University Press, 1977.

————. *Psyché: inventions de l'autre*. Paris: Galilée, 1987.

————. *Sauf le nom (Post-Scriptum)*. Paris: Galilée, 1993. Translated by John P. Leavey, Jr., as *On the Name*. Stanford, Calif.: Stanford University Press, 1995.

————. *Speech and Phenomena and Other Essays on Husserl's Theory of Signs*. Translated by David B. Allison. Evanston, Ill.: Northwestern University Press, 1973.

————. *La Voix et la phénomène*. Paris: Presses Universitaires de France, 1967.

Descartes, René. *Meditationes de Prima Philosophia. Ouvres de Descartes* VII. Paris: Librairie Philosophique Vrin, 1957.

Dionysius (the Aeropagite). *Corpus Dionysiacum*. 2 vols. Edited by Beate Regina Suchla, G. Heil, and A. M. Ritter. Berlin: Walter de Gruyter, 1990.

Dooley, Mark, ed. *A Passion for the Impossible: John D. Caputo in Focus*. Albany: State University of New York, 2003.

Douglass, Scot. "A Critical Analysis of Gregory's Philosophy of Language: The Linguistic Reconstitution of Metadiastemic Intrusions." In *Gregory of Nyssa: Homilies on the Beatitudes*. Proceedings of the Eighth International Colloquium on Gregory of Nyssa, Paderborn, September 14–18, 1998, ed. Hubertus R. Drobner and Albert Viciano, 447–465. Leiden: Brill, 2000.

Farrow, Douglas. *Ascension and Ecclesia: On the Significance of the Doctrine of the Ascension for Ecclesiology and Christian Cosmology*. Grand Rapids, Mich.: Eerdmans, 1999.

Felman, Shoshana, and Dori Laub. *Testimony: Crises of Witnessing in Literature, Psychoanalysis and History*. London: Routledge, 1992.

Flew, Anthony. "Theology and Falsification." In *The Philosophy of Religion*, ed. Basil Mitchell, 13–15. Oxford: Oxford University Press, 1971.

Florensky, Pavel. "Against Linear Perspective." In *Utopias: Russian Modernist Texts 1905–1940*, ed. Catriona Kelly, 70–75. London: Penguin Books, 2002.

————. *The Pillar and Ground of the Truth*. Translated by Boris Jakim. Princeton, N.J.: Princeton University Press, 1997.

Florovsky, Georges. *Bible, Church, Tradition: An Eastern Orthodox View. Collected Works*, vol. I. Vaduz: Belmont, 1987.

Gall, Robert. *Beyond Theism and Atheism*. Dordrecht: Martinus Nijhoff, 1987.

Gasché, Rodolphe. "God, for Example." In *Phenomenology and the Numinous*. Pittsburgh: Simon Silverman Phenomenology Center, 1988.

Gauchet, Marcel. *The Disenchantment of the World: A Political History of Religion*. Princeton, N.J.: Princeton University Press, 1997.

Giakalis, Ambrosios. *Images of the Divine: The Theology of Icons at the Seventh Ecumenical Council*. Leiden: Brill, 2005.

Golitzin, Alexander. "Suddenly Christ": The Place of Negative Theology in the Mystagogy of Dionysius Areopagites." In *Mystics: Presence and Aporia*, ed. Michael Kessler and Christian Sheppard, 8–37. Chicago: University of Chicago Press, 2003.

Gombrich, E. H. *Shadows: The Depiction of Cast Shadows in Western Art*. London: National Gallery Publications, 1995.

Greene, Brian. *The Elegant Universe*. New York: Vintage Books, 1999.

Gregor, Brian. "Eros That Never Arrives." *Symposium* 9, no. 1 (2005): 67–88.

Gregory of Nyssa. *Gregorii Nysseni Opera*. Edited by W. Jaeger. 13 vols. Leiden: Brill, 1960.

Greisch, Jean. "The Eschatology of Being and the God of Time in Heidegger." *International Journal of Philosophical Studies* 4, no. 1 (1996): 17–42.

———. "Nomination et révélation." *Archivo di Filosofia* 1–3 (1994): 577–598.

———. "La Pauvreté du 'Dernier Dieu' de Heidegger." In *Post-Theism: Reframing the Judeo-Christian Tradition*, ed. Henri A. Krop, Arie L. Molendijk, and Hent de Vries, 397–420. Leuven: Peeters, 2000.

Gurtler, Gary M., S.J. "Plotinus and Byzantine Aesthetics." *Modern Schoolman* 66 (1989): 275–284.

———. "Plotinus: Matter and Otherness, 'On Matter' (II 4[12])." *Epoché* 9, no. 2 (2005): 197–214.

Hallett, Garth. *A Companion to Wittgenstein's Philosophical Investigations*. Ithaca, N.Y.: Cornell University Press, 1977.

Hand, S., ed. *The Levinas Reader*. Oxford: Blackwell, 1996.

Harries, Karsten. *Infinity and Perspective*. Cambridge, Mass.: MIT Press, 2001.

Hart, Kevin. *Counter-Experiences: Reading Jean-Luc Marion*. South Bend, Ind.: University of Notre Dame Press, in press.

———. "The Kingdom and the Trinity." In *Religious Experience and the End of Metaphysics*, ed. Jeffrey Bloechl, 153–173. Bloomington: Indiana University Press, 2003.

———. "The Profound Reserve." In *After Blanchot: Literature, Criticism, Philosophy*, ed. Leslie Hill and Dimitris Vardoulakis, 35–57. Dover: University of Delaware Press, 2006.

———. *The Trespass of the Sign: Deconstruction, Theology and Philosophy*. New York: Fordham University Press, 2000.

Hegel, G. W. F. *Der Geist des Christentums und sein Schicksal*. Gerhard Ruhbach. Gütersloh: Gütersloher Verlagshaus G. Mohn, 1970.

———. *Glauben und Wissen: oder die Reflexionsphilosophie der Sujektivität, in der Vollstän-digkeit ihrer Formen, als Kantische, Jacobische, und Fichtische Philosophie*. Edited by Hans Brockard and Hartmut Buchner. Hamburg: Meiner, 1986.

Heidegger, Martin. *Aus der Erfahrung des Denkes 1910–1976. Gesamtausgabe* 13. Frankfurt: Klostermann.

———. *Beiträge zur Philosophie: vom Ereignis*. Edited by Friedrich-Wilhelm von Herrmann. *Gesamtausgabe* 65. Frankfurt: Klostermann, 1989. Translated by Parvis Emad and Kenneth Maly as *Contributions to Philosophy (From Enowning)*. Bloomington: Indiana University Press, 1999.

———. "Brief über den Humanismus." In *Wegmarken*, 311–360. Frankfurt: Klostermann, 1978.

———. *The End of Philosophy*. Translated by Joan Stambaugh. Chicago: University of Chicago Press, 2003.

———. *Four Seminars*. Translated by A. Mitchell and F. Raffoul. Bloomington: Indiana University Press, 2003.

———. *Die Grundprobleme der Phänomenologie. Gesamtausgabe* 24. Frankfurt: Klostermann, 1975.

———. *Holzwege*. Frankfurt: Vittorio Klostermann, 1950. Translated by Julian Young and Kenneth Haynes as *Off the Beaten Track*. Cambridge: Cambridge University Press, 2002.

———. *Identität und Differenz*. Pfullingen: Neske. 1978. Translated by Joan Stambaugh as *Identity and Difference*. New York: Harper & Row, 1969.

203

————. *An Introduction to Metaphysics.* Translated by Ralph Manheim. New Haven, Conn.: Yale University Press, 1959.

————. *Kant und das Problem der Metaphysik.* Bonn: F. Cohen, 1929.

————. *Nietzsche.* 4 vols. Pfullingen: Neske, 1961. Translated by David Farrell Krell as *Nietzsche.* 2 vols. New York: Harper & Row, 1984.

————. *Parmenides.* Translated by André Schuwer and Richard Rojcewicz. Bloomington: Indiana University Press, 1992.

————. *Phänomenologie des religiösen Lebens. Gesamtausgabe* 60. Frankfurt: Klostermann, 1995.

————."Phänomenologie und Theologie." In *Wegmarken*, 45–78. Frankfurt: Klostermann, 1978.

————. *Poetry, Language, Thought.* Translated by Albert Hofstadter. New York: Harper & Row, Perennial Classics, 2001.

————. *The Question Concerning Technology and Other Essays.* Translated by William Lovitt. New York: Harper & Row, 1977.

————. *Der Satz vom Grund.* Pfullingen: Neske, 1957. Translated by Reginald Lilly as *The Principle of Reason.* Bloomington: Indiana University Press, 1991.

————. *Sein und Zeit.* Tübingen: Max Niemeyer Verlag, 1953. Translated by Joan Stambaugh as *Being and Time.* Albany: State University of New York Press, 1996.

————. *Vorträge und Aufsatze.* Pfullingen: Neske, 1954.

————. *Was heisst Denken?* Tübingen: M. Niemeyer, 1954. Translated by J. Glenn Gray as *What Is Called Thinking?* New York: Harper & Row, 1968.

————. "Was ist Metaphysik?" In *Wegmarken*, 103–121. Frankfurt: Klostermann, 1978.

————. *Wegmarken. Gesamtausgabe* 9. Frankfurt: Klostermann, 1978. Translated as *Pathmarks*, ed. William McNeill. Cambridge: Cambridge University Press, 1998.

Henry, Michel. *L'essence de la manifestation.* Paris: Presses Universitaires de France, 1963.

————. *Incarnation: une philosophie de la chair.* Paris: Seuil, 2000.

————. *Phénoménologie matérielle.* Paris: Presses Universitaires de France, 1990.

————. *Philosophy and Phenomenology of the Body.* Translated by Girard Etzkorn. The Hague: Martinus Nijhoff, 1975.

Holler, Linda. *Erotic Morality: The Role of Touch in Moral Agency.* New Brunswick, N.J.: Rutgers University Press, 2002.

Hopkins, Gerard Manley. "On Personality, Grace and Free Will." In *The Sermons and Devotional Writings of Gerard Manley Hopkins*, ed. Christopher Devlin, S.J., 146–159. London: Oxford University Press, 1959.

Horner, Robyn. *Jean-Luc Marion: A Theo-Logical Introduction.* London: Ashgate, 2005.

————. *Rethinking God as Gift: Marion, Derrida and the Limits of Phenomenology.* New York: Fordham University Press, 2001.

Husserl, Edmund. *Cartesian Meditations: An Introduction to Phenomenology.* Translated by Dorion Cairns. The Hague: Martinus Nijhoff, 1970.

————. *Ideas Pertaining to a Pure Phenomenology and to Phenomenological Philosophy.* Book One. The Hague: Martinus Nijoff, 1983.

————. *Logische Untersuchungen.* Volume 2, Part 1, Section 2. Tübingen: Max Niemeyer Verlag, 1968.

Ihde, Dan. *Listening and Voice: A Phenomenology of Sound.* Athens: Ohio University Press, 1976.

————. "Some Auditory Phenomena." *Philosophy Today* 10, no. 4 (1966): 227–235.

————. "Studies in the Phenomenology of Sound." *International Philosophical Quarterly* 2 (1940): 232–251.

Janicaud, Dominique. *Heidegger en France.* Vol. I: *Récit.* Paris: Albin Michel, 2001.

————. *Le Tournant théologique de la phénoménologie française.* Combas: Éditions de l'Éclat, 1991.

Janicaud, Dominique, and Jean-François Mattéi. *Heidegger, from Metaphysics to Thought.* Translated by M. Gendre. Albany: State University of New York Press, 1995.

Janicaud, Dominique, et al. *Phenomenology and the "Theological Turn": The French Debate.* Translated by Bernard G. Prusak, Thomas A. Carlson, and Jeffrey L. Kosky. New York: Fordham University Press, 2000.

Jay, Martin. *Downcast Eyes: The Denigration of Vision in Twentieth-Century Thought.* Berkeley: University of California Press, 1993.

Kaegi, Dominic. "Die Religion in den Grenzen der blossen Existenz; Heideggers religionsphilosophische Vorlesungen von 1920/21." *Internationale Zeitschrift für Philosophie* 1 (1996): 133–149.

Kant, Immanuel. *Critik der reinen Vernunft. Werke in zehn Banden* III–IV. Edited by Wilhelm Weischedel. Darmstadt: Wissenschaftliche Buchgesellschaft, 1983. Translated by Norman Kemp Smith as *Critic of Pure Reason.* London: Macmillan, 1929.

———. *Die Religion innerhalb der Grenzen der blossen Vernunft. Werke in zehn Banden* VII. Darmstadt: Wissenschaftliche Buchgesellschaft, 1983.

———. "Von einem neuerdings erhobenen vornehmen Ton in der Philosophie" (1796). In *Werke in zehn Bänden* 5, 377–397. Darmstadt: Wissenschaftliche Buchgesellschaft, 1983.

Kearney, Richard. *The God Who May Be: A New Hermeneutics of Religion.* Bloomington: Indiana University Press, 2001.

———. *Poetics of Imagination.* London: Routledge, 1988.

———. *Poetics of Imagining: Modern to Postmodern.* New York: Fordham University Press, 1998.

———. *Poétique du possible.* Paris: Beauchesne, 1984.

———. *Strangers, Gods and Monsters: Interpreting Otherness.* London: Routledge, 2003.

———. *The Wake of Imagination.* London: Routledge, 1988.

Kerr, F. *Theology after Wittgenstein.* Blackwell: Oxford, 1986.

Kierkegaard, Søren. *The Concept of Anxiety. Kierkegaard's Writings* 8. Translated and edited by Reidar Thomte. Princeton, N.J.: Princeton University Press, 1980.

———. *Either/Or. Kierkegaard's Writings* 3. Translated and edited by Howard V. Hong and Edna H. Hong. Princeton, N.J.: Princeton University Press, 1987.

———. *Fear and Trembling. Kierkegaard's Writings* 6. Translated and edited by Howard V. Hong and Edna H. Hong. Princeton, N.J.: Princeton University Press, 1983.

———. *The Sickness unto Death. Kierkegaard's Writings* 9. Translated and edited by Howard V. Hong and Edna H. Hong. Princeton, N.J.: Princeton University Press, 1980.

———. *Works of Love. Kierkegaard's Writings* 16. Translated and edited by Howard V. Hong and Edna H. Hong. Princeton, N.J.: Princeton University Press, 1995.

Kloos, Kari. "Seeing the Invisible God: Augustine's Reconfiguration of Theophany Narrative Exegesis." *Augustinian Studies* 36, no. 2 (2005): 397–420.

Kripke, Saul A. *Naming and Necessity.* Cambridge, Mass.: Harvard University Press, 1972, 1980.

Lacan, Jacques. *L'Éthique de la psychanalyse, 1959–1960.* Translated by Dennis Porter as *The Ethics of Psychoanalysis, 1959–1960.* New York: W. W. Norton, 1992.

Lacoste, Jean-Yves. *Experience and the Absolute: Disputed Questions on the Humanity of Man.* Translated by Mark Raftery-Skehan. New York: Fordham University Press, 2004.

Lehmann, Karl. "Christliche Geschichtserfahrung und ontologische Frage beim jungen Heidegger." In *Heidegger: Perspektiven zur Deutung seines Werkes,* ed. Otto Pöggeler, 140–166. Königstein: Athenäum, 1984.

Levin, David M., ed. *Modernity and the Hegemony of Vision.* Berkeley: University of California Press, 1993.

Levinas, Emmanuel. *Autrement qu'être ou au-delà de l'essence.* The Hague: Martinus Nijhoff, 1974.

———. *De Dieu qui vient à l'idée.* Vrin: Paris, 1982. Translated by Bettina Bergo as *Of God Who Comes to Mind.* Stanford, Calif.: Stanford University Press, 1988.

Bibliography

————. *De l'existence à l'existant*. Paris: J. Vrin, 1978.

————. *Difficile liberté: essais sur le judaïsme*. 2nd rev. ed. Paris: A. Michel, 1976. Translated by S. Hand as *Difficult Freedom*. Baltimore: Johns Hopkins University Press, 1990.

————. *Du sacré au saint*. Paris: Éditions Minuit, 1977.

————. *Le Temps et l'autre*. Montpellier: Fata Morgana, 1979.

————. *Totalité et infini: essai sur l'extériorité*. 1961. The Hague: Martinus Nijhoff, 1961. Translated by Alphonso Lingis as *Totality and Infinity: An Essay on Exteriority*. Pittsburgh, Penn.: Duquesne University Press, 1969.

————. "La Trace de l'Autre." *Tijdschrift voor Filosofie* 3 (1963): 605–623.

Lyotard, Jean-François. *Le Différend*. Paris: Éditions de Minuit, 1983.

————. *The Hyphen: Between Judaism and Christianity*. Translated by Pascale-Anne Brault and Michael Naas. New York: Humanity Press, 1999.

————. *L'Inhumain: causeries sur le temps*. Paris: Galilée, 1988.

MacDonald, Michael J. "Jewgreek and Greekjew: The Concept of Trace in Derrida and Levinas." *Philosophy Today* (1991): 215–227.

Magee, Bryan. *The Tristan Chord: Wagner and Philosophy*. New York: Metropolitan Books, 2001.

Manoussakis, John Panteleimon. "From Exodus to Eschaton." *Modern Theology* 18, no. 1 (2002): 95–107.

————. "The Revelation According to Jacques Derrida." In *Other Testaments: Derrida and Religion*, ed. Kevin Hart and Yvonne Sherwood, 309–323. London: Routledge, 2005.

————, ed. *After God: Richard Kearney and the Religious Turn in Continental Philosophy*. New York: Fordham University Press, 2006.

Margel, Serge. *Le Tombeau du dieu artisan: sur Platon*. Paris: Éditions du Minuit, 1995.

Marion, Jean-Luc. "La Banalité de la saturation." In *Le Visible et le révélé*, 143–182. Paris: Cerf, 2005.

————. *De Surcroît: études sur les phénomènes saturés*. Paris: Presses Universitaires de France, 2001. Translated by Robyn Horner and Vincent Berraud as *In Excess: Studies of Saturated Phenomena*. New York: Fordham University Press, 2002.

————. *Dieu sans l'être: hors texte*. 1982. Paris: Quadrige, 1991. Translated by Thomas A. Carlson as *God without Being*. Chicago: University of Chicago Press, 1991.

————. "The End of the End of Metaphysics." *Epoché* 2, no. 2 (1994): 1–22.

————. "Une Époque de la métaphysique." In *Jean Duns Scot ou la revolution subtile*, ed. Christine Goémé, 87–95. Paris: FAC, 1982.

————. *Étant donné: essai d'une phénoménologie de la donation*. Paris: Presses Universitaires de France, 1997. Translated by Jeffrey L. Kosky as *Being Given*. Stanford, Calif.: Stanford University Press, 2002.

————. *L'idole et la distance: cinq études*. Paris: Grasset, 1977. Translated by Thomas A. Carlson as *The Idol and Distance*. New York: Fordham University Press, 2001.

————. "Metaphysics and Phenomenology: A Relief for Theology." Translated by Thomas A. Carlson. *Critical Inquiry* 20 (summer 1994): 573–591.

————. *Le Phénomène érotique*. Paris: Grasset, 2003.

————. *Prolegomena to Charity*. Translated by Stephen Lewis. New York: Fordham University Press, 2002.

————. *Réduction et donation: recherches sur Husserl, Heidegger et la phénoménologie*. Paris: Presses Universitaires de France, 1989.

————. "The Saturated Phenomenon." Translated by Thomas A. Carlson. *Philosophy Today* 40 (spring 1996): 103–124.

————. *Sur la théologie blanche de Descartes: analogie, création des vérités éternelles et fondement*. Paris: Presses Universitaires de France, 1989; Quadrige, 1991.

————. "They Recognized Him; and He Became Invisible to Them." *Modern Theology* 18, no. 2 (2002): 145–152.

Marrati-Guénoun, Paola. *La Genèse et la trace: Derrida lecteur de Husserl et Heidegger*. Dordrecht: Kluwer, 1998.

Martin, Jay. *Downcast Eyes: The Denigration of Vision in Twentieth-Century Thought*. Berkeley: University of California Press, 1993.

McDonough, Christopher M. "Carna, Proca and the *Strix* on the Kalends of June." *Transactions of the American Philological Association* 127 (1997): 315–344.

Menn, Stephen. "The Origins of Aristotle's Concept of Ἐνέργεια: Ἐνέργεια and Δύναμις." *Ancient Philosophy* 14 (1994): 73–114.

Merleau-Ponty, Maurice. "Eye and Mind." In *The Primacy of Perception*. Translated by Carleton Dallery and edited by James M. Edie. Evanston, Ill.: Northwestern University Press, 1964.

———. *L'Oeil et l'esprit*. Paris: Gallimard, 1964.

———. *Phénoménologie de la perception* (1945). Paris: Gallimard, 1976. Translated by Colin Smith as *Phenomenology of Perception*. London: Routledge, 2002.

———. *Union de l'âme et du corps chez Malebranche, Biran et Bergson*. Translated by P. B. Milan as *The Incarnate Subject: Malebranche, Biran, and Bergson on the Unity of Body and Soul*. Edited by P. Burke and A. G. Bjelland. New York: Humanity Books, 2002.

———. *The Visible and the Invisible*. Translated by Alphonso Lingis. Evanston, Ill.: Northwestern University Press, 1968.

Mitchell, W. J. T. *Iconology: Image, Text, Ideology*. Chicago: University of Chicago Press, 1986.

———. *Picture Theory; Essays on Verbal and Visual Representation*. Chicago: University of Chicago Press, 1994.

Mondzain, Marie-José. *Image, icône, économie: les sources byzantines de l'imaginaire contemporain*. Paris: Éditions du Seuil, 1996. Translated by Rico Franses as *Image, Icon, Economy: The Byzantine Origins of the Contemporary Imaginary*. Stanford, Calif.: Stanford University Press, 2005.

Mosshammer, Alden A. "Disclosing but Not Disclosed: Gregory of Nyssa as Deconstructionist." In *Studien zu Gregor von Nyssa und der Christlichen Spätantike*, ed. Hubertus R. Drobner and Christoph Klock, 99–123. Leiden: Brill, 1990.

Mulhall, S. *Inheritance and Originality*. Oxford: Clarendon Press, 2001.

Nancy, Jean-Luc. "La Déconstruction du Christianisme." *Les Études Philosophiques* 4 (1998): 503–519.

———. "Dies Illa: (From One End to the Infinite, or of Creation)." *Journal of the British Society for Phenomenology* 32 (October 2001): 257–276.

Nicholas of Cusa. *De Li non Aliud*. Translated by Jasper Hopkins. Minneapolis: Arthur J. Banning, 1987.

———. *De Visione Dei*. Translated by H. Lawrence Bond. In *Nicholas of Cusa, Selected Spiritual Writings*, 233–269. New York: Paulist Press, 1997.

———. *Opera Omnia*. Edited by Adelaida Dorothea Riemann. Hamburg: Felix Meiner, 2000.

Nietzsche, F. W. *Beyond Good and Evil*. Translated by Walter Kaufmann. New York: Vintage Books, 1966.

———. *Die fröhliche Wissenschaft*. Translated by Walter Kaufmann as *The Gay Science*. New York: Vintage Books, 1974.

———. *Götzen-Dämmerung oder Wie Man mit dem Hammer philosophiert*. Translated by Walter Kaufmann as *Twilight of the Idols* in *The Portable Nietzsche*. New York: Penguin Books, 1968.

———. *The Will to Power*. Translated by Walter Kaufmann and R. J. Hollingdale. New York: Vintage Books, 1968.

———. *Zur Genealogie der Moral*. 1887. *Sämtliche Werke* 5. Translated by Walter Kaufmann as *Genealogy of Morals*. New York: Vintage Books, 1967.

Norman, Malcolm. *Thought and Knowledge*. Ithaca, N.Y.: Cornell University Press, 1977.

Nussbaum, M. C. *The Fragility of Goodness*. Cambridge: Cambridge University Press, 1986.

Oliver, Harold H. *Relatedness: Essays in Metaphysics and Theology.* Macon, Ga.: Mercer University Press, 1984.

———. *A Relational Metaphysic.* The Hague: Martinus Nijhoff, 1981.

O Murchadha, F. *Zeit des Handelns und Möglichkeit der Verwandlung: Kairologie und Chronologie bei Heideger im Jahrzehnt nach Sein und Zeit.* Würzburg: Königshausen & Neumann, 1999.

Origen. *Die griechischen christlichen Schriftsteller der ersten drei Jahrhunderte: Origenes Werke.* Edited by E. Klostermann. Leipzig, 1941.

———. *On First Principles.* Translated by G. W. Butterworth. Gloucester: Peter Smith, 1973.

Ott, Hugo, and Giorgio Penzo, eds. *Heidegger e la teologia: atti del convegno tenuto a Trento l' 8–9 Febbraio 1990.* Morcelliana, 1995.

Otto, Rudolf. *Das Heilige: über das Irrationale in der Idee des Göttlichen und sein Verhältnis rum Rationalen* (1917). Munich: C. H. Beck, 1997.

Papagiannopoulos, Ilias. *Beyond Absence: Essay on the Human Person on the Traces of Sophocles's Oedipus Rex.* Athens: Indiktos, 2005.

Perella, Nicholas James. *The Kiss Sacred and Profane.* Berkeley: University of California Press, 1969.

Perl, Eric. "Signifying Nothing: Being as Sign in Neoplatonism and Derrida." In *Neoplatonism and Contemporary Thought,* vol. 2, ed. Harris R. Baine, 125–151. Albany: State University of New York Press, 2002.

Perotti, James L. *Heidegger on the Divine: The Thinker, The Poet, and God.* Athens: University of Ohio Press, 1974.

Phillips, D. Z. *Wittgenstein and Religion.* New York: St. Martin's Press, 1993.

Plato. *Opera: Tetralogiae IX. Scriptorum Classicorum Bibliotheca Oxoniensis I–V.* Edited by Ioannes Burnet. Oxford: Oxford University Press, 1900.

Pöggeler, Otto. *Der Denkweg Martin Heideggers* (1963). Pfullingen: Neske, 1983.

Prestige, G. L. *God in Patristic Thought.* London: S.P.C.K., 1959.

Proclus. Στοιχείωσις Θεολογική *(The Elements of Theology).* Edited by E. R. Dodds. Oxford: Clarendon Press, 1963.

Putman, Hilary. "Wittgenstein on Religious Belief." In *Renewing Philosophy.* Cambridge, Mass.: Harvard University Press, 1992.

Rahner, K. "Le Debut d'une doctrine des cinq sens spirituels chez Origène." *Revue d' Ascétisme et de Mysticisme* 13 (1932): 113–145.

———. *Hearers of the Word.* Translated by M. Richards. New York: Herder and Herder, 1969.

Reid, Duncan. *Energies of the Spirit.* Atlanta, Ga.: American Academy of Religion, 1997.

Richardson, William J. *Heidegger: Through Phenomenology to Thought.* Preface by Martin Heidegger (1962). The Hague: Martinus Nijhoff, 1974.

———. "Like Straw: Religion and Psychoanalysis." In *Eros and Eris: Liber Amicorum en homage à Adriaan Peperzak,* 93–104. The Hague: Kluwer, 1992.

———. "Psychoanalysis and the God-Question." *Thought* 61 (1986): 68–83.

Ricœur, Paul. *Le Conflit des interprétations: essais d'herméneutique.* Paris: Éditions du Seuil, 1969. Translated by Don Ihde as *The Conflict of Interpretations: Essays in Hermeneutics.* Evanston, Ill.: Northwestern University Press, 1974.

———. *Husserl: An Analysis of His Phenomenology.* Translated by Eduard G. Bollard and Lester E. Embree. Evanston, Ill.: Northwestern University Press, 1967.

Rilke, Rainer Maria. *The Book of Hours: Prayers to a Lowly God.* Bilingual edition. Translated by Annemarie S. Kidder. Evanston, Ill.: Northwestern University Press, 2001.

Rogozinski, Jacob. "It Makes Us Wrong: Kant and Radical Evil." In *Radical Evil,* ed. Joan Copjec, 30–45. London: Verso, 1996.

Rorty, Richard. *Contingency, Irony, and Solidarity.* Cambridge: Cambridge University Press, 1989.

———. *Philosophical Papers.* Vol. I: *Objectivity, Relativism, and Truth.* Vol. II: *Essays on Heidegger and Others.* Cambridge: Cambridge University Press, 1991.

Rosen, Stanley. "Thought and Touch: A Note on Aristotle's *De Anima.*" *Phronesis* 6 (1961): 127–137.

Said, Edward. *Musical Elaborations.* New York: Columbia University Press, 1991.

Sallis, John. *Being and Logos.* Bloomington: Indiana University Press, 1996.

———. *Chorology: On Beginning in Plato's Timaeus.* Bloomington: Indiana University Press, 1999.

———. *Delimitations: Phenomenology and the End of Metaphysics.* Bloomington: Indiana University Press, 1986.

———. *Shades: Of Painting at the Limit.* Bloomington: Indiana University Press, 1998.

Sartre, J. P. *L'Être et le néant: essai d'ontologie phénoménologique.* Paris: Gallimard, 1977. Translated by Hazel Barnes as *Being and Nothingness.* New York: Washington Square Press, 1956.

———. *The Psychology of Imagination.* Secaucus: Citadel Press, 1972.

———. *The Transcendence of the Ego.* Translated by Forrest Williams and Robert Kirkpatrick. New York: Hill and Wang, 1960.

Saussure, Ferdinand de. *Course in General Linguistics.* Translated by Wade Baskin. New York: McGraw-Hill, 1959.

Schopenhauer, A. *The World as Will and Representation.* 2 vols. New York: Dover, 1966.

Schürmann, Reiner. *Broken Hegemonies.* Bloomington: Indiana University Press, 2003.

———. *Heidegger on Being and Acting: From Principles to Anarchy.* Bloomington: Indiana University Press, 1987.

Sheehan, Thomas. "A Paradigm Shift in Heidegger Research." Unpublished paper presented at the XXXIV Heidegger Conference, Marshall University, Huntington, W.V., May 20, 2000.

Smith, James K. A. "Liberating Religion from Theology: Marion and Heidegger on the Possibility of a Phenomenology of Religion." *International Journal for Philosophy of Religion* 46 (1999): 17–33.

———. "Respect and Donation: A Critique of Marion's Critique of Husserl." *American Catholic Philosophical Quarterly* 71, no. 4 (1988): 523–538.

Sorabji, R., M. Schofield, and J. Barnes, eds. *Articles on Aristotle.* Vol. 4. London: Duckworth, 1979.

Stavrakakis, Y. "Lacan and History." *Journal for the Psychoanalysis of Culture and Society* 4, no. 1 (1999): 99–118.

———. *Lacan and the Political.* London: Routledge, 1999.

Stenstad, Gail. "The Last God: A Reading." *Research in Phenomenology* 24 (1994): 172–184.

Underwood, A. *The Kariye Djami.* 3 vols. New York: Bollingen Foundation, 1966.

Ventis, Haralambos. *The Reductive Veil: Post-Kantian Non-representationalism versus Apophatic Realism.* Katerini: Epektasis Publications, 2005.

Verghese, T. Paul. "Διάστημα and διάστασις." In *Gregor von Nyssa und die Philosophie*, ed. Heinrich Dörrie et al., 243–260. Leiden: Brill, 1976.

Vlastos, Gregory. "The Individual as Object of Love in Plato." In *Platonic Studies.* Princeton, N.J.: Princeton University Press, 1981.

Volf, Miroslav. *After Our Likeness: The Church as the Image of the Trinity.* Grand Rapids, Mich.: William B. Eerdmans, 1998.

Vries, Hent de. *Philosophy and the Turn to Religion.* Baltimore: Johns Hopkins University Press, 1999.

Wahl, Jean. *Sur l'interprétation de l'histoire de la métaphysique d'après Heidegger.* Paris: Centre de Documentation Universitaire, 1951.

Ware, Kalistos Timothy. "The Transfiguration of the Body." In *Sacrament and Image*, ed. A. M. Allchin. London: Fellowship of S. Alban and S. Sergius, 1967.

Westphal, Merold. *Overcoming Onto-theology: Toward a Postmodern Christian Faith.* New York: Fordham University Press, 2001.

Bibliography

———. *Transcendence and Self-transcendence.* Bloomington: Indiana University Press, 2004.

Wickham, L. R. "*Syntagmation* of Aetius the Anomean." *Journal of Theological Studies* 19 (1968): 537.

Wittgenstein, Ludwig. *Culture and Value.* Translated by Peter Winch. Chicago: University of Chicago Press, 1980.

———. *Lectures and Conversations on Aesthetics, Psychology, and Religious Belief.* Notes published by Yorick Smythies, Rush Rhees, and James Taylor. Edited by Cyril Barrett. Berkeley: University of California Press, 1966.

———. *Philosophical Investigations.* 1953. Translated by G. E. M. Anscombe and R. Rhees. Oxford: Blackwell, 1997.

———. *Tractatus logico-philosophicus.* Werkausgabe I. Frankfurt: Suhrkamp, 1989.

———. *Vermischte Bemerkungen.* Bilingual edition. Translated by Peter Winch as *Culture and Value.* Edited by G. H. von Wright. Chicago: University of Chicago Press, 1984.

———. *Wittgenstein's Lectures in Cambridge 1932–1935.* Edited by Alice Ambrose. Oxford: Blackwell, 1979.

———. *Zettel.* Berkeley: University of California Press, 1967.

Wood, David. *Thinking after Heidegger.* Cambridge: Polity Press, 2002.

Yannaras, Chrestos. *Προτάσεις Κριτικής Οντολογίας* (Sentences of Critical Ontology). Athens: Domos, 1985.

———. *Σχεδίασμα Εισαγωγής στην Φιλοσοφία* (Sketch of an Introduction to Philosophy). Athens: Domos, 1988.

———. *Το Πρόσωπο και ο Έρως* (The Person and Eros). Athens: Domos, 1987.

Yu, N., M. S. Kruskall, J. J. Yunis, et al. "Disputed Maternity Leading to Identification of Tetragametic Chimerism." *New England Journal of Medicine* 346 (May 16, 2002): 1545–1552.

Zagzebski, Linda. "The Uniqueness of Persons." *Journal of Religious Ethics* 29 (2001): 401–423.

Zahavi, Dan. *Husserl's Phenomenology.* Stanford, Calif.: Stanford University Press, 2003.

Ziogas, Yiannis. *The Byzantine Malevitch.* Athens: Stachy Publications, 2004.

Zizioulas, J. (Metropolitan of Pergamon). *Η Κτίση ως Ευχαριστία* (Creation as Eucharist). Athens: Akritas, 1992.

———. *Being as Communion.* New York: St. Vladimir's Seminar Press, 1985.

———. "Church and the Eschaton." In *Church and Eschatology,* ed. Pantelis Kalaitzidis, 27–45. Athens: Kastaniotis, 2001.

———. "Communion and Otherness." *St. Vladimir's Theological Quarterly* 38, no. 4 (1994): 347–361.

———. "Eucharist and the Kingdom of God." *Synaxis* 52 (1994): 81–97.

———. "Human Capacity and Human Incapacity." *Scottish Journal of Theology* 28 (1975): 401–448.

———. "On Being a Person: Towards an Ontology of Personhood." In *Persons, Divine and Human,* 33–46. Edinburgh: T&T Clark, 1991.

Žižek, Slavoj. *The Fragile Absolute — or, Why Is the Christian Legacy Worth Fighting For?* London: Verso, 2000.

———. *The Puppet and the Dwarf: The Perverse Core of Christianity.* Cambridge, Mass.: MIT Press, 2003.

———. *The Sublime Object of Ideology.* London: Verso, 1989.

INDEX

Page numbers in italics indicate illustrations.

Index

JOHN PANTELEIMON MANOUSSAKIS teaches philosophy at Boston College and the American College of Greece. He is author of *Theos Philosophoumenos* (in Greek), editor of *After God*, and co-editor (with Drew Hyland) of *Heidegger and the Greeks* (Indiana University Press). He has also translated Heidegger's *Sojourns*. He is an ordained deacon in the Orthodox Archdiocese of Athens.